A FORTRAN IV Primer

RICHARD A. MANN

MECHANICAL ENGINEERING DEPARTMENT
UNIVERSITY OF NEW HAVEN

INTEXT EDUCATIONAL PUBLISHERS
COLLEGE DIVISION OF Intext
SCRANTON SAN FRANCISCO TORONTO LONDON

I-QN-RI

ISBN 0-7002-2412-2

Preface

This book is intended for the use of students without any previous knowledge of programming. A brief description of computation procedures, the use of flow diagrams, and the operation of digital computers including machine-language and symbolic machine-language programming is given in the first three chapters. While a student might master the techniques of FORTRAN programming without any of this background knowledge, he will find the details of FORTRAN programming more meaningful with this knowledge than if he regards the computer merely as a "black box" that accepts FORTRAN programs as input and produces a printed or punched output.

An effort is made to explain points that are often assumed to be obvious but give many beginning programmers difficulty. The student is warned about many errors he might ordinarily make.

The material covered is not presented in the usual order. Most textbooks present all the ramifications of a particular FORTRAN statement in one section or chapter. This is ideal for a reference book but does not provide the optimal learning sequence for the beginning programmer. In this book the most simple and basic aspects of a topic are presented first, and the student is given sample programs to help him master these concepts. The more complex aspects of the topic are then delayed to later chapters. A few topics that might well be omitted in a first elementary programming course are briefly presented in appendixes.

The author sincerely believes that a mastery of FORTRAN programming may be achieved only by writing programs and attempting to run them on a computer. The book is written so that a student may write complete, meaningful programs almost from the beginning. The student will thus be made aware of the fact that he must pay attention to many small details if he wishes his programs to make the required computations successfully. One misplaced comma will prevent the program from achieving the desired results. The programmer must learn that while the computer will make very rapid calculations, he must provide the thinking. The computer will do what it is told to do, but will give meaningless results unless supplied with the correct logic.

This book is not intended for the "hot-shot" programmer, nor is it a complete definitive description of FORTRAN IV. Rather it is intended as a primer for the student who wishes to use the digital computer as a very useful tool that will permit him to make numerical computations and manipulate alphabetic information.

RICHARD A. MANN

West Haven, Connecticut
February, 1972

CONTENTS

INTRODUCTION

Ever since the development of number systems man has been making calculations. At first they were relatively simple, but as society, commerce, and technology became more complex, calculations became more numerous and involved. For centuries man has been developing new methods and equipment to help him make these calculations. The devices used in making numerical computations, whether abacus, slide rule, adding machine, or "electronic brain," may be called *computers*.

Computers are usually classified as either "analog" or "digital" computers. An analog computer represents numbers by continuously varying quantities such as lengths, angles, or voltages. When a problem is to be solved with the help of an analog computer, electrical or mechanical connections are made in such a way that some measurable quantities in the computer satisfy the same mathematical relationships that govern the variables in the problem to be solved. Your slide rule is an analog computer on which lengths proportional to the logarithms of numbers are added or subtracted to give a distance proportional to the logarithm of the product or quotient. Electronic analog computers are available and are used primarily to solve problems involving differential equations.

Problems involving algebraic equations are usually more readily solved by the use of digital computers. A digital computer represents numbers by a sequence of digits. When you count on your fingers you are using the first digital computer. Many mathematicians and inventors provided ideas and developed computing devices that led to the modern electronic digital computer.

The abacus was one of the first digital computers and was in common use in China as early as 600 B.C. It uses the positions of beads on wires to represent digits. John Napier (1550–1617) was one of the first mathematicians in Western culture to devise a mechanical digital computer in 1617. In 1620 William Oughtred (1575–1660) discovered that computations could be made by holding two straight logarithmic scales together by hand and sliding one of the scales along the other. He may thus be considered the inventor of the slide rule. Many others, including Sir Isaac Newton (1642–1727), later added improvements and refinements to the slide rule. Blaise Pascal (1623–62) invented the mechanical adding machine in 1642, and Gottfried Wilhelm Leibnitz (1646–1716) devised a multiplying machine in 1671.

Charles Babbage (1792–1871) is credited with the development of many of the basic concepts that led to the development of the modern computer. A professor of mathematics at Cambridge University, in 1812 he devised a "difference engine" to aid him in developing trigonometric and logarithmic tables. From 1834 to 1854 he attempted to build a mechanical "analytic engine" which was to execute a preset arbitrary sequence of arithmetic operations on internally stored data. Babbage's concept of a digital computing device in which instructions and numbers could be stored is the basis of modern electronic digital computers. His "engine," however, was never completed because the technology of his time could not provide the necessary precision machining. Later, advances in technology made it possible to convert the ideas of these early developers into modern adding machines and desk calculators making use of gears and linkages.

It was not until development of electrical and electrical-mechanical devices in the twentieth century that many of these early concepts could be practically applied. Telephone relays were used to build a series of computers at the Bell Telephone Laboratories and at Harvard University in the 1940's. The first computer using electron tubes was built at the University of Pennsylvania. Other early computers were developed at Massachusetts Institute of Technology, at Cambridge University in England, and at the National Bureau of Standards all before 1950. Although IBM punched-card machines were introduced in the early 1930's, the modern era of electronic digital computers is usually considered to have started about 1950 when such computers first became commercially available. The development of transistors around 1960 and the recent advent of integrated microelectronic circuits produced further advances.

The modern digital computer is thus about twenty years old, but computers and computing science have reached a stage where they greatly affect the business and technology of the world. The development is continuing rapidly, and more sophisticated computers with larger capacity and higher speed are continually being designed.

CHAPTER 1

Setting Up a Calculation, Flow Charts, Indexes, and Loops

1-1. Setting Up a Computation Procedure

Electronic digital computers cannot make any calculations that could not theoretically be made by a man using pencil and paper, given enough time. The advantage of the computer is that it is many times faster (the IBM 1130, a small computer, can perform 120,000 additions per second) and almost never makes a mistake.

Suppose we have a clerk who is not very intelligent but who can follow simple instructions and do simple arithmetic with the help of a desk calculator. If we ask this clerk to do the calculations for a problem we wish to solve, we must furnish him with step-by-step instructions. We might want a table giving the value of x from the equation $x = 3t - 2t^2 + 50$ for $t = 0$, $t = 0.5$, $t = 1.0$, $t = 1.5$, etc., for all such values of t that yield a positive value of x.

One way of calculating the value of x for a particular value of t is to multiply t by 3, multiply t by t to obtain t^2, multiply t^2 by 2 to obtain $2t^2$, subtract $2t^2$ from $3t$, and add 50. This requires three multiplications, one subtraction, and one addition.

The number of multiplications could be reduced by writing the equation in the form

$$x = (-2t + 3)t + 50$$

The value of x may now be obtained by multiplying -2 by t, adding 3 to this product, multiplying this sum by t, and adding 50 to this product; two multiplications and two additions. This method of evaluating polynomials is called *nesting*.

The equation

$$x = 6t^5 + 4t^4 - 5t^3 - 3t^2 + 7t - 8$$

could be written as

$$x = (\{[(6t + 4)t - 5]t - 3\}t + 7)t - 8$$

Evaluation of this nested expression requires five multiplications and five additions or subtractions. Evaluation of the original expression without nesting would have required nine multiplications and five additions or subtractions.

Minimizing the number of arithmetic operations required—whether the operations are performed longhand, with a slide rule, on a desk calculator, or on an electronic digital computer—is always desirable.

Let us suppose that the clerk has a blackboard ruled in such a manner that its surface is divided into rectangles. Each of these rectangles has an identifying number printed in one of its corners. The clerk has been told that he must erase anything written in a rec-

3

tangle before he writes something new in it. We could hand the clerk one sheet of paper ruled in two columns and another sheet containing the following instructions:

1. Write 0.0 in the rectangle numbered 429.
2. Multiply the number in rectangle 429 by −2.0 and write the product in rectangle 430.
3. Add the number in rectangle 430 to 3.0 and write the sum in rectangle 431.
4. Multiply the number in rectangle 431 by the number in rectangle 429 and write the product in rectangle 432.
5. Add the number in rectangle 432 to 50.0 and write the sum in rectangle 433.
6. If the number in rectangle 433 is positive or zero, go to instruction 7; if this number is negative, go to instruction 10.
7. Put the numbers in rectangles 429 and 433 into columns 1 and 2 respectively of the first blank line of the two-column table on the piece of paper.
8. Go back to the blackboard, add 0.5 to the number in rectangle 429 and write the sum in rectangle 429. (Note that this instruction tells the clerk to replace the number in the rectangle by another number 0.5 larger than the number being replaced.)
9. Go back to instruction 2.
10. Bring the two-column table to my office and see if I have another job for you.

Such a series of instructions is known as a *program*.

Figure 1-1 shows the numbers that the clerk would write on the blackboard. Of course not more than one number would be written in any one rectangle at any one time. The final two-column table is not shown.

Follow the procedure given in the list of instructions to calculate the first several lines of the table to see how computations are carried out and that they yield the desired results. Note that if we omit instruction 6 the desired two-column table would never be brought to the office. If we went to the clerk's desk later on we might have found him calculating with $t = 328$ and obtaining $x = -214.134$; a result that has absolutely no application in

Rectangle 429	Rectangle 430	Rectangle 431	Rectangle 432	Rectangle 433
0.0	0.0	3.0	0.0	50.0
0.5	−1.0	2.0	1.0	51.0
1.0	−2.0	1.0	1.0	51.0
1.5	−3.0	0.0	0.0	50.0
2.0	−4.0	−1.0	−2.0	48.0
2.5	−5.0	−2.0	−5.0	45.0
3.0	−6.0	−3.0	−9.0	41.0
3.5	−7.0	−4.0	−14.0	36.0
4.0	−8.0	−5.0	−20.0	30.0
4.5	−9.0	−6.0	−27.0	23.0
5.0	−10.0	−7.0	−35.0	15.0
5.5	−11.0	−8.0	−44.0	6.0
6.0	−12.0	−9.0	−54.0	−4.0

FIG. 1-1.   Numbers on clerk's blackboard.

our problem. Thus some instruction should always be included that tells the clerk or the computer that this job is finished.

Going over these instructions, we find that it might have been desirable to give the clerk additional instructions as to how we wanted the numbers written. Should he write 50.0 or just 50? If the calculations had involved decimals (divide 45.658 by 2.3759) it might be necessary to tell him what precision is required in the calculations. We might give him special instructions for each job or standing instructions to carry all calculations to five significant figures unless specifically instructed otherwise.

Our clerk is very much like an electronic digital computer in that he is a "whiz" at arithmetic and follows the instructions to the letter. On the other hand, neither the clerk nor the computer has a very large vocabulary and has no understanding of higher mathematics. We could not give the clerk our problem in the form $x = 3t - 2t^2 + 50$, since he does not understand algebra. He and the computer follow the instructions exactly if they are written in a form that they can understand. If we try to shorten the list of instructions, however, by not including everything or lumping several steps into a more complex instruction, both the clerk and computer will be confused and will say "I don't know what this instruction means." We can't tell a computer "You know what I mean." We must always remember that the computer will do precisely what we tell it to and not what we "obviously meant."

The calculation which we asked the clerk to perform was very simple and required only one decision (instruction 6). Our clerk could perform much more complicated calculations involving many decisions if his instructions specifically informed him what to do in every eventuality. If instruction 6 had been

> 6. If the number in column 5 is positive, go to instruction 7; if this number is negative go to instruction 10.

he would have said, "I can't do this calculation because you haven't told me what to do if the number is zero." It does no good to tell him "The number will never be zero." since the meaning of this statement is not included in his limited vocabulary. We might say "Then add 'go to instruction 3 if this number is zero' to instruction 6." This procedure would of course have no meaning in the calculation, but since our clerk would never obtain zero for the number he would sit down with his list of instructions that now tell him what to do in every "possible" situation and happily carry out the assignment.

Suppose you wanted the value of x from the equation $x = 5 - 3t + 4t^3$ for the one value $t = 27$. Wouldn't it be more efficient to make the calculation yourself instead of writing out the detailed instructions for the clerk? Only when a set of instructions must be carried out many times is it desirable to have our clerk (or a digital computer) make the calculation.

1-2. Flow Charts

We have seen that before a computation is carried out we must break it down into small steps and decide the order in which the steps are to be performed. The problem that we looked at was so simple that it was easy to decide what steps were to be taken and in what order they should be made. Our thought processes may have included the following ideas. Before any calculations for a specific value of x can be made, one of the required values must be assigned to t. A value of x for a particular t must be found before it is known whether a larger value of t must be used.

The procedure to be followed in carrying out the calculations may be shown in a diagram called a *flow chart*. A flow chart for our problem is shown in Fig. 1-2.

Rectangular boxes are used on the flow charts to group segments of the procedure. All of the information necessary to make the calculations included in any one box must be available each and every time we reach the box in tracing out the process of computation. The information given in a box may be given in great detail or may only be briefly sum-

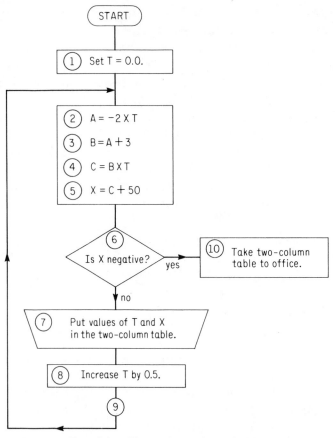

FIG. 1-2. Flow chart for clerk's
problem.

marized. Figure 1-2 specifically includes every one of the instructions that we wrote for the clerk. This is not necessary, and we might only say "Calculate X" in the second rectangular box in Fig. 1-2. On long and involved computations it is sometimes helpful to first lay out the computation procedure in very large segments and then later go back and tackle the boxes one at a time, making a detailed flow chart for each.

Trapezoids are often used for instructions pertaining to reading or writing. Such processes concerned with the transmission of information are referred to as *input* and *output* by computer programmers.

Diamond-shaped boxes are used where a question is asked. A properly labeled line must come from the diamond to show what procedure should be followed next for every possible answer to the question asked. Since the possible answers to the question "Is X negative?" are "yes" and "no" lines labeled "yes" and "no" come from the diamond containing this question in Fig. 1-2. One of the common tests made by a computer is to ask whether a quantity is negative, zero, or positive. This test is usually indicated on flow charts as shown in Fig. 1-3.

Fig. 1-3 asks the clerk or the computer to look at quantity Z and then to proceed to step 7 if the quantity is negative, to step 3 if the quantity is zero, or to step 9 if it is positive.

Flow diagrams are often used for planning many other procedures in addition to computation. The flow chart shown in Fig. 1-4 is an illustration of the decisions and procedures that a student (male) might follow on the doorstep of his girl's home after a date.

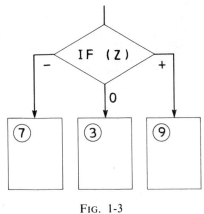

FIG. 1-3

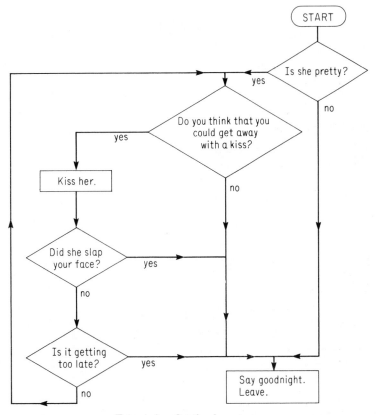

FIG. 1-4.   On the doorstep.

Some students might wish to follow a different flow chart, thinking that the test (Is she pretty?) and/or the test (Is it getting too late?) are not needed. Any other variations after the answer "No" to the question (Did she slap your face?) are left to the student.

1-3. INDEXES AND LOOPS

The following is a recipe for cooking an omelet.

Mix 3 eggs lightly with fork and add ½ teaspoon salt. Heat omelet pan over high heat and in it melt 1 teaspoon butter. Immediately pour in the eggs and stir them briskly with a fork, shaking the pan constantly. When the fork makes a visible track through the eggs, the omelet is set. As each omelet is cooked keep it warm in a slow oven (200°F) until the others are finished.

Since the eggs are broken one at a time, we want some way to count how many eggs have been used. This may be done by use of an "index." The quantity that we call J in Fig. 1-5 is used as an index.

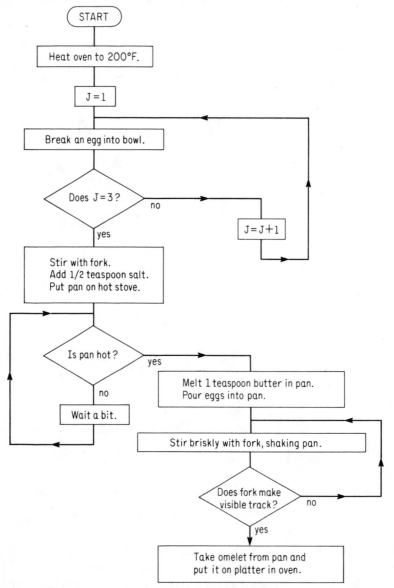

Fig. 1-5.   Cooking an omelet.

Since the instructions for breaking an egg, testing the value of J, and incrementing J are executed several times before any other instructions are carried out, we have created a loop. Note the difference between this loop and the series of instructions (Is the pan hot?) and (Wait a bit) or the series (Stir briskly with fork, shaking pan) and (Does fork make visible track?). These other series are also loops, but we have not preset the number of times that they will be carried out. The number of times depends on the results of the process just as the number of lines that the clerk had to calculate until he obtained a negative value of X depended on the results of the calculations.

Note the instruction $J = J + 1$. This is obviously not an algebraic equation, since there is no value of J for which J and $J + 1$ are equal. Here the "$=$" means replace. The instruction says take the value that J has had up until this instruction was reached, add one, and assign J this new value which it will retain until the next time an instruction is found that modifies the value of J.

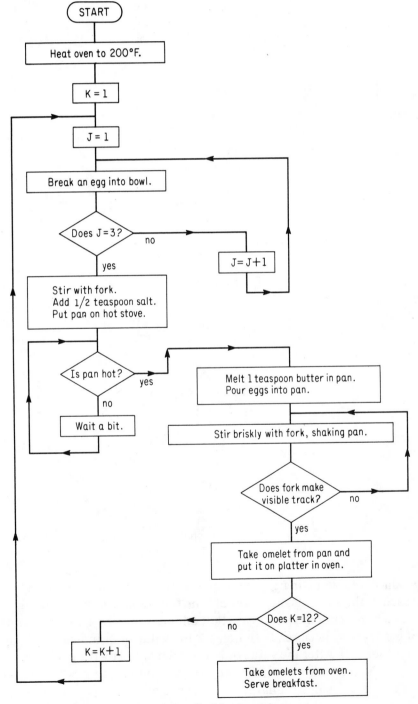

Fig. 1-6. Cooking breakfast.

Suppose the cook preparing omelets according to our flow chart wishes to serve breakfast to a large group and wishes to make twelve omelets. Another index such as K could be added to produce the flow chart shown in Fig. 1-6. This chart includes loops within a loop, called *nested loops*.

If an instructor has the table shown in Fig. 1-7 which contains the student identification number and three examination grades for each of the ten students in a class and

Student Identification Number	Grade Exam 1	Grade Exam 2	Grade Exam 3
1036	80	85	83
1076	57	60	62
1145	100	94	97
1189	79	82	74
1204	83	90	92
1233	47	39	50
1260	76	75	79
1348	92	100	100
1419	85	90	88
1523	65	69	64

FIG. 1-7

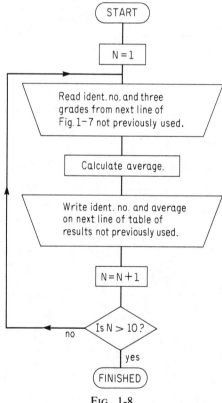

FIG. 1-8

wishes to produce a table giving the student identification number and the examination average for each of the students, he might use the flow diagram shown in Fig. 1-8.

There are a number of different ways that an index may be used to keep track of how many sets of grades have been read. In Fig. 1-8 the value of N indicates which row of Fig. 1-7 is being considered. After the value of N is incremented by the instruction N = N + 1, the new value of N will indicate which line is to be considered next. The index J in the flow diagram of Fig. 1-9 will be equal to the number of lines used only *after* the index has been incremented. Note that the tests to determine whether or not all lines have been

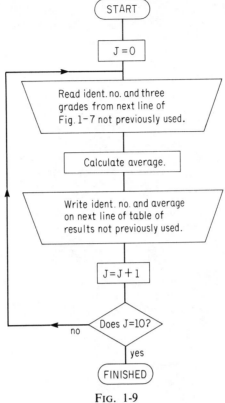

Fig. 1-9

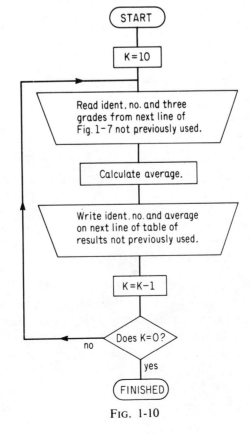

Fig. 1-10

read are different in Figs. 1-8 and 1-9. The flow diagram shown in Fig. 1-10 uses an index K that will be equal to the number of lines which are still to be read. Figure 1-11 shows a diagram that is similar to Fig. 1-8 except that the value of the index is tested *before* it is incremented.

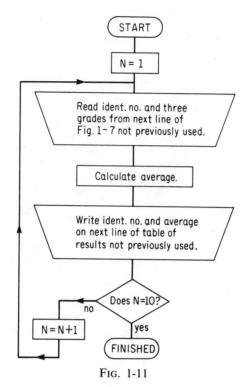

FIG. 1-11

PROBLEMS

1-1. The instructions on a can of frozen orange juice read:

> Empty contents of can into pitcher.
> Add three cans of cold water.
> Stir until well mixed.

Draw a flow diagram for this process.

1-2. A city government taxes incomes according to the following table.

Income	Tax
Less than $3,000.00	0
$3000.00 to $9,999.99	0.5%
$10,000.00 or more	$50.00 + 1% of income over $10,000.00

Draw a flow chart to calculate the tax on an income of X dollars.

1-3. A baseball player hits the ball so that the horizontal distance from the plate to the ball in feet is given by the equation $x = 80t$, where t is the time in seconds since the ball was hit. The height of the ball above the ground is given by the equation $y = 4 + 70t - 16.1t^2$. Draw a flow chart to produce a three-column table giving values of t, x, and y at $\frac{1}{2}$-sec intervals as long as the ball has not hit the ground (as long as y is greater than zero) or has not gone over the fence (x is less than 355 feet).

1-4. Write a set of instructions that the clerk may use to produce the table of t, x, and y described in Prob. 1-3.

1-5. Draw a flow chart for finding the value of $N!$ where N is a positive integer.

1-6. Write a set of instructions that the clerk may use to find the value of $N!$ where N is a positive integer.

1-7. Draw a flow chart to find the total amount of money in a piggy bank after deposits have been made in this bank for 30 days; one cent the first day, two additional cents the second day, four additional cents the third day, and so on for 30 days (the size of the deposit doubles each day).

1-8. In 1627 Manhattan Island was sold for the equivalent of \$24. Draw a flow chart to find what the bank balance would have been after the interest had been paid this year if that money had been placed in a bank with 4% interest compounded annually (first interest paid in 1628).

1-9. Write a set of instructions that the clerk may use to calculate the bank balance described in Prob. 1-8.

1-10. Draw a flow chart to calculate the first 30 values of y from the equation

$$y = 5x^3 + 7x^2 - 4x + 10$$

for $x = 0.0$, $x = 0.1$, $x = 0.2$, $x = 0.3$, etc. The output desired is a table of values of x and y.

1-11. The sine of an angle may be obtained from the series

$$\sin x = x - \frac{x^3}{3!} + \frac{x^5}{5!} - \frac{x^7}{7!} + \frac{x^9}{9!} - \cdots$$

where x is measured in radians. Draw a flow chart for a computation that uses the first five terms of this series to calculate the sine of 0.3 radian.

1-12. Draw a flow chart using the series in Prob. 1-11 to obtain a table of angles and sines of angles $0.1, 0.2, 0.3, 0.4, \ldots, 2.0$ radians. Use as many terms of the series as necessary to insure that the absolute value of the quantity obtained by dividing the last term used by the sum of the terms is less than 0.000001.

1-13. Draw a flow diagram to produce a table giving the diameter and area of circles with diameters of $5, 10, 15, 20, \ldots, 50$.

1-14. Draw a flow diagram to produce a table of x and y where $y = x + x^2$ for $x = 0.5$, $x = 1.0$, $x = 1.5$, $x = 2.0$, etc., for all such values of x that yield a value of y less than 120.

1-15. Draw a flow diagram to produce a table of q and p where $q = p^2$ if $p < 2.5$ and $q = p^2 - p$ if $p \geq 2.5$ for $p = 0.0$, $p = 0.5$, $p = 1.0$, $p = 1.5, \ldots, p = 6.0$.

CHAPTER 2

THE COMPUTER AND ITS LANGUAGE—FORTRAN

2-1. BINARY NUMBERS

Most of the devices used for storing numbers in digital computers have two possible conditions: a spot on a magnetic material may be either magnetized or not, a transistor is either in the "on" or "off" condition, the small doughnut-shaped magnets known as cores may be magnetized in either of two directions. Because of this duality, most electronic digital computers store numbers as binary numbers and execute arithmetic operations in a binary "mode." This should cause no difficulty to a student learning to program in FORTRAN, since the computer will accept "input" numbers in the decimal form and automatically convert them to binary numbers for storage and computation. The computer also automatically converts the answers back to a decimal form before printing them or punching them on cards. A slight knowledge of binary numbers is, however, helpful in understanding certain characteristics of computer operation.

The decimal system we usually use for writing numbers uses the ten decimal digits 0, 1, 2, 3, 4, 5, 6, 7, 8, and 9. When we write a number such as 372.6, we mean

$$3 \times 10^2 + 7 \times 10^1 + 2 \times 10^0 + 6 \times 10^{-1}$$

The binary system uses the two binary digits 0 and 1. The term "binary digit" is often shortened to "bit." The binary number 101.011 means

$$1 \times 2^2 + 0 \times 2^1 + 1 \times 2^0 + 0 \times 2^{-1} + 1 \times 2^{-2} + 1 \times 2^{-3}$$

and would be equal to the decimal number

$$4 + 1 + \tfrac{1}{4} + \tfrac{1}{8} = 5.375$$

2-2. THE COMPUTER MEMORY—THE STORAGE OF NUMBERS

One of the important parts of a computer is its memory, often called the *storage unit*. This memory takes the place of the blackboard the clerk used for his table. The main part of the memory in most computers is made up of thousands of small doughnut-shaped magnets known as *cores*. These cores are arranged in a rectangular pattern with wires strung through them in such a manner that any one wire goes through many cores and any one core has three wires through it. A positive pulse of electric current passed through two of the wires through a core causes this core to become magnetized in a certain direction. A negative pulse through the same wires causes magnetization in the opposite direction. These two states of magnetization are used to represent zero and one. The third wire through the core is used as a *sense wire* so that it is possible to tell which of the two magnetization states the core is in. A group of these cores is needed to hold one number and is called one "word" of storage.

Each of the numbered rectangles on the clerk's blackboard is known as a *word*. Suppose that each of these words is divided into ten small compartments. The clerk may write one sign (plus or minus) or one digit in each of these small compartments. There are several ways that the clerk may write (store) numbers on this blackboard. The simplest way is used for writing integer numbers (numbers that have no decimal part). The clerk is told to put a sign in the left compartment of each word and to write one digit in each of the other compartments filling all compartments with zeros that do not contain a sign or some other digit. Figure 2-1 shows some integer numbers written on the blackboard.

000	001	002
+ 0 0 0 0 0 5 7 2 8	− 0 0 0 0 0 0 0 0 7	+ 0 0 0 0 0 0 0 0 0
003	**004**	**005**
− 0 0 0 0 0 0 1 0 9	+ 8 6 5 4 3 0 2 0 8	− 0 0 3 2 5 0 7 4 1
006	**007**	**008**
− 0 0 0 9 8 0 9 3 2	− 5 0 3 7 0 2 5 1 4	+ 0 0 0 0 0 0 0 5 6
009	**010**	**011**
− 0 0 0 0 0 0 0 9 2	+ 0 0 0 0 9 3 4 5 3	− 0 0 0 0 0 0 1 4 4
012	**013**	**014**
+ 0 0 0 5 2 9 0 0 0	− 0 2 0 2 0 0 0 5 6	− 0 0 0 8 0 9 7 0 9

FIG. 2-1.   Integers on blackboard.

The integer numbers stored in words **000**, **001**, and **002** in Fig. 2-1 would of course be +5728, −7, and zero. The clerk would not be able to write any number in this table whose value is smaller than −999,999,999 or is larger than +999,999,999. The magnitude of the largest number that could be written on the blackboard of course depends on the number of small compartments in each word. If each word had been divided into six compartments the clerk would not have been able to write any number in the table whose value was smaller than −99,999 or was larger than +99,999.

Digital computers use a similar method for storing integer numbers. Most computers use one core to store a zero or a one and therefore store numbers in a binary form. The range permitted for the size of integer numbers depends on the number of cores used to store one word. The IBM 1130 computer can store integers from −32768 to +32767, while the NCR Century 100 is able to store numbers from −2,147,483,648 to +2,147,-483,647.

This method of storing numbers is simple but imposes several limitations on the numbers that can be stored. The limit on the magnitude of the numbers has already been mentioned. Another limitation is that numbers containing a fractional or decimal part may not be written on the clerk's blackboard or stored in the computer memory by this method.

Numbers that may be larger than this limit or may contain a decimal part are stored by a method similar to the so-called scientific notation. We may write the number 186,000 as 0.186×10^6. Similarly, 0.000567 could be written as 0.567×10^{-3}. The clerk could be told to convert a number to be stored by this method into a number between 0.1 and 1.0 times ten raised to the required integer power. He would then store the number by writing a sign in the first compartment of a word, writing the first six significant digits of the number in the next six compartments, the sign of the exponent in the next compartment, and two digits representing the exponent in the last two rectangles. It is not necessary for him to take space to write the "0." or the "× 10," since he is told that **—567000—03** means −0.567000 × 10⁻⁰³. Numbers stored in this manner are called *real numbers*. Note that the term "real" when used in conjunction with computers does not refer to the absence of imaginary quantities, but refers to a method of storing numbers that may contain decimal parts. A section of the clerk's blackboard using this notation is shown in Fig. 2-2.

015	016	017
+|5|6|7|0|0|0|-|0|3	+|2|7|9|5|6|4|+|0|5	+|1|8|6|0|0|0|+|1|2
018	**019**	**020**
-|9|2|8|3|0|7|-|1|1	+|5|0|0|0|0|0|+|0|0	+|3|6|0|9|7|1|-|0|2
021	**022**	**023**
-|5|2|5|8|0|0|+|0|8	+|6|3|2|7|0|0|+|0|9	-|5|2|5|3|0|0|+|0|1
024	**025**	**026**
+|3|1|4|1|5|9|+|0|1	-|9|3|5|2|0|0|+|0|3	-|6|2|6|0|0|0|-|0|1
027	**028**	**029**
+|5|2|8|0|0|0|+|0|4	+|3|1|7|4|5|9|-|0|6	+|5|0|0|0|0|0|+|1|3

FIG. 2-2.   Real numbers on blackboard.

The number in word **022** of Fig. 2-2 represents the real number

$$+0.632700 \times 10^9 = 632,700,000$$

and the number in word **028** represents

$$+0.317459 \times 10^{-6} = 0.000000317459$$

The number of significant digits that may be stored for each number is limited by the number of compartments provided in the table. If we asked the clerk to write a number on his blackboard equal to

$$3.1415926536$$

he would have to write

$$+314159+01$$

as shown in word **024** of Fig. 2-2 and represents the number

$$+0.314159 \times 10^1 = +3.14159$$

He could not store more than six significant digits for any one number.

Electronic digital computers store real numbers in a very similar manner except that in most computers both the number and the exponent are stored in a binary form. The number of significant digits in the number and the maximum size of exponent depend upon the number of cores provided in the memory to store these items. The IBM System/360 permits numbers to be stored with approximately seven significant decimal digits (it is *approximately* seven, not *exactly* seven, since the numbers are stored using a specific number of binary digits and not a specific number of decimal digits). This permits the storage of a real number equal to zero or a number whose absolute value is not greater than 10^{75} or less than 10^{-79}.

Different computers have different size memories. There are some small computers that contain enough cores to hold 16,384 words. Slightly larger computers may have 32,768 word memories. Many computers permit additional memory to be added at additional cost. Usually these additions are in multiples of 16,384 words. These numbers may sound strange to students who are used to thinking in terms of decimal numbers. Numbers such as 1,000 or 100,000 may seem more logical to these students since 1,000 is equal to 10^3 and 100,000 is equal to 10^5. The logic of the computer is based on binary numbers and 2^{14} and 2^{15} are equal to 16,384 and 32,768 respectively. These sizes are often shortened to 16K and 32K respectively.

The group of cores that hold one word each are numbered **00000, 00001, 00002, 00003**, etc., and these numbers are called *addresses*. We refer to words by giving their "address." We can instruct the computer to multiply the number in location **00028** by the number in location **03025** and put the result in location **12067**.

The cost of such core storage has greatly decreased as mass production methods have been developed, but such storage remains one of the most expensive parts of the computer. There are several different types of *mass storage* devices used that cost less than core storage. We may think of the clerk having several filing cabinets full of papers covered with numbers. It takes the clerk a much longer time to look up a number or to write a new number using these pages than to read or write a number on his blackboard, but the filing cabinets will hold millions of numbers while he has room on his blackboard for only several thousand. This mass storage is sometimes known as *auxiliary memory*.

This auxiliary memory is provided in some computers by the use of one or more disk cartridges that usually provide additional storage of over a half-million words each. A disk is like a heavy phonograph record that rotates at 1,500 revolutions per minute. As the disk rotates, access arms move radially across the top and bottom of the disk in order to read or write the information which is stored as magnetized spots in the thin metallic coating on the surface of the disk. A very large amount of information may be written on or read from the disk in a fraction of a second. Access to information on the disk is, however, much slower than access to information in the core storage. The spelling of this term has not been standardized in the computer industry, one computer manufacturer using the spelling *disk* where another uses *disc*.

Magnetic-tape units are often used for mass storage. A plastic tape with a ferrous oxide coating passes over a read-write head as it is wound from one reel to another. The information is stored on the tape in the form of magnetized bands in the ferrous oxide.

2-3. OTHER PARTS OF THE COMPUTER

ARITHMETIC UNIT

The computer has a unit, called an *arithmetic unit*, consisting of electronic circuits. This unit unit is wired so that it is able to perform simple arithmetic operations such as addition or multiplication. This is analogous to the desk calculator that the clerk may be using to work the problem.

INPUT-OUTPUT DEVICES

Data and instructions must be put into the computer and the results gotten out. We may think of the information on the pieces of paper we hand to the clerk as the input and the pencil and paper the clerk uses to make the final two-column table as the output device.

There are a number of input-output devices (often called I/O devices) used on a computer. Most often information is read into the computer by a card reader. A punched card is fed into the card reader, and as the card passes the "read station" the location of the punched holes in the card is sensed by the card reader, and the information contained on the card is fed into the memory. Modern card readers use photoelectric cells to sense light rays passing through the punched holes. Older card readers used wire brushes that electrically sensed the punched holes.

The results of the computation (the output) are usually "printed out" by a printer onto a continuous sheet of paper. Sometimes a card punch is used to punch the output information into cards.

Almost all computers have a typewriter keyboard electrically connected to the computer; information may be entered directly from this keyboard, or the computer may be instructed to type the output on a sheet of paper in the typewriter. This typewriter is much slower than the card reader or the printer and is used only when very small amounts of information are to be fed in or read out.

Some small computers use a narrow strip of punched paper tape for the primary input and output. The input tape must first be punched by the use of a special typewriter, and the output tape must be run through a typewriter to obtain the results on a piece of paper.

Some of the larger computers use magnetic-tape devices for input and output in addition to using them as auxilliary memory.

THE CONTROL UNIT

The clerk himself had to decide which rectangle was referred to and had to keep track of which instruction on the list was to be executed next. The control unit in the computer has these functions. The instructions are stored in the memory of the computer. The control unit "looks" at an instruction, tells the arithmetic unit what operation to perform, locates the information required from memory, and locates the next instruction to be executed. The control unit executes the instructions in the order in which they are stored in the memory unless an instruction gives an out of order address for the next instruction.

THE ACCUMULATOR

In order to multiply two numbers on a desk calculator the clerk would first have to enter the first number into the calculator and then perform the multiplication by the other number. The product would appear in a register of the calculator. The arithmetic unit of the computer contains a register called the *accumulator* to perform this function.

2-4. MACHINE LANGUAGE

It is not necessary to completely understand the internal workings of a digital computer to make use of it, just as it is not necessary to understand thermodynamics and mechanics to drive an automobile. Some knowledge, while not necessary, is helpful. The driver must know that turning the steering wheel causes the car to turn; it is helpful for him to know that the steering wheel turns the front wheels.

The concepts of machine language and symbolic language are briefly presented here to give the student a useful background.

We have seen that the instructions for the computer are stored in the memory of the computer, interpreted by the control unit, and usually executed by the arithmetic unit. Since the instructions are stored in the memory they must be coded as numbers. In many computers the first several digits or bits of a word that is to represent an instruction are coded to give the operation and the remaining digits or bits refer to an address. Let us imagine that we have a computer that has a memory of one thousand words. The addresses of these words would be $000, 001, 002, \ldots, 999$. We might have the computer use the operation codes given in Table 2-1.

TABLE 2-1   Operation Codes

Code	Operation	Meaning
16	Add	Add the number stored at the address given to the number in the accumulator; put sum in accumulator.
18	Subtract	Subtract the number stored at the address given from the number in the accumulator; put difference in accumulator.
20	Multiply	Multiply the number in the accumulator by the number stored at the address given; put product in accumulator.
21	Divide	Divide the number in the accumulator by the number stored at the address given; put the quotient in accumulator.
24	Load	Load the number stored at address given into the accumulator.
26	Store	Store the number in the accumulator in the address given.

Any actual computer would have a larger number of operation codes (some computers may have as many as 150 different operation codes), and these codes differ from one computer to another.

The following instructions would be required by our imaginary computer in order to add the number in location **028** to the number in location **194** and put the sum in location **035**. Such a group of instructions is called a *program*.

Code	Address
24	**194**
16	**028**
26	**035**

These three instructions might be stored in the memory of the computer as five-digit numbers (**24194**, **16028**, and **26035**) at addresses **007**, **008**, and **009**. We would have to give an instruction to the computer that causes it to start computation with the instruction at address **007**.

2-5. Symbolic Machine Languages—Assembly Programs

Our original problem may have included the formula $X = Y + Z$. We could have used the program given above to make this calculation if the preceding portion of our program had stored the values of **Y** and **Z** in locations **194** and **028**. We would then remember that **X** will be stored in **035** when we need it later in the program. We might have found it easier to first write the program using letters instead of digits in the instructions.

Code	Address
LD	**Y**
A	**Z**
STO	**X**

Such a program that uses alphabetic symbols to stand for numbers is called a *symbolic program*.

We could give this type of program to the clerk and tell him to translate our symbolic machine program into a machine-language program. He would be told to write **24** in the operation code part of the instruction every time he found **LD** in this portion on our program, write **16** when he found **A**, etc., and to assign an unused numerical address in the place of a letter in the address part of the instruction, being sure to assign the same address to any one symbol no matter how often it appeared in the address column. If we wished to multiply a number by **X** later on in the program, the instruction:

Code	Address
M	**X**

would have to be translated as

Code	Address
20	**035**

so that **X** would have the same address **(035)** in the **(STO X)** instruction and the **(M X)** instruction.

Since the job of translating a symbolic program into a machine-language program consists of recognizing certain letter symbols and substituting certain numerical symbols for them in a predefined systematic way, a clerk could easily be given the instructions required to carry out this translation even if he did not know what **LD** or **24** meant. In practice a program is written for a computer that uses the symbolic program as input and produces the machine language program as output. Such a program is known as an *assembly program* and is usually written and supplied by the manufacturer of the computer as "software."

Each of the assembly programs has a list of the instructions that the computer is wired to perform together with the *mnemonic symbols* to be used for each instruction. Mnemonic symbols or mnemonics are names that suggest the meaning of a quantity or the function of the instruction. Thus if what we were calculating were a payroll, we could use the symbols **PY = RT X HRS**, where **PY** stands for pay, **RT** for rate, and **HRS** for the number of hours worked. The **LD** that we used for the operation "load the accumulator" is a mnemonic for load. Different computers are wired to perform a different list of instructions, and the assembly programs are written by different programmers. Therefore the form that must be followed in the writing of a symbolic program must conform to that prescribed by the assembly program written for the particular computer on which it is to be used. The mnemonic "A" used for add in the example above is used in the assembly programs for some computers, while the assembly programs for other computers may use "AD" or "ADD" for the same instruction.

2-6. FORTRAN

The original problem given in Sec. 1-1 could be solved by writing a machine-language program and running it on the computer or by writing a program in a symbolic machine language, having this program translated by the computer into a machine-language program, and finally running this program on the computer. Either of these procedures would involve writing the instructions in a form rigidly specified for the particular computer to be used. A program written in either language for the IBM 1130 could not be run on the General Electric 635, or even on the IBM 7090. A programmer who knows how to program for one computer would have to learn a new language in order to program in machine language for a different computer. A programming language that could be used on a number of different computers would be very useful.

It would also be helpful if there were a language available that could understand instructions for more complicated operations written in a form similar to the original statement of the problem. It would have been a great help if our clerk understood what the equation $x = 3t - 2t^2 + 50$ meant. Several languages have been devised that can be used on many different computers and will accept instructions similar to the equations and formulas that mathematicians, scientists, and engineers are used to using. One of the most widely used languages is called FORTRAN. The name FORTRAN comes from the name FORmula TRANslation. There are several different FORTRAN languages, the latest being FORTRAN IV. The FORTRAN IV languages used on different computers are not completely identical, since the FORTRAN compiler—the program that translates the program written in a FORTRAN language into a machine-language program—must consider the limitations caused by the special characteristics of the particular computer on which the machine-language program is to be run. The differences between the FORTRAN languages used by different computers are slight. A programmer who knows FORTRAN IV for one computer would be able to learn these differences very easily and be able to write a FORTRAN IV program for another computer after a small amount of study.

The expression "running a FORTRAN program on a computer" is often used. This is not really correct. A FORTRAN program is loaded into the computer and translated into a machine-language program by use of a program called a FORTRAN compiler, and this machine-language program is then run on the computer.

The term FORTRAN IV is usually shortened to FORTRAN, and the term FORTRAN as used in this book will refer to FORTRAN IV unless otherwise specified.

PROBLEMS

2-1. Write all the real numbers represented in Fig. 2-2. Write both forms for the numbers as they are written for words **022** and **028** following the figure.

2-2. Show how the clerk would write numbers equal to the following in a table similar to Fig. 2-2.

5.287 in **030**	−829.2 in **031**	−0.003208 in **032**
28.92 in **033**	5028.01 in **034**	64.021 in **035**
−0.007 in **036**	−60.37 in **037**	0.000092 in **038**

2-3–2-12. Write a program using the machine language given in Sec. 2-4 to calculate the value of the expression given and store the result in the location specified. Assume that the values of the variables used in the expressions have already been stored in the following locations.

Variable	Location
U	059
V	128
W	129
X	260
Y	412
Z	677

Use the location in which the result is to be stored and/or location **999** for temporary storage when intermediate results must be stored.

2-3.	$X - Y$	Result in **028**
2-4.	$W + Z$	Result in **099**
2-5.	$V(U - Z)$	Result in **113**
2-6.	$Z(X^2 - Y)$	Result in **154**
2-7.	$\dfrac{(X - Y)}{(W + Z)} - U$	Result in **200**
2-8.	$\dfrac{(U - V)(W + X)}{Z}$	Result in **230**
2-9.	$V(X^2 - YZ)$	Result in **281**
2-10.	$\dfrac{(X - Y)}{(W + Z)} - \dfrac{U}{V}$	Result in **319**
2-11.	$\dfrac{(Z - W)}{X} + \dfrac{(Z - Y)}{(W + U)}$	Result in **512**
2-12.	$X^2 - XY + UVW$	Result in **690**

2-13–2-18. Write a program using the symbolic machine language discussed in Sec. 2-5 to calculate the value of the expression given on the right-hand side of the equals sign in the formula given and store the result in the location specified by the letter on the left-hand side of the equals sign. Assume that values for all the variables on the right-hand side have already been stored in memory. Use the location in which the result is to be stored and/or location **T** for temporary storage when intermediate results must be stored. Use the following mnemonic codes for the operations.

A	add
S	subtract
M	multiply
D	divide
LD	load
STO	store

2-13.	$A = B - C$
2-14.	$D = E(F + G)$
2-15.	$P = Q(R^2 - S)$
2-16.	$U = \dfrac{(B - C)}{(E + G)}$
2-17.	$V = \dfrac{(Q - R)}{S} + \dfrac{(E + F)}{(R - Q)}$
2-18.	$W = \dfrac{(Q + R)(B - C)}{(G - F)} + \dfrac{Q}{S}$

CHAPTER 3

CONSTANTS, VARIABLES, AND ARITHMETIC STATEMENTS

3-1. CONSTANTS

Computer programs (or any calculations) generally include both constants and variables. The term *variable* is used in FORTRAN to denote any quantity that is refered to by name and whose value may be changed. In the equation

$$x = 4.3y + 2.5$$

x and y are variables and 4.3 and 2.5 are constants.

The value of each constant or variable is a number and is stored in a specific location in the computer. The computer must be told which of these numbers are to be stored as "integer numbers" and which as "real numbers."

When the clerk finds a number in his instructions written without a decimal point

+73

he writes this number on his blackboard as an integer number as he did in Fig. 2-1.

+000000073

A constant that is to be stored as an integer is written as a number without a decimal point. Commas are not permitted within any FORTRAN constants. A preceding plus sign is optional for positive numbers—any unsigned constant is assumed to be positive.

The following examples are valid integer constants.

```
      0
     57
 -21254
  +684
```

The following are *not* valid integer constants.

```
    5.3  (contains a decimal point)
    47.  (contains a decimal point)
  5,280  (contains a comma)
8000000000  (too large for most computers)
```

Remember that the maximum size permitted for an integer number to be stored in memory depends on the specific computer being used. The number

54692

would be a valid integer constant if used on the IBM 360 but would be invalid on the IBM 1130 since it is larger than the 32767 limit for this computer.

When the clerk finds a number written with a decimal point

$$+73.$$

he converts it to a number between 0.1 and 1.0 times ten raised to a power

$$+73. = +0.73 \times 10^2$$

and writes the constant as a real number storing the number and the exponent in the form he used in Fig. 2-2.

$$+730000+02$$

Any constant in a FORTRAN program that is written as a number containing a decimal point is stored as a real number by the computer. In some other versions of FORTRAN integer is called *fixed-point* and real is called *floating-point*.

The clerk knows that when he sees a letter E with a real number he is to read the E as "times ten to the." He would read

$$+73.2E+02$$

as $+73.2$ times ten to the 2nd power, convert the number

$$+73.2 \times 10^2 = +0.732 \times 10^4$$

and write

$$+732000+04$$

This form used in FORTRAN is called E format and is written as a number including a decimal point followed by the letter E and a one- or two-digit integer constant (signed or unsigned without a decimal point) indicating the power of 10. For example, 0.0000528 could be written **5.28E-5** (showing that the number is equal to 5.28×10^{-5}). This same constant could be written in many different ways; for example

$$0.0000528$$
$$.0000528$$
$$+0.0000528$$
$$0.528E-4$$
$$.5280E-04$$
$$+52.8E-6$$

are all valid ways of writing the same constant. The clerk would see that any of these numbers could be converted to the form

$$+0.528 \times 10^{-4}$$

and would put

$$+528000-04$$

on his blackboard regardless of which of the above forms was used in the FORTRAN program.

The following are valid examples of other real constants.

$$2.067$$
$$3.1416$$
$$-584.$$
$$0.0$$
$$0.$$
$$-57.6E05$$
$$+.789403E+6$$
$$2.E-18$$

The following are *not* valid real constants.

    573   (no decimal point; however this is a valid integer constant)
    573E06   (no decimal point—not accepted by most computers)
    5.0E003   (exponent contains three digits)
    5.3E4.0   (decimal not permitted in exponent)
    E-23   (the letter E must be preceded by a real number)
    5.2E87   (too large for most computers)

The FORTRAN compiler, the program that uses the FORTRAN instructions as input and produces machine-language instructions as output, converts the constants written in the FORTRAN program to the binary equivalents of the forms used by the clerk for storage in the memory.

3-2. Variables

The variable names used in FORTRAN consist of one or more alphameric characters, the first of which must be alphabetic. The term *alphameric characters* refers to the 26 letters of the alphabet and the digits **0, 1, 2, 3, 4, 5, 6, 7, 8,** and **9**. Only capital letters may be used, since there are no lowercase letters on the keypunch, console typewriter, or the printer. Several of the smallest computers permit variable names with a maximum of five characters, many computers have a maximum of six characters, and a few permit a larger number of characters. The variable name may therefore be one letter, or one letter followed by one or more characters any one of which may be either a letter or a digit. Some examples of valid variable names are

X,A,B2,BETA,NEXT,X5B42,GG24G,ETC

It is often helpful to use mnemonic variable names—names that remind us what the variable stands for. **BETA** and **NEXT** in the examples might be mnemonic names. Names such as **RATE1**, **RATE2**, and **RATE3** could be used; **X2Y** could be used for the name of a variable that is equal to x^2y. Superscripts and subscripts may not be used in variable names, and special characters such as periods, commas, apostrophes, or parentheses may not be used in variable names. Imbedded blanks (blanks occurring anywhere between the first and last characters) may not be included in many versions of FORTRAN.

The computer will assign a storage location in its memory for each different variable name used in a program. A number that represents the value of the variable is stored in this location. The first character in the variable name tells the computer whether the number is to be stored as a real or integer number. If the first character of the variable name is **I, J, K, L, M,** or **N** the variable is an integer variable and any number stored in its location will be stored as an integer number. If the first character of the variable name is *not* **I, J, K, L, M,** or **N** the variable is a real variable and any number stored in its location will be real. For example, **NEXT, I, JABE, NUTS, N63** and **MR2X** would be names of integer variables, and **X, A, B2, BETA, X5N42, RATE,** and **ETC** would be names of real variables.

The following are *not* valid variable names.

    3XAR   (does not begin with a letter)
    RAYMOND   (too many characters for many computers)
    RT+3F   (contains a character other than a letter or digit)

3-3. WRITING CHARACTERS

Since digits and letters are used together, the programmer must be sure to print his characters so that there is no trouble in distinguishing between these characters. Suppose a programmer wrote a variable name as

$$X10$$

A keypunch operator or the programmer himself, after a period of time, might wonder if the last two characters are letters or numerals. Different keys on the keypunch and console typewriter are used for the letter I and the numberal 1. The usual method when writing by hand is

Letter I Numeral 1

There are several different methods used to differentiate between the letter **O** and zero. This book will use the following:

Letter $\emptyset$ Numeral 0

This method is used by many computer installations, but other installations slash the numeral, and some underline the alphabetic O. The programmer must be aware of the system used at the particular installation where he is working.

Another pair of characters that may cause confusion are Z and 2, particularly with careless handwriting. A cross bar is sometimes made on the letter Z to avoid confusion.

Letter Z Numeral 2

3-4. ARITHMETIC STATEMENTS

A FORTRAN program is made up of *statements*, each of which is either an order to carry out some particular operation or a source of information about the program. The most common statement is the *arithmetic statement* sometimes called an *assignment statement*. This is of the form $a = b$, where a is the name of a variable written without a sign, and b is an expression that may include constants, variable names, and operation symbols.

The simplest arithmetic statement consists of a variable name, an equals sign, and a constant. For example,

J = 5

is a statement which tells the computer to replace any number that is stored in a location called **J** with a number five. **J** is one of the letters used for integer variable names. Therefore any number stored in **J** must be stored in integer form. The execution of the statement

J = 5

would result in the integer **5** being stored in location **J**.

The statement

XM7 = 4.63

tells the computer to replace any number that is stored in **XM7** by the real number **4.63**.

Since **X** is not one of the letters used to indicate integer variable names, only real numbers may be stored in **XM7**.

The statement

    XM7=4

is a valid statement, but the statement

    XM7=4.

or the statement

    XM7=4.0

is much preferred. Remember that a constant written without a decimal point is considered to be an integer constant by the computer, therefore the statement

    XM7=4

would require the computer to convert the integer **4** into a real number **4.0** before it could be stored in **XM7**. Think of the clerk having to convert his integer number **+000000004** to the real form **+400000+01** before he could write it into location **XM7**.

Similarly, the statement

    J=5.0

is permitted, but would require the computer to convert the real number **5.0** into the integer number **5** before it could be stored in location **J**. Note that the number will be stored in a mode (integer or real) indicated by the variable name and not by the mode of the constant.

Since integer numbers may not contain decimal parts, the statement

    KZ=6.25

would result in the integer number **6** being stored. The statement

    NEXT=2.99

would store the integer number **2** in location **NEXT**. The statement

    L=0.95872

would store the integer number zero in location **L**.

The conversion of a real number into an integer number truncates the number by cutting off the decimal part and does not round to the nearest integer.

The **E** format is permitted for real numbers:

    WET=-5.97E-16

is a valid arithmetic statement.

Another simple type of arithmetic statement consists of a variable name, an equals sign, and another variable name.

    CAR=AUTO

would cause the real number stored in **AUTØ** to be stored in **CAR** and would leave the number stored in **AUTØ** unchanged.

Remember that this is not an equation. The arithmetic statement

    AUTO=CAR

is not equivalent to the statement

CAR=AUTO

If **4.56** were stored in **CAR** and **−.97** stored in **AUTØ,** the execution of the statement

CAR=AUTO

would leave **−0.97** stored in both **CAR** and **AUTØ,** while the statement

AUTO=CAR

would leave **4.56** in both locations.

A statement such as

RATE=JOKE

is often used to obtain a real number numerically equal to an integer number. A statement of the type

JOKE=RATE

is valid but is less often used, and the programmer must be aware that the real number stored in **RATE** will be unchanged by the execution of this statement but that the integer number stored in **JØKE** will be truncated and will not be numerically equal to the original number if the original number had a decimal part.

Only a single variable name may appear on the left-hand side of the equals sign in an arithmetic statement, but any number of variable names and/or constants may be combined on the right side by use of operation symbols. The plus sign (+) and the negative sign (−) have the same meanings in FORTRAN that they have in ordinary algebra. The statement

FOOD=MUSH+MILK

tells the computer to add the integer numbers found in locations **MUSH** and **MILK** and store the sum in location **FØØD** (in this case the sum would have to be converted to a real number for storage). Some other valid examples of this type of statement are

```
X = Z − Y
R5 = R4 − R3
I = J + K
P = 7.16 − S
W8J = −R
Z = W + 4.987ε2
J = J + 1
```

The last statement in the list was mentioned in Sec. 1-3. This statement tells the computer to take the integer number stored in location **J,** add one, and store this new integer number in **J.**

In all arithmetic statements the only number in storage changed by the execution of the statement is the number indicated by the variable name on the left of the equals sign. All other variables on the right-hand side of the equals sign remain unchanged. The clerk may read a number from his blackboard and use it in a calculation without erasing, but he must erase a number before he can write a new number in a space that he had already used.

Multiplication in FORTRAN is indicated by an asterisk (∗). The statement

X2=RED∗TX

tells the computer to multiply the number in location **RED** by the number in location **TX** and store the product at location **X2**. The following statements are valid examples of arithmetic statements

```
M2=N7*L
BIG=TALL*WIDE
X=5.4*Z
ZAPP=-5.97*YEGG
J=J*7
```

Multiplication in a FORTRAN arithmetic statement must always be indicated by the asterisk. We may write an algebraic[1] multiplication with or without a symbol for the multiplication

$$k = 7 \times m$$

or

$$k = 7 \cdot m$$

or

$$k = 7m$$

The FORTRAN arithmetic statement used to carry out this multiplication *must* contain the multiplication symbol (*)

```
K=7*M
```

The statement

```
K=7M
```

would *not* be a valid FORTRAN arithmetic statement. The compiler would think that **7M** was supposed to be a variable name and would give an error indication since the first character in a variable name may not be numeric. A programmer might think that he could get around this by

```
K=M7
```

But this statement only tells the computer to find a number in location **M7** and to store this number in location **K**. No multiplication would be performed.

Division in FORTRAN is indicated by a slash (/). The statement

```
RT5=X/YL
```

tells the computer to divide the number stored in location **X** by the number stored at **YL** and to store the quotient at **RT5**. The following statements are valid examples of arithmetic statements

```
G6=.924E-4/Y
J=560/K
W=W/X
DIA=CIR/3.1416
```

Two asterisks (**) are used in FORTRAN arithmetic statements to indicate exponentiation. The statement

```
Z=X**Y
```

[1]Algebraic formulas and expressions are set in lowercase italic letters in this book and FORTRAN statements and expressions are set in roman capital letters.

tells the computer to raise the number in location **X** to a power given by the number stored in **Y** and to store the result in location **Z**—in other words, to set **Z** equal to **X**^{Y}.

```
J=M**2
```

tells the computer to square the number stored in **M** and to store the result in **J**. Other examples of exponentiation are

```
X=2.54**Z
R=Z**J
BIG=.9867**DAB
```

The combination of constants, variable names, and operation symbols on the right of the equal sign is known as an *arithmetic expression*. An arithmetic expression may contain many constants, variable names, and operation symbols

```
Z=X-Y*R+Y**3-W/X
```

is a valid arithmetic statement equivalent to the algebraic equation

$$z = x - y \cdot r + y^3 - \frac{w}{x}$$

The five arithmetic operation symbols and their meanings are

Symbol	Operation
+	Addition
−	Subtraction
*	Multiplication
/	Division
**	Exponentiation (or the process of raising a number to a power)

The operations called for in an arithmetic expression are carried out according to a specific hierarchy. Exponentiations are given the highest preference—all exponentiations in an expression are carried out before any other operations are performed. When more than one exponentiation appears in an expression they are carried out in the order that they appear from left to right. Multiplications and divisions are both given the second level of preference and are all carried out after every exponentiation has been completed but before any additions or subtractions. Additions and subtractions are thus given the lowest level and are not carried out until all other operations have been performed.

The leftmost exponentiation would thus be the first operation performed followed in order by the other exponentiations from left to right. Next the leftmost multiplication or division would be performed followed by the remaining multiplications and divisions in the order in which they appear. Finally all additions and subtractions are carried out from left to right. Note that multiplications and divisions are given the same preference. The multiplication would be performed first and the division second in the statement

```
Q=R*S/T
```

which is equivalent to the algebraic

$$q = \frac{rs}{t}$$

This left-to-right preference would cause the division in the statement

W=X/Y*Z

to be performed before the multiplication giving the equivalent of

$$w = \frac{x}{y} z$$

Thus the expression

X-Y*R+Y**3-W/X

would be evaluated in the following order:

> **Y** would be cubed
> **Y** would be multiplied **R**
> **W** would be divided by **X**
> **Y** times **R** would be subtracted from **X**
> **Y**^{3} would be added to this difference
> **W/X** would be subtracted from this sum

Parentheses may be used in arithmetic expressions, as in algebra, if some other order than that given above is required. For example, the algebraic expression

$$\frac{a + b}{c + d}$$

would be evaluated by the FORTRAN arithmetic expression

(A+B)/(C+D)

The algebraic expression

$$a + \frac{b}{c} + d$$

would require the FORTRAN expression

A+B/C+D

Any number of pairs of parentheses may be used in a FORTRAN expression, but they must appear in *pairs*—each use of a left parenthesis "(" must be balanced by the use of a right parenthesis ")" and vice versa. For example,

(A*(B-C)

is not valid because of the unbalanced parenthesis.

Extra parentheses that do not change the normal order of the operations are permitted as long as they are balanced in pairs. The expression

W*X+Y*Z

and

(W*X)+(Y*Z)

would be equivalent in that they would cause the computer to perform the same operations in the same order. Beginning programmers usually use more parentheses than are used by experienced programmers. It is reasonable for the beginner to use parentheses in a place where he is not sure if they are needed, since they will cause no error if not needed.

If a beginning programmer wished to write a FORTRAN arithmetic expression to evaluate the algebraic expression

$$\frac{a \cdot b}{c \cdot d}$$

he might note that the expression

A*B/C*D

would not give the desired result, because the prescribed order of operations would be: Multiple A by B, divide this result by C, multiply this result by D. The final result would be equivalent to the evaluation of the algebraic expression

$$\left(\frac{a \cdot b}{c}\right) d$$

The beginner might therefore write the expression as

(A*B)/(C*D)

which would give the correct result. An experienced programmer would probably write

A*B/(C*D)

which would give the same result.

When sets of parentheses are completely contained within another set of parentheses, they are called *nested parentheses*. The operations required within the innermost set of parentheses would be performed first in the prescribed order, then the result of this evaluation would be treated as a single quantity as the operations in the next outward set of parentheses were performed. This procedure would be continued until all operations contained in a set of parentheses had been performed, and finally the operations not contained in any parentheses would be performed in the usual order. For example,

$$\frac{t^{(y-z)} + \dfrac{r}{s}}{\dfrac{a}{b} + \dfrac{c}{d}}$$

would require the FORTRAN arithmetic expression

(T**(Y-Z)+R/S)/(A/B+C/D)

Multiplication in FORTRAN is *not* implied by parentheses. The arithmetic expressions

A(B-C)

and

(A-B)(C+D)

are incorrect in FORTRAN. An asterisk is always needed to indicate multiplication.

A*(B-C)
(A-B)*(C+D)

The algebraic formula

$$x = (\{[(6t + 4)t - 5]t - 3\}t + 7)t - 8$$

given in Sec. 1-1 could be written as the FORTRAN statement

$$X=((((6.*T+4.)*T-5.)*T-3.)*T+7.)*T-8.$$

The algebraic formula was written using several sequences of parentheses, brackets, and braces ({[(, to help the reader recognize the pairs. This cannot be done in FORTRAN since the keypunch and printer have only one type of group symbols, ( ). Pairs of parentheses must be recognized by their positions in the expression.

Two operation symbols must not appear together.

$$Y*-Z$$

is not a valid expression, but

$$Y*(-Z)$$

is.

If all the variable names in an arithmetic expression are names of integer variables (names starting with the letters **I, J, K, L, M,** or **N**) and all the constants are integer constants (constants written without decimals), the expression is said to be in the *integer mode*. The results of all operations will be integers.

Remember that the term *expression* refers to the part of an *arithmetic statement* that is to the right of the equals sign. The expression

$$(A-B)*(C+D)$$

is part of the arithmetic statement

$$X=(A-B)*(C+D)$$

The integer mode is used primarily for counting operations; most computations are made in the real mode because of the limitations placed on integer numbers. Integer numbers may not contain decimal parts and are more limited in magnitude than real numbers. The operations performed in the evaluation of integer expressions will be done in integer mode, and the results of these operations will be integer numbers. Particular care must be taken if division is made in the integer mode. The evaluation of the expression

$$J/3$$

would yield an integer result that would only be equal to one third **J** if **J** were evenly divisible by three. If **J** were equal to **8**, the results would be truncated to **2**, which of course is not equal to one third of **8**. This is not always a handicap. An easy way to determine if an integer is even or odd is to write the arithmetic statement

$$K=J/2*2$$

and then test to see if **K** is equal to **J**. The student should calculate what value of **K** would be produced if **J** is equal to **37** and what value would be produced if **J** is equal to **48**.

If all the variable names in an arithmetic expression are names of real variables (names *not* starting with the letters **I, J, K, L, M,** or **N**) and all the constants are real constants (constants written with a decimal including the **E** format), the expression is said to be in the *real mode*.

If an arithmetic expression contains both integer and real quantities it is said to be a *mixed mode.* Most FORTRAN systems will not accept mixed-mode expressions, and even with the few computers that will accept them they are to be avoided in most cases.

A statement such as

$$X = 5 * J - L / 4$$

does not contain a mixed-mode expression, since all the constants and variable names on the right-hand side of the equals sign are integer even though the variable name on the left is real. The statement

$$X = 2 * Y$$

does contain a mixed-mode expression, since **2** is an integer constant and **Y** is a real-variable name. Most computers would reject this statement giving the programmer a message that this contains a mixed-mode expression. The programmer would then have to correct the statement to

$$X = 2 . * Y$$

which would be accepted by the computer. This is the commonest error made by beginning programmers—omitting the decimal point after a whole number in an otherwise real expression.

Exponentiation is one of the exceptions of mixing modes. Real quantities may be raised to either real or integer exponents. Thus all the following expressions are valid:

$$X ** 2$$
$$Y ** 4 . 5$$
$$X ** J$$
$$W ** P$$
$$3 . 52 ** L$$
$$41 . 7 ** Q$$
$$J ** 4$$
$$N ** J$$
$$45 ** J$$

The exponents themselves may be expressions; for example,

$$K ** (2 * J + 3)$$

It is usually preferable to use integer exponents regardless of the mode of the quantity being raised to the indicated power. The expressions

$$X ** 2 . 0$$

and

$$X ** 2$$

are mathematically equivalent, but the second is preferred. Most computers evaluate an expression written with an integer exponent by multiplying; that is,

$$X ** 3$$

would be evaluated as though it had been written

$$X * X * X$$

When a real exponent is used, the evaluation is done by an expansion of a series and requires more computer time. Incidently, the evaluation of the expression

$$X*X$$

usually takes less computer time than the evaluation of the expression

$$X**2$$

and is therefore preferred.

Of course a real exponent is required if the exponent is not a whole number:

$$Q**2.52$$

cannot be done with an integer exponent.

Roots may be taken by raising the required quantity to a decimal power. The statements

$$Y=(Q-R)**0.5$$

and

$$T=4.5*D**0.25$$

are equivalent to

$$y = \sqrt{q - r}$$

and

$$t = 4.5 \sqrt[4]{d}$$

Arithmetic statements are thus made up of a variable name, an equals sign, and an arithmetic expression. Only one variable name without any constants or operation signs may appear on the left of the equals sign. The expression on the right of the equals sign will be evaluated in a mode dependent on the mode of the constants and variable names in the expression. The number obtained by this evaluation will then be stored at the location specified by the variable name on the left of the equals sign with the mode of the number being stored being converted *at the time of storage* if the mode of the variable name on the left is different than the mode of the expression.

The characters of the arithmetic statement are written in columns 7 through 72 of the coding form and are punched in these columns of the punched card. Every character, including the decimal point, requires a space of its own, since the card will be punched on a keypunch which has a keyboard similar to that of a typewriter. If you type 0.5 on a typewriter, the decimal point requires a space, and it will require a space when this number is punched on the keypunch.

Blank spaces left in the arithmetic statements (except in the middle of variable names or constants) are ignored by the compiler. The computer would consider the list of statements given in Fig. 3-1 to be equivalent to those given in Fig. 3-2. Blank spaces in most of the other types of statements discussed later are also ignored by the computer.

FIG. 3-1

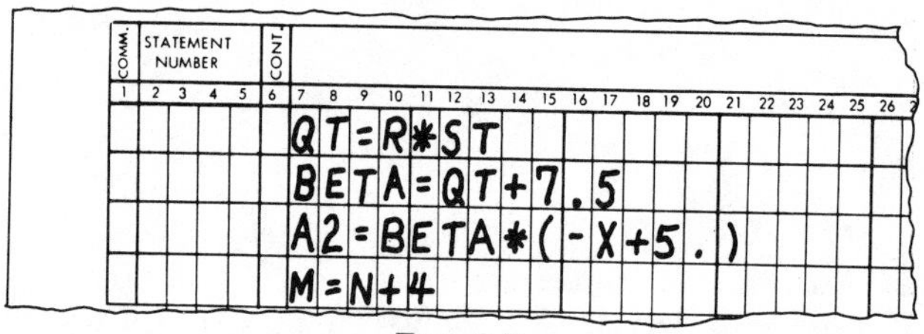

Fig. 3-2

Problems

3-1. A programmer has written a program that included the following as *integer* constants. Indicate for each whether or not it is a valid *integer* constant.

(a) −4658
(b) 12,658
(c) 3562.
(d) 24E02

(e) 5000000000
(f) −5460
(g) 40.00
(h) 0

3-2. A programmer has written a program that included the following as *real* constants. Indicate for each whether or not it is a valid *real* constant.

(a) +546.24
(b) 0
(c) 0.
(d) −256

(e) −283.8E−3
(f) 432E5
(g) 543.E2.0
(h) +23.4E19

3-3. Identify each of the following as a valid integer constant, a valid real constant, or an invalid constant.

(a) 356
(b) +356.0
(c) 896027
(d) 896027.

(e) 5,280
(f) −5.28E+03
(g) 528E01
(h) 6.39E−182

3-4. Write real constants using the **E** format that represent the following numbers.

(a) −0.0000768
(b) 2.96×10^{14}
(c) 7.8903×10^{-4}
(d) 890,700,000

(e) −298.7
(f) 7689.4×10^{5}
(g) 0.0000000476
(h) 5000

3-5. A programmer has written a program that included the following constants. He intended to have them represent the number given in the right-hand column. Correct any errors.

FORTRAN	Intended Values
(a) 5286E−2	5.286
(b) 0.678E+5	67800.
(c) .38E3	−380.
(d) 6.7E4	0.00067
(e) 428E−05	4.28×10^{-4}.
(f) 5.29E	5.29

3-6. Identify each of the following as a valid integer variable name, a valid real-variable name, or an invalid variable name.

(a) JOE
(b) DICK
(c) M63
(d) 7K8X
(e) X2K4

(f) BETA
(g) IBETA
(h) TANGENT
(i) J5.8
(j) MARY

3-7. Each of the FORTRAN arithmetic statements below contain at least one error. Identify the errors.

(a) `+X=A+B`

(b) `(X+Y)*(A+BETA/2.))`

(c) `4.3=X`

(d) `P=(P-5)(A7-3)`

(e) `X=5,280.*Y`

3-8. Write FORTRAN arithmetic statements corresponding to each of the following algebraic statements.

(a) $x = \dfrac{a + b}{c}$

(b) $x = \dfrac{a - 7}{6 - b}$

(c) $x = a + \dfrac{b}{c - d}$

(d) $\text{Area} = \pi r^2$

(e) $x = \dfrac{-b + \sqrt{b^2 - 4a \cdot c}}{2a}$

3-9. Determine the number that will be stored in **X** as the result of each of the following arithmetic statements if **2.5** has been stored in **Y, 7.0** in **Z, 3** in **J,** and **−4** in **M.**

(a) `X=2.0*Y+5.0`

(b) `X=-Y*(Z-2.)`

(c) `X=2*J+M`

(d) `X=(4.*Y*(Z-5.)+(Y+3.)/2.)*2.`

(e) `X=J**2/M`

(f) `X=Z/J`

3-10. A programmer has written a program that included the following arithmetic statements. He intended these statements to correspond to the algebraic statements given in the right-hand column. Correct any errors.

(a) `X=(A+B)/G*P` $x = \dfrac{a + b}{gp}$

(b) `K=(3J/4M)**2+3(N+I)/M` $k = \left(\dfrac{3j}{4m}\right)^2 + \dfrac{3(n + i)}{m}$

(c) `Z=(5.*A+B)/4.*C*C` $z = \dfrac{5a + b}{4c^2}$

(d) `B=(A**3-C/(3.*D)/(4.*E**4)` $x = \dfrac{5a - \dfrac{c}{3d}}{4e^4}$

3-11. Write algebraic statements corresponding to each of the following FORTRAN arithmetic statements.

(a) `X=7.0*(Y+Z**3)**2.0/3.0`

(b) `J=L*M/N*K`

(c) `R=4.*(A-3.*B)/7.*C**3`

(d) `P=Q*(2.5+3.2*Q*(W-1.2*Z)/7.4)+8.9`

(e) `B=E/(W*W+(3.1416*Z-1.0/(2.5*Q*R)**2)**.5)`

(f) `M=3*(J+K)/((4-L)*N)`

3-12.   Are the two real numbers in each pair below equal?
  (a) +0.0682   .0682
  (b) 5280.   0.528E3
  (c) -.0006971   -69.71E-04
  (d) .008092E+4   809.20E-01
  (e) -9292.0   0.9292E+04
  (f) 728.92   7.2892E2

3-13.   Determine the number that will be stored in **L** as the result of each of the following arithmetic statements if **3.5** has been stored in **Y**, **7.0** in **X**, **6.5** in **Z**, **4** in **J**, and −**3** in **M**.
  (a) L = 5*M+J
  (b) L = J/M+4
  (c) L = Y**2
  (d) L = X*Y
  (e) L = (4.*Y*(Z-5.))*2.
  (f) L = Z/J

CHAPTER 4

STATEMENT NUMBERS, CONTROL STATEMENTS, INTRODUCTION TO OUTPUT

4-1. STATEMENT NUMBERS

The statements in a FORTRAN program are executed in the order in which they are written unless a statement tells the computer to follow a different order. The clerk would execute the instructions in his list in the order they are written until he reached instruction 6 (see Sec. 1-1) which tells him to go to either instruction 7 or instruction 10, depending on the result of his calculation up to this point. After he has reached instruction 7, he will continue executing the instructions in order until he reaches instruction 9, which tells him to go back to instruction 2. Instructions 6 and 9 do not tell the clerk to make any calculations but indicate what instruction to execute next. Statements in a FORTRAN program similar to the clerk's instructions 6 and 9 are called *control statements*.

All of the instructions given to the clerk were numbered, but the clerk could have carried out the calculation if only instructions 2, 7, and 10 had been numbered. Any FORTRAN statement may be given a statement number and all FORTRAN statements that are referred to by a control statement must be given a statement number.

FORTRAN statement numbers are integer numbers which are written without a sign in the first five columns on the coding sheet. When the program is punched into punched cards, the statement numbers are punched into the left-hand five columns of the card to the left of the statement. It is physically possible to punch any integer number from **1** to **99999** in five or less columns, and many computers will accept any of these numbers as a statement number. There are several computers, for example the IBM 7090, which will not accept statement numbers larger than **32767**. When the statement number has less than five digits, it may be written or punched anywhere in the five columns as shown in Fig. 4-1.

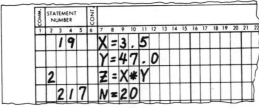

FIG. 4-1

Most programmers either right-justify or left-justify the statement numbers (write the numbers as far to the right or left as possible) as shown in Figs. 4-2 and 4-3.

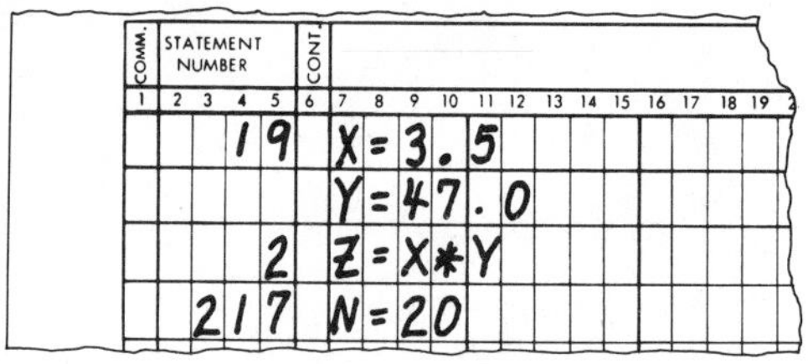

FIG. 4-2

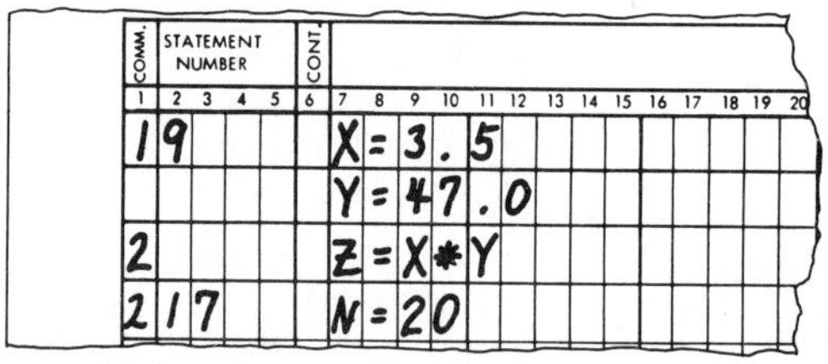

FIG. 4-3

The statement numbers may be assigned arbitrarily (in Figs. 4-1, 4-2, and 4-3 number **2** comes between numbers **19** and **217**), but no two statements may have the same statement number.

The statements are executed in the order they are written on the page unless a control statement causes a transfer to a particular statement number, and not in any order determined by the magnitude of the statement numbers.

4-2. CONTROL STATEMENTS

THE ARITHMETIC **IF** STATEMENT

The arithmetic **IF** statement is a control statement that enables the computer to "decide" what statement is to be executed next based on whether a number is negative, zero, or positive. This statement *always* consists of the word "IF," a FORTRAN arithmetic expression contained in a pair of parentheses, and *three* statement numbers separated by commas. The **IF** statement tells the computer to compute the value of the expression in the parentheses; if the computed value is negative go to the statement indicated by the first statement number, if the value is zero go to the statement indicated by the second statement number, if the computed value is positive go to the statement indicated by the third statement number. For example,

$$IF(J-3)40,37,60$$

tells the computer to calculate the value of **J-3**; go to statement **40** if the value is negative, to statement **37** if the value is zero, or to statement **60** if the value is positive.

A FORTRAN arithmetic **IF** statement equivalent to instruction 6 on the clerk's list would be

$$IF(X)10,7,7$$

All three statement numbers in the arithmetic **IF** statement may be different, or any two of them may be the same.

The requirement that there be three statement numbers in this type of **IF** statement holds even when the programmer knows that one of the three conditions (negative, zero, of positive) will never occur. This was discussed in Sec. 1-1 in connection with the clerk's problem. If the programmer is confident that the value of **X** will never be zero, he could use the number of any executable statement used anywhere in the program for the central statement number in the arithmetic **IF** statement. He could write

        IF(X)10,10,7

or

        IF(X)10,2,7

or

        IF(X)10,3,7

if there are executable statements somewhere in the program numbered **10**, **2**, and **3**. If he is not quite positive that the value of **X** will never be zero, he should use a statement number that will send the computer to the statement he wants the computer to execute next if **X** is zero. Since it would take some computations to discover that **X** would never be zero, the statement

        IF(X)10,7,7

would be the logical one to use. The expression in the parentheses may be any valid **FORTRAN** arithmetic expression. It may be a single variable name such as **X** or **J** or it may be a more complicated expression including variable names, constants, operation symbols, and parentheses. All the rules concerning the formation of arithmetic expressions including the mode of the expression discussed in Sec. 3-4 apply to expressions used in arithmetic **IF** statements.

If a complicated arithmetic expression such as

        ((((6.*T+4.)*T-5.)*T-3.)*T+7.)*T-8.

is used in an **IF** statement an additional pair of parentheses must be used to enclose the expression

        IF(((((6.*T+4.)*T-5.)*T-3.)*T+7.)*T-8.)3,56,9

Note that the two statements

        X=((((6.*T+4.)*T-5.)*T-3.)*T+7.)*T-8.
        IF(X)3,56,9

would cause the same calculation and decision as would be caused by the single **IF** statement containing the complicated expression. These latter two statements would, however, do one additional operation that would not be performed by the single **IF** statement. The first of the two statements would cause the number found by the evaluation of the expression to be stored at location **X**; the single **IF** statement would not cause any number to be stored, another arithmetic statement would have to be written, and the calculation would have to be performed again if the value of **X** was needed later in the computation. The two statement form should be used if the value of the expression is to be used again at any point in the computation.

The arithmetic **IF** statement (as well as all other types of statements) must be written in exactly the form specified. If one of the two commas or one of the parentheses were omitted or an extra comma or other character included, the program would not be translated into a machine-language program, and the computer would print a comment telling the programmer that there was an error in this statement.

The computer is particularly useful when a statement or a set of statements are to be executed many times. For example, suppose we wished to write a FORTRAN program to calculate w, where

$$w = y_1 y_2 y_3 y_4 y_5 y_6 y_7 y_8$$
$$y_n = x_n^3 + 7$$
$$x_1 = 0.5, \quad x_2 = 1.0, \quad x_3 = 1.5, \quad x_4 = 2.0, \quad x_5 = 2.5, \quad \text{etc.}$$

We could write a program repeating several statements eight times as shown in Fig. 4-4.

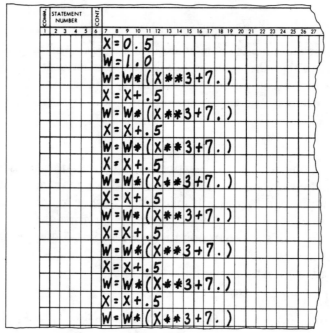

FIG. 4-4

This program would correctly solve the problem, but is much longer than necessary in that the statements

$$W = W * (X**3 + 7.)$$

and

$$X = X + .5$$

appear a number of times. The program could be shortened by using an integer variable as an "index" to count the number of times a group of statements have been executed and an arithmetic **IF** statement to determine whether they have been executed the correct number of times. Such a program is shown in Fig. 4-5. (Remember each character takes up one space, including even commas and decimal points.)

```
        X = 0.5
        N = 8
        W = 1.0
      2 W = W * (X**3+7.)
        N = N - 1
        X = X + .5
        IF (N) 4, 4, 2
```

FIG. 4-5

The last four statements in Fig. 4-5 would be executed eight times (for **N = 8, 7, 6, 5, 4, 3, 2, 1**). Such a series of statements which the computer will execute a number of times with different values of the variables is called a *loop*. The first three statements in the program would be executed only once and would set the variables to the values they should have when the loop is executed the first time. This presetting of the variable values is known as *initializing*.

The **IF** statement would send the computer to statement **4** after the loop had been executed eight times. Statement **4** might tell the computer to print the value of **W**, the answer to the problem.

There are many slightly different programs that could be written to solve this problem. Figure 4-6 shows a program in which statement **2** would be executed eight times while N increased (while N had the values of **1, 2, 3, 4, 5, 6, 7, 8**).

The index **N** is only used for counting the number of times the loop is executed in the programs of Figs. 4-5 and 4-6. The index may also be used as a factor in the calcula-

COMM.	STATEMENT NUMBER				CONT.	7 8 9 10 11 12 13 14 15 16 17 18 19 20 21 22
1	2 3 4 5				6	
						X=0.5
						N=1
						W=1.0
	2					W=W*(X**3+7.)
						N=N+1
						X=X+.5
						IF(N-8)2,2,4

FIG. 4-6

tion. The program shown in Fig. 4-7 makes use of the fact that the value of **X** may be takes as one half N as N takes the values 1, 2, 3, 4, 5, 6, 7, and **8**. Note that the

COMM.	STATEMENT NUMBER				CONT.	7 8 9 10 11 12 13 14 15 16 17 18 19 20 21 2
1	2 3 4 5				6	
						N=1
						W=1.0
	2					Q=N
						X=Q/2.
						W=W*(X**3+7.)
						N=N+1
						IF(N-8)2,2,4

FIG. 4-7

statement

$$Q = N$$

is used to obtain a real number numerically equal to the integer number **N**.

The type of **IF** statements discussed in this section are known as *arithmetic* **IF** statements. Many FORTRAN systems also include another type of **IF** statement known as a *logical* **IF** statement. The logical **IF** statement will be discussed in Chapter 7.

THE GØ TØ STATEMENT

The **GØ TØ** statement is used for "unconditional branching" or "unconditional transfer," since no decision is made by the computer with this statement. The **GØ TØ** statement consists of the two words "**GØ TØ**" followed by a single statement number. The statement

$$GO\ TO\ 14$$

tells the computer to execute statement **14** next instead of the statement written immediately after this **GØ TØ** statement. The **GØ TØ** statement is often used at the end of a sequence of statements that represent one option of some other control statement such as an arithmetic **IF** statement, and directs the computer to skip the statements that represent the other option or options. For example, suppose that we are told to calculate the value of w given by one of the two formulas:

$$w = 7.5y - 0.85 \quad \text{if} \quad y \leq 4.5$$
$$w = 8.4y - 1.25 \quad \text{if} \quad y > 4.5$$

and then to calculate the value of u given by the formula

$$u = 3w^2 - 5w + 8 = (3w - 5)w + 8$$

The choice of which formula should be used may be determined by an **IF** statement since the quantity $y - 4.5$ will be negative if y is less than 4.5, will be zero if y is equal to 4.5, and will be positive if y is greater than 4.5. A beginning programmer might write a program such as that shown in Fig. 4-8 to solve this problem. This program would not

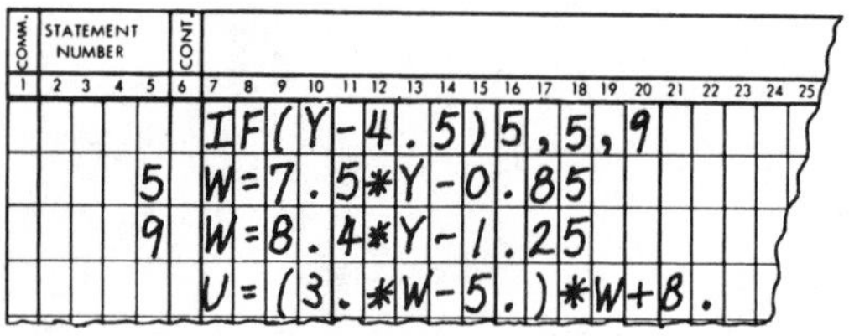

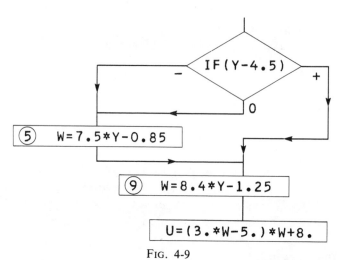

FIG. 4-8

give the correct answer when y is not greater than 4.5. The reason for incorrect calculation may be seen if we draw a flow diagram for the program. This flow diagram is shown in Fig. 4-9.

FIG. 4-9

The computer would be sent to statement **5** if y is less than or equal to 4.5, and a correct value for w would be calculated by statement **5**, but then the computer would go on to statement **9** since it has not been told to follow any order other than the usual. A new value of *w* would be calculated by statement **9,** and this new value will replace the correct value in memory.

COMM.	STATEMENT NUMBER				CONT.																					
1	2	3	4	5	6	7	8	9	10	11	12	13	14	15	16	17	18	19	20	21	22	23	24	25	26	2
						I	F	(	Y	-	4	.	5	)	5	,	5	,	9							
				5		W	=	7	.	5	*	Y	-	0	.	8	5									
						G	O		T	O		7														
				9		W	=	8	.	4	*	Y	-	1	.	2	5									
				7		U	=	(	3	.	*	W	-	5	.	)	*	W	+	8	.					

FIG. 4-10

Figure 4-10 shows a program that would correctly solve the problem. The statement

GO TO 7

tells the computer that it is not to go to statement **9** after using statement **5** but is to skip to statement **7.**

Note that the statements are written starting in column **7** using one column for each character. The number **4.5** takes three columns, and the number **3.** takes two. Any one character whether letter, digit, comma, decimal point, or operation symbol must be given a column to itself.

Figure 4-11 is a flow diagram for the program given in Fig. 4-10.

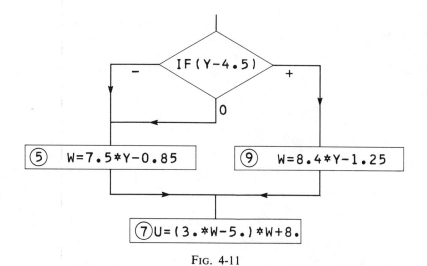

FIG. 4-11

Every arithmetic or control statement in a FORTRAN program must be executable. There are two ways in which a statement may be reached by the computer: by being written immediately following a statement that is being executed (but which does not send the computer to some other statement), or by having a statement number to which a control statement sends the computer. The statement

R=8.2*X+Y

in the part of a program shown in Fig. 4-12 could never be executed. The FORTRAN compiler would give an error indication for this program. *Every* statement written im-

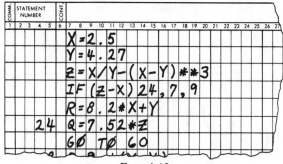

FIG. 4-12

mediately after an arithmetic **IF** statement or a **GØ TØ** statement must have a statement number which is usually refered to by a control statement somewhere in the program.

A control statement, like any FORTRAN statement, may have a statement number of its own to be referred to by *other* control statements. A control statement is not allowed to refer to itself. If **X** were positive when the computer reached the statement

$$25 \quad IF(X)16,15,25$$

the computer would keep testing **X** over and over, finding it positive until the operator intervened.

THE STØP STATEMENT

The last instruction on the clerk's list was:

10. Bring the two-column table to my office and see if I have another job for you.

A FORTRAN program must include a control statement that tells the computer that it has completed the job. A statement that consists of the single word **STØP** is often used for this purpose. The **STØP** statement normally does not have exactly the same meaning as instruction **10** given above; it is approximately equivalent to the instruction:

10. Leave all final output tables you have produced in the basket labeled "out" and sit there doing nothing until someone tells you to do another job.

The last statement the computer would reach going through the program must be either a **STØP** statement or a **CALL EXIT** statement that is described below. Most FORTRAN systems require that there be at least one **STØP** or **CALL EXIT** statement in each program. If control statements in the program cause *branching*, each possible path that the computer might take going through the calculation should terminate in a **STØP** or **CALL EXIT** statement. Figure 4-13 shows a program using three **STØP** statements to

FIG. 4-13

C O M	STATEMENT NUMBER				C O N T																														
1	2	3	4	5	6	7	8	9	10	11	12	13	14	15	16	17	18	19	20	21	22	23	24	25	26	27	28	29	30	31	32	33	34	35
						X	=	5	.	3																								
						Y	=	7	.	*	X	*	*	3	+	5	0	.	-	4	9	.	/	(	X	-	3	.	)					
						I	F	(	Y	)	2	,	9	,	7																			
			7			Z	=	Y	+	6	0	.																						
						G	Ø		T	Ø		5	2																					
			2			Z	=	Y	-	4	5	.	5																					
						G	Ø		T	Ø		5	2																					
			9			Z	=	2	.	*	Y																							
		5	2			S	T	Ø	P																									

Fig. 4-14

terminate the three possible paths created by the **IF** statement. Figure 4-14 shows a program in which the three paths are brought back together by **GØ TØ** statements and is terminated by one **STØP** statement.

THE **CALL EXIT** STATEMENT

Most computers must be restarted by the computer operator after a computation has been terminated by a **STØP** statement. This operator intervention between programs is not necessary if the program is terminated by a statement consisting of the two words **CALL EXIT.** This statement is equivalent to giving the clerk the instruction:

10. Leave all final output tables you have produced in the basket labeled "out" and start work on the next set of instructions in the basket labeled "in."

When the **STØP** statement brings the computer to a complete halt the computer sits doing nothing, and the fraction of a minute it may take for the operator to realize that the computer has halted and walk across the room to the computer console may represent many dollars worth of wasted computer time. A few FORTRAN compilers reject any program containing a **STØP** statement, while in others a **STØP** statement has the same "terminate this program and proceed to the next job" effect normally provided by the **CALL EXIT** statement.

A programmer should check with the computer center that will run his programs to determine if his programs should contain **STØP** statements or **CALL EXIT** statements. The example programs in this book will normally use **STØP** statements.

THE **END** STATEMENT

The first thing that the computer must do when a FORTRAN program is fed into it is to translate this FORTRAN program into a machine-language program. The statements of the FORTRAN program are fed into the computer one at a time and the computer must be told when it has been given the entire list of statements so it may proceed to the job of translating the program. This is done by making the *last* statement of *every* FORTRAN program a statement consisting of the one word "END". The **END** statement is different from the other control statements discussed in that it is not "executed" but is a specification statement that tells the computer "You have the entire FORTRAN program. Go ahead and write a machine-language program to make this calculation."

COMMENTS

The programmer may insert any identifying or explanatory comments into a FORTRAN program by means of a comments card. If the character **C** is placed in column 1, anything written in columns 2 through 72 of that line will be printed on the listing of the program. The comments (as well as blank cards) are ignored by the FORTRAN compiler. It is good practice to make the first card of every program a comments card giving the name of the programmer and identifying the program. Additional comments cards are often used for documentation of the program. These give information so that someone reading the listing of the program will be informed as how to use a program; what input information is necessary, what procedure is used to make the calculation, and what output is produced.

4-3. INTRODUCTION TO OUTPUT

The clerk's computations would be useless to us unless he produced a table of results that we could read. We must know how to tell the computer to give us the answers as well as how to make the computation. Results are obtained from the computer by means of a **WRITE** statement consisting of three parts: the word **WRITE** (starting in column 7), two integer numbers enclosed in parentheses and separated by a comma, and a list of the variable names whose values are to be printed, typed, or punched. If more than one variable name appears in the list, the names are separated by commas. The statement

COMM	STATEMENT NUMBER	CONT	
1	2 3 4 5	6	7 8 9 10 11 12 13 14 15 16 17 18 19 20 21 22 23
			W R I T E (3 , 1 6) X , Y

tells the computer to print the numbers stored in locations **X** and **Y**. The first of the two integer numbers in the parentheses (the **3** in the example) tells the computer which of the several output devices available it is to use. A programmer use determine how output unit numbers are assigned at the computer installation he is using. The IBM 1130 computer assigns particular output unit numbers to particular pieces of hardware. A FORTRAN program written for an IBM 1130 computer must refer to a model number 1132 printer as output unit **3**, to a model 1442 card-read punch as output unit **2**, and to the console printer (the typewriter) as output unit **1**. Therefore, the statement

```
WRITE(3,16)X,Y
```

used on the IBM 1130 would tell the computer to print the numbers stored in locations **X** and **Y** on the 1132 printer. The statement

```
WRITE(2,16)X,Y
```

would tell the IBM 1130 to punch these two numbers using the 1442 card-read punch.

Other computers may use different numbers to refer to the various output units, for example, some computers use

```
WRITE(6,16)X,Y
```

when refering to the printer.

Some computers permit the programmer to decide for himself what unit numbers he will use. He must feed a *monitor control card* into the card reader ahead of his FORTRAN program to tell such a computer what output unit numbers he is going to use in refering to the printer and to the other output units.

Some hardware units (particularly some magnetic tape units) have switches which must be manually set to the unit numbers by which they are to be referred in the FORTRAN program.

The second integer number in the parentheses of the **WRITE** statement is a statement number referring to a **FØRMAT** statement that specifies where on the line of printing and in what form the numbers are to be printed (or where on the card and in what form the numbers are to be punched). The **FØRMAT** statement is a specification statement which gives information to the computer telling it how the **WRITE** statement is to be executed. A **FØRMAT** statement may be placed anywhere in the program. Many programmers place the **FØRMAT** statement next to the **WRITE** statement which refers to it, but this is not necessary. Some programmers place all of the **FØRMAT** statements at the end of the program. Actually the **FØRMAT** statements may be placed anywhere in the program, not necessarily in the order in which they are referred to. Since the **FØRMAT** statement is not executed, does not tell the computer to do anything, the statement number of a **FØRMAT** statement may not be referred to by any control statement (its statement number must *not* be one of the statement numbers in an arithmetic **IF** statement or **GØ TØ** statement).

The letter **I** is used with an integer number in the **FØRMAT** statement for typing, printing, or punching integer numbers. If the computer being used refers to the console printer (the typewriter) as output unit **1**, the statements

```
     STATEMENT
     NUMBER
1  2  3  4  5  6  7  8  9 10 11 12 13 14 15 16 17 18 19 20 21 22
               WRITE(1,57)J
        5 7    FØRMAT(I5)
```

tell the computer to set up a five-space field and to type the number stored in memory location **J** right-justified in this field. If **528** were stored at location **J** at the time this **WRITE** statement were executed, three spaces would be required to type this number, and the console printer would leave two blank spaces and type the three digits **528** in the three spaces at the right-hand end of the field.

```
|   |   | 5 | 2 | 8 |
```

⌐ first column on the page

If **−372** were stored in **J**, execution of this **WRITE** statement would leave one blank space in the first column on the page and cause **−372** to be typed in the next four columns.

```
|   | − | 3 | 7 | 2 |
```

Note that a space is required to type the minus sign for a negative number. Usually no sign is typed if the number is positive; however, many computers require a space to be reserved for the sign whether the number is positive or negative.

When the **FØRMAT** statement does not provide a large enough field width to hold the number involved, some computers will place asterisks in the spaces provided. If **82** were stored at location **K2Z**, the statements

```
     STATEMENT
     NUMBER
1  2  3  4  5  6  7  8  9 10 11 12 13 14 15 16 17 18 19 20 21 22 23
               WRITE(1,4)K2Z
          4    FØRMAT(I2)
```

would cause the two digits **82** to by typed in the first columns of the page. If, however, the number stored in **K2Z** were **365**, the two spaces provided would not be able to hold the three characters required, and many computers would type two asterisks in the first two columns.

*	*

There are computers which do not fill a field with asterisks when asked to type, print, or punch a number requiring more spaces than are required. These computers fill the spaces provided with as many of the characters as possible and ignore the other characters. Most such computers ignore the leftmost characters; the computer would type **65** when asked to type **365** in two spaces, giving no indication that part of the number was missing. The statements

COMM.	STATEMENT NUMBER				CONT.																								
1	2	3	4	5	6	7	8	9	10	11	12	13	14	15	16	17	18	19	20	21	22	23	24	25	26	27	28	29
						W	R	I	T	E	(	1	,	3	5	)	K	,	L	X	5	,	M	Z				
		3	5			F	Ø	R	M	A	T	(	I	5	,	I	3	,	I	4	)							

tell the computer to type the numbers stored in locations **K, LX5,** and **MZ** in fields of five, three, and four spaces respectively. Each number will be right-justified in its field. If **−328, 6,** and **113** were stored in **K, LX5,** and **MZ** respectively,

	−	3	2	8			6		1	1	3

would be typed. If any number requires more spaces than the **FØRMAT** provides, the field provided for that number would either be filled with asterisks or would be filled with some of the digits of that number. If the numbers stored in **K, LX5,** and **MZ** were **−328, 17482,** and **113** respectively, either

	−	3	2	8	*	*	*		1	1	3

or

	−	3	2	8	4	8	2		1	1	3

would be typed depending on what computer is being used. In either case the numbers **−328, 17482,** and **113** would remain unchanged in their memory locations.

Regardless of what numbers are stored in the locations, the above statements would use three fields with widths of five, three, and four spaces, a total of twelve spaces, and the remainder of the line would be left blank. One line of typing on most console printers may type a maximum of 120 spaces.

Space should be left between numbers so that the individual numbers may be distinguished. If the numbers stored in **M, NUT,** and **L23** were **156, 29,** and **−372,** the statements

```
      WRITE(1,802)M,NUT,L23
  802 FORMAT(I3,I2,I4)
```

would produce the output

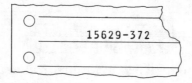

This is the actual output from the computer. The "boxes" that show fields are not typed, and it is impossible to tell that there are supposed to be three numbers. Space could be left between the numbers by making the fields larger than necessary to hold the numbers. The statements

```
    WRITE(1,803)M,NUT,L23
803 FORMAT(I5,I4,I5)
```

would type these same numbers as

Spaces may also be left in the output by using the letter **X** preceded by an integer number. The statements

```
    WRITE(1,804)M,NUT,L23
804 FORMAT(2X,I3,2X,I2,1X,I4)
```

tell the computer to set up fields of 2, 3, 2, 2, 1, and 4 spaces, to put blanks in the first field (the **2X** field), type the value stored in the location indicated by the first variable name in the variable-name list of the **WRITE** statement, **M**, as an integer in a field three spaces wide, put blanks in a two space field, type the value of the second variable, **NUT**, in a field with a field width of two, put a blank in a one space field, and type the value of the third variable, **L23**, in a field with a field width of four:

		1	5	6			2	9		−	3	7	2

The actual typed output would look exactly the same as the output obtained using the **FØRMAT** with statement number **803**.

```
                    156   29 -372
```

Use of the console printer has been discussed first since its operation is simpler than that of the printer normally used for output. The console printer is a character printer—output is produced one character at a time. The printer regularly used is a line printer printing one entire line at a time. The console printer is so slow that it is seldom used; a few computers do not even have a console printer.

Most of the output of a computer is produced on the printer. When the term *printer* is used alone without a modifying adjective such as console or character, the output unit referred to is the line printer. The use of this printer is slightly complicated by the fact that the first character described by the **WRITE** and **FØRMAT** statements is not printed and is not directly associated with any column of printing. This character is used for "carriage control" to instruct the printer to single space, double space, to skip to the top of a new page, or to print more than one **WRITE** statement on one line of printing.

After the printer has printed a line, the paper is not moved forward to a new line until the next **WRITE** statement that calls for this same output unit is executed. If the carriage control character provided by this **WRITE** statement in conjunction with the **FØRMAT** statement is a blank, the printer will single space before printing, and the remainder of the material requested by these two statements will be printed on the new line. If the printer is output unit **6** on the computer system being used, the statements

```
     WRITE(6,17)K,KH
  17 FORMAT(1X,I4,I4)
```

would set up the line

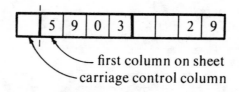

if **5903** and **29** were stored in locations **K** and **KH**.

One widely used method of leaving a blank in the control column is to provide a field width wider than necessary for the first variable to be printed. If **5903** and **29** were stored in **K** and **KH**, the statements

```
     WRITE(6,18)K,KH
  18 FORMAT(I5,I4)
```

would set up the line

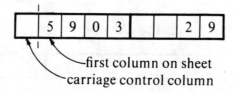

If the character in the carriage control column is zero, the printer will double-space before printing, leaving one blank line on the printed sheet. The zero will not be printed, and the first character printed will be the second character provided by the **WRITE** and **FØRMAT** statements. One method of placing the zero in the control character is by setting an integer variable equal to zero and including this variable name in the list in the **WRITE** statement with an **I1** in the statement.

The statements

```
     N=0
     WRITE(6,19)N,K,KH
  19 FORMAT(I1,I4,I4)
```

would set up the line

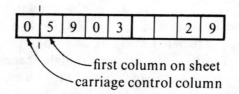

if **K** and **KH** had the values given above. The zero would not be printed but would cause a blank line to be left on the sheet.

The actual output produced by the statements

```
      N=0
      K=5903
      KH=29
      WRITE(6,17)K,KH
   17 FORMAT(1X,I4,I4)
      WRITE(6,18)K,KH
   18 FORMAT(I5,I4)
      WRITE(6,19)N,K,KH
   19 FORMAT(I1,I4,I4)
```

would be

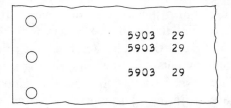

Many times the programmer does not know what value the number to be printed will have. There would be no need to make a computation when the answer is known. A large enough field width should be used to permit the printing of the maximum size answer expected. A programmer expecting the answer to be a four-digit number should use an **I5** or even **I6** specification to be sure to provide space for the answer and a blank in the control column (or space between numbers).

Remember that the character in the control column is *not* printed. The statements

```
      MISS=2937
      WRITE(6,9)MISS
    9 FORMAT(I4)
```

would cause the printer to print

Note that the **2** of the **2937** was not printed. This character was lost in the control column and was not printed (the number stored in location **MISS** would, however, remain **2937**). One common error is to forget that a minus sign requires a column. The statements

```
      NIX=-3760
      WRITE(6,11)NIX
   11 FORMAT(I5)
```

would print

with the three in the first column; the minus sign being lost in the control column.

The use of characters other than blank and zero in the control column will be discussed in Chapter 9.

Note that a group of characters is set up by the **WRITE** statement. What these characters are depends on the **WRITE** statement, on the **FØRMAT** statement, and on what numbers are stored at the locations specified in the variable name list of the **WRITE** statement. Many printers have 120 printing wheels and so may print 120 characters on one line. The statements used to print using these printers may describe a line of 121 characters including blanks. The first of these characters is not printed but is used as a signal to the printer as to what spacing between lines of printing is desired; the remaining 120 characters are printed. The first character, the control character, is normally made a blank to provide single-spaced printing. The safest and surest way to make this character a blank is to make the first specification in the **FØRMAT** statement a **1X**. Other printers are used on some computers with the maximum number of characters per line varying from 100 to 144.

There is no control column on other output units. The **FØRMAT** statement used with the console printer may describe a maximum of 120 characters per line all of which will be printed. Most punched cards permit a maximum of 80 characters per card; all characters described are punched. There are a few card punches that punch 72 or 90 characters per card.

The **I** specification is only used for integer numbers. Real numbers are printed, punched, or typed using either an **E** specification or an **F** specification. The use of the **E** specification will be discussed in Chapter 5. If the number **−2.91835** were stored in location **X** and the console printer is unit **1**, the statements

```
      WRITE(1,42)X
   42 FORMAT(F8.2)
```

would cause the computer to type the number **−2.918** right-justified in an eight-space field. The integer number between the letter **F** and the decimal point (the **8** in the example) indicates the field width, and the integer number after the decimal point in the specification indicates the number of digits to be typed after the decimal point of the typed number. A space is used for typing the decimal point, and a space will be used for a minus sign if the number is negative.

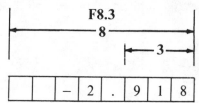

In the example given, the number **−2.91835** is nearer **−2.92** than it is to **−2.91**. Some computer systems take this into account and round the number while others truncate.

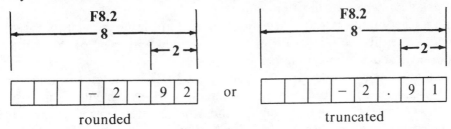

rounded   truncated

When programming for a computer that truncates it is desirable to have one more digit typed or printed than the number of significant digits required for the answer. If two significant digits after the decimal point are required in the answer to a certain problem, the **F8.3** specification should be used with a computer system that truncates while the **F8.2** specification would be satisfactory with a system that rounds.

The list of variable names in the **WRITE** statement tells the computer the order from left to right it is to use in typing, punching, or printing the numbers. The **FØRMAT** statement describes the form and field widths these numbers are to take; the specifications also being given from left to right. Both real and integer variable names may be included in one **WRITE** statement. The statements

```
      WRITE(6,79)K,BETA,JQ,RATE
   79 FORMAT(I7,3X,F6.2,I6,2X,F7.1)
```

would cause the values stored in **K**, **BETA**, **JQ**, and **RATE** to be printed with **I7**, **F6.2**, **I6**, and **F7.1** specifications respectively. The **3X** and **2X** would leave extra spaces between the designated values. The output would be

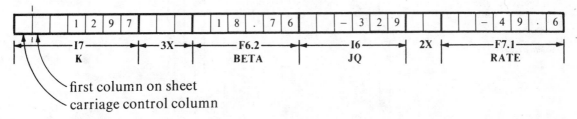

first column on sheet
carriage control column

if the numbers **1297**, **18.7625**, **−329**, and **−49.6037** had been stored in the designated locations. All the numbers are right-justified in their fields. The value of **BETA** is printed with two digits (**76**) after the decimal point because the **2** in the **F6.2** calls for two digits. The value of **RATE** is printed with one digit (**6**) after the decimal point because of the **1** in **F7.1**.

The statements

```
      X23K=-.037541
      QU=0.628
      WRITE(6,657)X23K,QU
  657 FORMAT(F10.4,F8.4)
```

would result in

The computer always supplies any additional zeros needed to fill out the required number of digits after the decimal point. Most computer systems supply a zero in front of numbers whose absolute values are less than one.

As with integer numbers, any **F** sepcification field not large enough to hold the value to be printed will either be filled with asterisks or filled with part of the digits wanted, depending upon the computer system being used.

No numbers in the memory are changed by the **WRITE** statement, and these numbers may be used later in the program in arithmetic or **IF**-statements or may be written by other **WRITE** statements. All the digits—those not printed as well as those printed—remain in the computer memory at the locations specified by the variable names.

The mode of the **FØRMAT** specification, must agree with the mode of the variable name to be printed. No integer variable may be typed, printed, or punched with an **E** or **F** specification, and no real variable with an **I** specification.

The statements

```
    WRITE(6,28)M,Z
 28 FORMAT(I5,I6)
```

would be incorrect since these statements tell the computer to print the value of the real number **Z** using the integer specification **I6**.

More than one **WRITE** statement may refer to the same **FØRMAT** statement as in the example program shown in Fig. 4-15.

```
      N=1
      K=7
      X=50.
      WRITE(6,5)N,X
    5 FØRMAT(I5,F7.1)
   10 J=K+2*N
      Z=J
      R=5.2*X+Z
      M=M+1
      WRITE(6,5)J,R
      IF(M-6)10,10,15
   15 STØP
      END
```

FIG. 4-15

An integer constant in front of the letter **I** or **F** indicates that the specification is to be repeated this number of times. The statement

```
 17 FORMAT(4I8)
```

is equivalent to writing

```
 17 FORMAT(I8,I8,I8,I8)
```

and

```
  6 FORMAT(2X,F10.2,2I5,3F12.5)
```

is equivalent to writing

```
  6 FORMAT(2X,F10.2,I5,I5,F12.5,F12.5,F12.5)
```

All the examples shown have provided the number of **FØRMAT** specifications in the **FØRMAT** statement necessary to justify the number of variable names in the list of the **WRITE** statement. The use of more or less specifications than the number of variable names, thus:

```
      WRITE(6,16)X,Y
   16 FORMAT(F6.2,F10.3,F8.6,F9.4)

      WRITE(6,63)W,X,Y,Z
   63 FORMAT(F12.4)
```

or

is discussed in Sec. 10-3.

Some large computer systems use magnetic-tape units in producing the output. For economic reasons results are first recorded on the magnetic tape at the time the program is run on the computer, and then afterwards the magnetic tape is used as input for a smaller less expensive computer which is programmed to print the results on a printer. This process need not trouble the beginning programmer since he only needs to use the unit number of the output magnetic tape unit in his **WRITE** statements to obtain the same results he would have obtained directly from a printer.

In earlier versions of **FØRTRAN** the output unit to be used was not indicated by a unit number but by a word or phrase

```
      PRINT 17,X,Y
```

or

```
      PUNCH 146,X,Y
```

or

```
      WRITE OUTPUT TAPE 2,X,Y
```

Some computer systems, for example the IBM 7090, still accept these "old-fashioned" statements as well as accepting the "newer" forms described above.

4-4. A FORTRAN Program to Solve the Clerk's Problem

There are many details about writing FORTRAN programs that have not as yet been mentioned, but enough of the fundamentals have been covered to permit us to write FORTRAN programs to solve many problems. Later chapters will introduce several others types of statements, functions, and subroutines, but the lack of knowledge concerning these topics does not prevent us from writing FORTRAN programs to solve simple problems.

A list of instructions to be given the clerk and a flow diagram for the solution of his problem have been given in Chapter 1. There are many details that must be remembered as we write the program—distinguishing integer and real-variable names and integer and real constants, writing arithmetic statements, branching by the use of an arithmetic **IF** statement, **WRITE** and **FØRMAT** statements, telling the computer that it has finished the computation with a **STØP** or **CALL EXIT**, telling the computer it has been given all of the program by writing **END**.

We may write a FORTRAN program by writing a FORTRAN statement for each of the instructions included in the flow diagram shown in Fig. 1-2. Such a program is shown in Fig. 4-16. Note that a comment card has been used at the beginning of the program so that a listing of the punched cards will be identified.

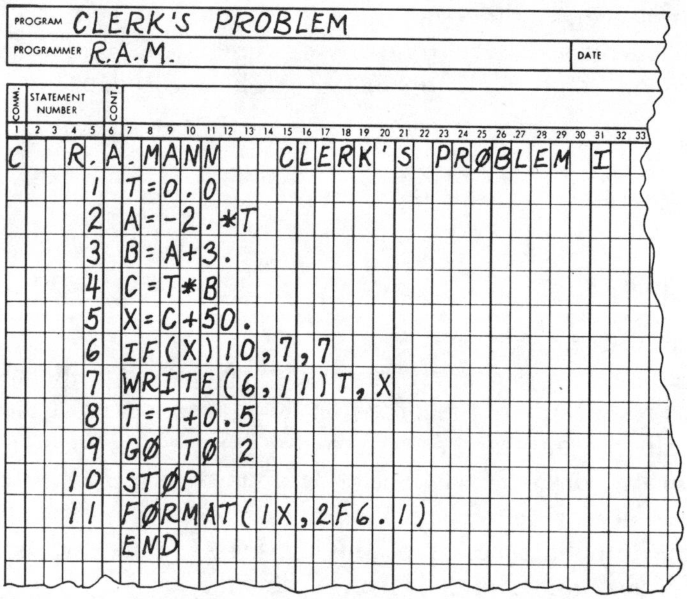

```
PROGRAM   CLERK'S PROBLEM
PROGRAMMER  R.A.M.                                                    DATE

C    R.A.MANN     CLERK'S PRØBLEM I
     1   T=0.0
     2   A=-2.*T
     3   B=A+3.
     4   C=T*B
     5   X=C+50.
     6   IF(X)10,7,7
     7   WRITE(6,11)T,X
     8   T=T+0.5
     9   GØ TØ 2
    10   STØP
    11   FØRMAT(1X,2F6.1)
         END
```

FIG. 4-16

This program will correctly solve the problem, but several simplifications could be made. Statement numbers are needed only on statements **2, 7, 10,** and **11,** since these are the only statement numbers referred to by number in the program. Writing numbers on the other statements will not cause trouble but will require more computer time for the compiling of the program. The **END** statement is normally not given a statement number since it is not executable and therefore may not be referred to by a control statement. Figure 4-17 shows the program after the unneeded statement numbers have been removed.

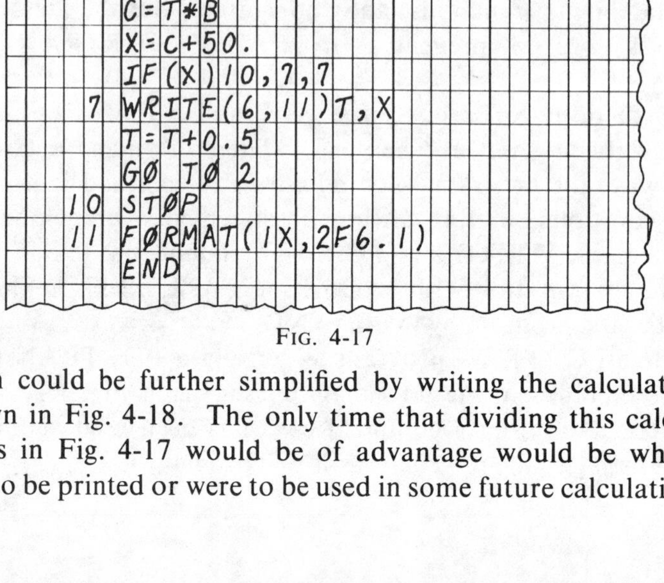

```
PROGRAM   CLERK'S PROBLEM II
PROGRAMMER  R.A.M.                                                    DATE

C    R.A.MANN     CLERK'S PRØBLEM II
         T=0.0
     2   A=-2.*T
         B=A+3.
         C=T*B
         X=C+50.
         IF(X)10,7,7
     7   WRITE(6,11)T,X
         T=T+0.5
         GØ TØ 2
    10   STØP
    11   FØRMAT(1X,2F6.1)
         END
```

FIG. 4-17

The program could be further simplified by writing the calculation of **X** as one statement as shown in Fig. 4-18. The only time that dividing this calculation into several statements as in Fig. 4-17 would be of advantage would be when the quantities **A, B,** and **C** were to be printed or were to be used in some future calculation.

```
PROGRAM  CLERK'S PROBLEM III
PROGRAMMER  R.A.M.                                          DATE

C     R.A.MAMM    CLERK'S  PRØBLEM  III
         T=0.0
      2  X=(-2.*T+3.)*T+50.
         IF(X)10,7,7
      7  WRITE(6,11)T,X
         T=T+0.5
         GØ TØ 2
     10  STØP
     11  FØRMAT(1X,2F6.1)
         END
```

FIG. 4-18

All three programs (those shown in Figs. 4-16, 4-17, and 4-18) will correctly solve the problem and will give printer output shown in Fig. 4-19.

T   X

T	X
0.0	50.0
0.5	51.0
1.0	51.0
1.5	50.0
2.0	48.0
2.5	45.0
3.0	41.0
3.5	36.0
4.0	30.0
4.5	23.0
5.0	15.0
5.5	6.0

FIG. 4-19

4-5. MONITOR CONTROL CARDS

Since early computers had a very limited amount of memory it was necessary to load a deck of cards containing the compiler program into the computer each time a FORTRAN program was to be compiled. After the FORTRAN compiler program had been loaded, the deck of cards containing the FORTRAN program to be compiled, known as the *source deck*, was used as input to the compiler program producing an *object deck*, a deck of cards in which the machine-language instructions were punched, as output. This object deck then had to be loaded into the computer in order that the computation could be made. Some small computers required several steps of loading programs and receiving punched cards that must be reloaded before the actual computation could be made.

The introduction of mass storage permitted the same result being obtained without the physical handling of great masses of punched cards. The same programs still have to be loaded into the computer memory and other instructions produced as output, but now these programs are normally kept in the mass storage units—on a disk or on magnetic tape where they may be loaded into the core memory very quickly without the casual observer being aware that any such process is occurring. An *object program* is still produced, but the machine-language instructions of this program are not punched into cards but are stored, usually in one of the mass-storage units.

The calling of the various programs into action is usually controlled by a supervisory program often called a *monitor program*. A deck of cards containing the entire FORTRAN compiler is no longer loaded for each job. One or more cards are placed in front of the source program to activate the monitor program and give it the information necessary for it to carry out the required procedure. The first card used is typically a **JØB** card that tells the monitor to prepare the computer to receive a new program and often contains identification of the program about to be compiled and run. Other information may be included on this card or on following monitor control cards telling the monitor that the FORTRAN compiler will be needed (the computer system probably also accepts programs written in languages other than FORTRAN such as assembly language or COBOL), what input-output units must be readied, that a listing of the source program is or is not wanted, etc. The programmer must consult the computing center he is using to determine what monitor control cards must be included with his FORTRAN program. These cards often have a particular character or characters punched in their leftmost columns to identify them as monitor control cards. Some systems use **$** as this character; others use // or *. Most computer centers have a supply of prepunched control cards available for the programmer. Some systems require a control card after the **END** card of the FORTRAN program and before any date cards used with the program.

4-6. ERROR MESSAGES

Certain types of errors in FORTRAN programs are detected by the FORTRAN compiler. These are usually errors in form. If a programmer had punched the program shown in Fig. 4-20 into cards and fed these cards with the proper monitor control cards into the computer no calculation would be made.

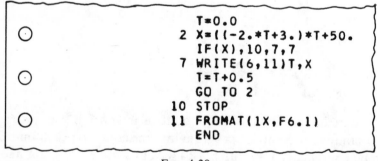

```
                    T=0.0
                  2 X=((-2.*T+3.)*T+50.
                    IF(X),10,7,7
                  7 WRITE(6,11)T,X
                    T=T+0.5
                    GO TO 2
                 10 STOP
                 11 FROMAT(1X,F6.1)
                    END
```

FIG. 4-20

Statement number **2** contains two left parentheses and only one right parenthesis. Someone looking at this statement would realize that there is something wrong but would have no way of telling whether the programmer had put in an extra left parenthesis or had omitted a right parenthesis. The computer not knowing what formula should be used had omitted a right parenthesis. The computer not knowing what formula should be used to calculate **X** will print a message that in effect says to the programmer, "I am unable to write machine-language instructions that will make the computations you desire until you correct statement number **2** to a form that tells me unambiguously exactly what computation you want made. If there is a parenthesis missing in this statement where should it be?" The message is usually given as an error code:

C 36 ERROR AT STATEMENT NO 2

This message tells the programmer that there is an error in statement number **2**. The code (**C36** in the example) informs the programmer of the type of error detected. The codes used are different for different computer systems, but the code used with a particular system is listed in the manuals issued by the computer manufacturer and is often posted in the computer center. The amount of detail given in describing the error found (the *diagnostics*) varies greatly from system to system. One computer may give an error code for the error in statement **2** that refers to unbalanced parentheses while another computer may merely give a code that says that there is an error in form (a syntax error) in the arithmetic statement.

There is also an error in the **IF** statement since the correct form for an **IF** statement does not include a comma between the right parenthesis and the first statement number. The statement should be

```
IF(X)10,7,7
```

and not

```
IF(X),10,7,7
```

The computer is unable to identify the location of this error by printing the statement number of the **IF** statement since it has no statement number. Most computers would print a message of the form

```
C 37 ERROR AT STATEMENT NO 2     +001
```

showing that the error occurs in the first statement after statement number **2**.

A common form of typing error is the transposition of two letters. This is also often found in computer programs because the operation of the keypunch is very similar to typing. Statement number **11** in Fig. 4-20 contains such an error. The programmer no doubt wrote **FØRMAT** on the coding sheet, but he or some other keypunch operator made a "typing" error while punching the cards. (The other two errors in this program may also have been the result of keypunch errors.) Almost any one at all familiar with FORTRAN would realize that the programmer had meant **FØRMAT**; in fact many programmers might overlook this error while proof reading the cards they have punched. The computer, however, is more exacting and will say in effect, "The word '**FRØMAT**' is not in my vocabulary. I don't know what it means."

```
C 04 ERROR AT STATEMENT NO 11
```

One error in the FORTRAN program may cause more than one error comment. Since the computer was unable to recognize statement number **11** as a **FØRMAT** statement it will produce a message stating that statement number **7** is a **WRITE** statement which does not refer to a valid **FØRMAT** statement. The entire error listing then might appear as

```
INVALID STATEMENTS

C 36 ERROR AT STATEMENT NUMBER 2
C 37 ERROR AT STATEMENT NUMBER 2     +001
C 46 ERROR AT STATEMENT NUMBER 7
C 04 ERROR AT STATEMENT NUMBER 11


COMPILATION DISCONTINUED
```

The exact form of these messages varies from computer to computer.

Many beginning programmers are troubled by the fact that an error message may be given for a statement in which no error occurs. Statement number **7** is perfectly correct *if statement number* **11** *is a valid* **FØRMAT** *statement.* Correction of the spelling in statement number **11** would remove two error messages.

There are some types of errors that the computer cannot find. The statement

```
AREA=0.5*B*H
```

would give the correct result if **B** was the base length of a triangle and **H** was the altitude and the result that was wanted was the area of the triangle, but if **B** and **H** were dimensions of a rectangle the statement would not cause the calculation of the area of the rectangle. The computer cannot check your logic. It can say, "You have not given me adequate instructions to permit me to make any computation," but since it is not a mind reader it cannot say, "The computation you have asked me to make is not really the computation you meant to ask me to do."

The computer is very unlikely to make a mistake, but programmers often do. It is desirable for the programmer to check the results produced by the computer where practical. He might not want to check all of the calculations made by the computer in solving the clerk's problem, but an inspection of Fig. 4-19 would show that the variable **T** was stepped in the proper intervals. It would also be desirable to check the computation for several particular values of **T**. If the value of **X** is correct for **T=1.5** and **T=4.0** it will probably be correct for the other values.

PROBLEMS

4-1. What final value would be stored in **J** by each of the following programs?

(a)	(b)	(c)
J=2	J=0	J=0
N=4	N=16	N=1
3 J=J+N	5 J=J*N	6 J=J+N
N=N-1	N=N-2	N=N+1
IF(N-1)4,4,3	IF(N)7,5,5	IF(N-3)6,2,2
4 J=J+5	7 J=J+3	2 J=J/2

4-2. The programs given below are intended to solve the same problem solved by the program in Fig. 4-5. What statement numbers (i, j, k) should be used in each of the **IF**-statements if statement **4** is to be executed after the loop has been executed eight times?

(a)	(b)	(c)
X=0.5	X=0.5	X=0.5
N=0	N=0	N=50
W=1.0	W=1.0	W=1.0
2 W=W*(X**3+7.)	2 W=W*(X**3+7.)	2 N=N-5
N=N+1	N=N+1	W=W*(X**3+7.)
X=X+.5	X=X+.5	X=X+.5
IF(N-7)i,j,k	IF(N-8)i,j,k	IF(N-15)i,j,k

4-3. Write FORTRAN statements that will set *a* and *b* equal to **50.5** and **39.75** respectively, compute *w* such that

$$w = a^2 - b \quad \text{if} \quad a \geq b \qquad \text{and} \qquad w = a + b^2 \quad \text{if} \quad a < b$$

and then set x equal to

$$\frac{w^3}{a}$$

4-4. If **8.24310** and **−592** were stored in locations **X** and **N**, what printed output would be obtained when the statement **WRITE(6,5)X,N** was used with the following **FØRMAT** statement? Show in what columns on the sheet the numbers would be printed.

   (a)   5 FORMAT(F7.3,I5)
   (b)   5 FORMAT(F7.0,2X,I3)
   (c)   5 FORMAT(3X,F6.4,3X,I6)
   (d)   5 FORMAT(I6,F9.4)

4-5. Write **WRITE** and **FØRMAT** statements that will produce the printed values shown if **X = −6.7823** and **N = 542**:

(a)		−	6	.	7	8		5	4	2			
(b)	5	4	2			−	6	.	7	8	2		
(c)		−	6	.	7	8	2		5	4	2		
(d)		5	4	2		−	6	.	7	8		5	4	2

↖ first column on sheet (not the control column)

4-6. Write a FORTRAN program that calculates and prints the amount of money in a piggy bank after deposits have been made in this bank for 30 days; one cent the first day, two cents the second day, four cents the third day, and so on for 30 days (the size of the day's deposit doubles each day). Real arithmetic is to be used. Make the computation in dollars (the first deposit will be 0.01) and use **F15.2** for the output **FØRMAT** specification. Note that the result wanted is the amount of money in the bank after 30 days not the size of the deposit on the 30th day.

4-7. Write a FORTRAN program to solve the following problem. In 1627 Manhattan Island was sold for the equivalent of $24. If that money would have been placed in a bank at 4% interest compounded annually (first interest paid in 1628), what would the bank balance be after the interest had been paid this year? Use **F15.2** for the output.

4-8. Write a FORTRAN program to calculate the first 30 values of y from the equation

$$y = 5x^3 + 7x^2 - 4x + 10$$

for $x = 0.0$, $x = 0.1$, $x = 0.2$, $x = 0.3$, etc. The output desired is a table of values of x and y.

4-9. The sine of an angle may be obtained from the series

$$\sin x = x - \frac{x^3}{3!} + \frac{x^5}{5!} - \frac{x^7}{7!} + \frac{x^9}{9!} - \cdots$$

where x is measured in radians. Write a FORTRAN program to compute and print the sine of 0.3 radian using the first five terms of this series.

4-10. Write a FORTRAN program to compute and print the sine of 0.3 radian using the series given in Prob. 4-9. Use as many terms as necessary to insure that the absolute value of the quantity obtained by dividing the last term used by the sum of the terms is less than 0.000001.

4-11. Write a FORTRAN program to determine whether or not 127 is prime (not exactly divisible by any positive integer other than one or itself). Have the computer print zero if 127 is not prime or one if it is.

4-12. Write a FORTRAN program that will add all odd integers from 1 to 75 and print the sum.

$$J = 1 + 3 + 5 + 7 + \cdots + 71 + 73 + 75$$

4-13. Write a FORTRAN program to produce a table giving the diameter and area of circles with diameters of 5, 10, 15, 20, ..., 50.

4-14. Write a FORTRAN program to produce a table of x and y where $y = x + x^2$ for $x = 0.5$, $x = 1.0$, $x = 1.5$, $x = 2.0$, etc., for all such values of x that yield a value of y less than 120.

4-15. Write a FORTRAN program to produce a table of q and p where $q = p^2$ if $p < 2.5$ and $q = p^2 - p$ if $p \geq 2.5$ for $p = 0.0$, $p = 0.5$, $p = 1.0$, $p = 1.5$, ..., $p = 6.0$.

4-16. Write a FORTRAN program using the series in Prob. 4-9 to obtain a table of angles and sines of angles 0.1, 0.2, 0.3, 0.4, ..., 2.0 radians. Use as many terms of the series as necessary to insure that the absolute value of the quantity obtained by dividing the last term used by the sum of the terms is less than 0.000001.

CHAPTER 5

Accuracy, E Format, Input

5-1. Accuracy

Any calculation, whether made by hand or by a digital computer, may be exact but is more often approximate. Approximations are brought into the calculations when digits are omitted by rounding or truncation, or when the "input" numbers of the calculation are only approximately known. Suppose that we give the clerk instructions to write real numbers equal to **4.78296** and **31.6526** into locations **028** and **136** on his blackboard. He would convert these numbers to the required form and write them as

028									
+	4	7	8	2	9	6	+	0	1

and

136									
+	3	1	6	5	2	6	+	0	2

If we now asked him to multiply the number in location **028** by the number in location **136** and put the product in location **203** he could make the multiplication

$$4.78296 \times 31.6526 = 151.393119696$$

but when he attempted to write this product into location **203** he would have to write it as

203									
+	1	5	1	3	9	3	+	0	3

The number he must write into location **203** is approximately but not exactly equal to the correct product since he has space to write only six significant digits whereas the exact product contains twelve digits. He must discard the last six digits (119696) of the product. Computers normally calculate using binary arithmetic, but are often required to discard binary digits (bits) when the number of bits produced by an arithmetic operation exceeds the number of cores provided for the storage of the number. Inaccuracies caused by the discarding of the excess decimal digits or bits are known as *round-off errors*.

Round-off errors may cause unexpected results. Suppose that the clerk is asked to carry out the simple computation shown in the flow chart of Fig. 5-1. We might expect the clerk to write numbers approximately equal to zero, one third, two thirds, and one, and then to stop. This would not be entirely correct since the numbers he would store in a location representing **Y** would be

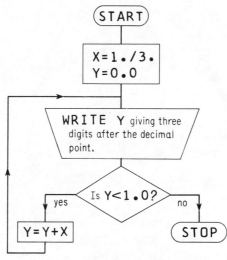

Fig. 5-1

```
+000000+00
+333333+00
+666666+00
+999999+00
+133333+01
```

The number he stored on his blackboard (in memory) that was approximately equal to one would be equal to **+0.999999.** He would write this number on the output sheet as **1.000** or as **0.999** depending on whether his standing orders were to round or truncate output, but in either case the number in memory would be less than one, and the question

Is **Y** < **1.0**?

would send him on for one more addition producing a number approximately equal to one and one third. Note that if the flow chart had attempted to end the computation with the question

Does **Y** equal **1.0**?

the computation would never be finished since the clerk would never produce a number exactly equal to one. When such an event occurs in a computer program we say that we have created an *endless loop*. The computer would continue go around and around on the loop, making the computation until the computer operator intervened.

This type of round-off complication may occur unexpectedly due to the fact that the computer does use binary arithmetic. When we write a decimal number such as **372.6,** we mean

$$3 \times 10^2 + 7 \times 10^1 + 2 \times 10^0 + 6 \times 10^{-1}$$

Some fractions may be represented exactly as decimal numbers:

$$^3/_4 = 7 \times 10^{-1} + 5 \times 10^{-2} = 0.75$$

There are fractions that may not be represented *exactly* as decimal numbers:

$$^1/_3 = 0.333333333\ldots$$

and
$$^4/_7 = 0.5714285714\ldots$$

In the same manner, there are fractions that may be represented exactly in a binary form:

$$^5/_8 \text{ (decimal)} = {}^1/_2 + {}^1/_8 = 1 \times 2^{-1} + 0 \times 2^{-2} + 1 \times 2^{-3}$$
$$= 0.101 \text{ (binary)}$$

There are, however, many fractions that may not be represented exactly in a binary form including $^1/_{10}$ (decimal). Therefore when a real constant that includes a decimal part is fed into a binary computer (as for example by the arithmetic statement $X = 6.891$) the decimal number will be converted into a binary number and stored in the computer as a number that may not be exactly equal to the number we attempted to store.

This may cause trouble if the programmer does not take it into account just as the clerk's calculation might be incorrect if the person giving him his instructions had planned on his ending the computation with Y equal to one. The program shown in Fig. 5-2 is very

```
        Y=0.
   1    WRITE(6,10)Y
        IF(Y-1.0)3,5,5
   3    Y=Y+0.1
        GØ TØ 1
   5    STØP
  10    FØRMAT(1X,F10.3)
        END
```

FIG. 5-2

similar to the program used to solve Fig. 5-1. The clerk or a decimal computer would not be bothered by round-off with this program and would end the computation with Y being exactly equal to one. A binary computer (which means most computers) would end the computation with Y being approximately equal to 1.1.

Figure 5-3 shows the printed output produced when the program of Fig. 5-2 is run on

```
        0.000
        0.100
        0.200
        0.300
        0.399
        0.499
        0.599
        0.699
        0.799
        0.899
        0.999
        1.099
```

FIG. 5-3

a computer system that truncates output. Figure 5-4 shows the output produced by the same computer system using the output FØRMAT statement

```
10 FORMAT(1X,F10.1)
```

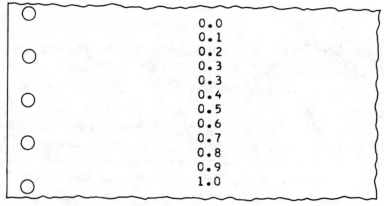

FIG. 5-4

The output produced by a computer system that rounds output is shown in Fig. 5-5. The results obtained look less startling than those in Fig. 5-4, but the final number obtained is still not approximately equal to one. The numbers produced by the computation and stored internally by the computer would be the same in all cases. The difference arises only when the binary numbers are converted to decimal numbers for printing.

```
                    0.000
                    0.100
                    0.200
                    0.300
                    0.400
                    0.500
                    0.600
                    0.700
                    0.800
                    0.900
                    1.000
                    1.100
```

FIG. 5-5

The program shown in Fig. 5-6 illustrates one method that may be used to obtain rounded results on a computer system that truncates output. This program would produce output identical to that of Fig. 5-5.

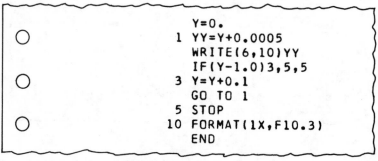

```
      Y=0.
   1  YY=Y+0.0005
      WRITE(6,10)YY
      IF(Y-1.0)3,5,5
   3  Y=Y+0.1
      GO TO 1
   5  STOP
  10  FORMAT(1X,F10.3)
      END
```

FIG. 5-6

Computations made in the integer mode will be exact unless division causes truncation or an integer number is produced that is larger than the maximum that may be stored, and integer numbers printed are of course neither truncated nor rounded.

5-2. E FØRMAT SPECIFICATION FOR OUTPUT

Printing or punching of integer numbers always makes use of an **I FØRMAT** specification. The output of real numbers may use either an **F FØRMAT** specification or an **E FØRMAT** specification. Using **I** and **F** specifications for output was discussed in Sec. 4-3. The **F** specification yields results in a very readable form if the numbers involved are not very large or very small. Large numbers such as

$$513502000000.0$$

or small numbers like

$$0.0000000000000365892$$

are not easy to interpret, since it is necessary to count digits or zeros to evaluate these numbers. The **F** specification is only practical when the programmer has a close knowledge of the magnitudes of the results to be printed. If a program included the statements

```
WRITE(6,5)Q
5 FORMAT(2X,F4.1)
```

used for printing successive values of **Q**, a readable table would be produced:

```
50.1
48.7
46.1
97.3
```

However, if a positive value of **Q** was **100** or larger or a negative value was **10** or larger, the number would not fit into the spaces provided, and some or all of the characters would not be printed. If the number were **0.59832,** only one significant digit would be printed

```
0.5
```

and any number less than **0.1** would be printed as

```
0.0
```

The **F** specification is usually used for the output of real numbers if the magnitude of the numbers is approximately known. This specification may not be desirable when the absolute value of the numbers involved is very large or very small, since such numbers printed with this format may be difficult to interpret.

The **E FØRMAT** specification is used for the output of real numbers that may not be readily written using the **F** specification because their magnitudes are too large, too small, or unknown. The **E FØRMAT** specification consists of the letter **E** followed by two numbers separated by a decimal point. If **−4678.9** were stored in location **W,** the statements

```
WRITE(6,9)W
9 FORMAT(E14.5)
```

would produce

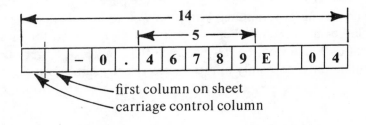

first column on sheet
carriage control column

This output indicates that the number is equal to

$$-0.46789 \times 10^4 = -4678.9$$

The number between the letter **E** and the decimal point in the **FØRMAT** specification (the **14** in the example) gives the field width. The number after the decimal point (the **5** in the example) indicates the number of significant digits that are to be printed. The statements

```
        QR=0.0005072378
        WRITE(6,17)QR
    17 FORMAT(E15.4)
```

would produce

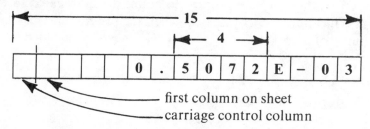

The output indicates that the number stored in **QR** is equal to

$$0.5072 \times 10^{-3} = 0.0005072$$

to the number of significant digits printed.

Section 3-1 described how a programmer could write a constant in a number of different ways using a letter **E**. Any one of the statements below would result in a number equal to **0.0000528** being stored in location **X**.

```
        X=0.528E-04
        X=+52.80E-6
        X=.52800E-4
        X=528.E-5
```

The programmer has an option as to how he may write the constant, but the computer is given no option. It is told that when it receives instructions to print a number using a **FØRMAT** specification of the form Ew.d (where w and d are integer constants) it is to print a minus sign if the number is negative (no plus sign is to be printed on most computer systems if the number is positive); a zero and a decimal point; the number of significant digits specified (the first digit after the decimal is not be zero); the letter **E**; a minus sign if the exponent is negative or a blank space if the exponent is positive; and last of all a two digit exponent. All of these characters are to be right-justified in a field whose width is given in the specification. The field width should be at least seven spaces larger than the number of significant digits in order to leave space for the sign, the zero, the decimal point, the letter **E**, and the exponent. It is desirable to leave a blank space for the control column when the printer is the output unit being used, and when more than one number is printed on a line it is desirable to leave space between numbers to improve readability. The beginning programmer would do well to always make the field width at least eight digits larger than the number of significant digits asked for in an **E** specification. The specification **E10.6** would not work since **10** is only four larger than **6**.

Many computers may store only approximately seven significant digits for each real number, and when the **WRITE** and **FØRMAT** statements ask for more than this number of significant digits to be printed, the computer will supply meaningless digits to fill the required spaces. The statements

```
      X=513527000000.0
      WRITE(6,23)X
   23 FORMAT(E18.10)
```

would produce the output

```
0.5135270551E 12
```

Note that the first seven significant digits are those expected, but that the remaining three digits are meaningless. The same effect will be noted when an **F** specification would produce more than seven significant digits. The statements

```
      X=513527000000.0
      WRITE(6,24)X
   24 FORMAT(F16.1)
```

yield

```
513527055103.9
```

The form of the output produced using an **E** specification may be modified by the use of a scale factor. The use of such a factor is not necessary for utilization of the computer and is described in Appendix G.

5-3. INPUT

There are two methods by which the given numerical data may be entered into a FORTRAN computation. The program that solved the clerk's problem (Fig. 4-18) included the given data as constants (**2.**, **3.**, **50.**, and **0.5**) in the two arithmetic statements

```
    2 X=(-2.*T+3.)*T+50.
```

and

```
      T=T+0.5
```

All numerical data may be entered as constants in arithmetic statements, but this method is tedious if a very large amount of input data is required. Many if not most FORTRAN programs are executed more than once requiring a new set of data for each execution. It would be a time-consuming task to rewrite the statements that contain the data and repunch the cards for each execution. Usually the quantities whose values change from "run" to "run" are given variable names, and the program is set up to read numerical data from cards at the time the program is executed, and constants are used only for the quantities that are really constant.

Input is in many respects very similar to output. A **READ** statement refers to a particular piece of input equipment and to a **FØRMAT** statement that indicates the form of the data. The statement

READ(5,92)JUG,INK,L

tells the computer to read numbers from the next card in the input hopper of the card reader (if input unit number **5** is the card reader), that **FØRMAT** statement number **92** gives the form and location of the numbers on the card, and that these numbers are to be stored at locations **JUG**, **INK**, and **L**. Storing a number in or at a location means replacing whatever number had been stored in that location by the new number.

The letter **I** in a **FØRMAT** specification used with a **READ** statement tells the computer that it will find an integer number punched in the indicated columns. The statements

READ(5,92)JUG,INK,L
92 FORMAT(I7,I13,I6)

tell the computer to take the next card, read the integer number it finds in the first seven columns and store this number in location **JUG**, find an integer number punched in the next thirteen columns (columns 8 through 20) and replace whatever number is in location **INK** with this new number, and finally find an integer number in the next six columns (columns 21 through 26) and replace the old number in location **L** with this new number. If the card shown in Fig. 5-7 were read by the above statements the integer numbers **328**,

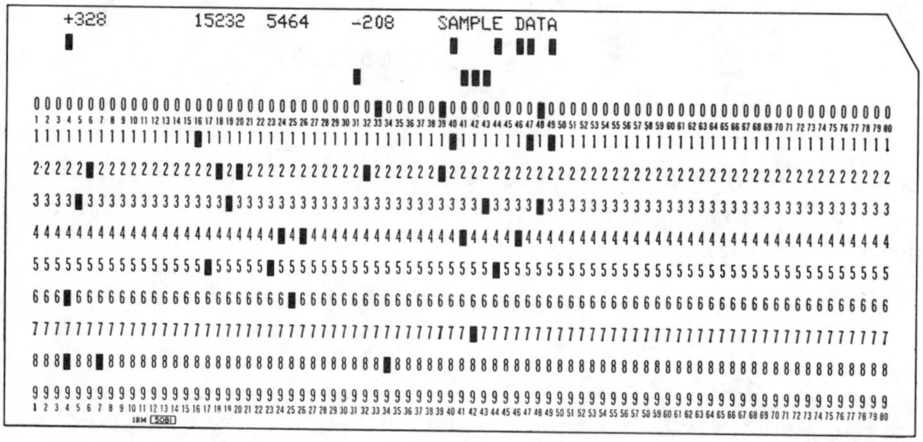

Fig. 5-7

−15232, and **5464** would be stored in **JUG**, **INK**, and **L** respectively. The number **−208** and the letters **SAMPLE DATA** would be completely ignored since the **READ** and **FØRMAT** statements tell the computer to examine columns 1 through 26, and anything punched in any column other than these 26 columns will be ignored. If the programmer had wished the number **−208** to be read he would have had to include another variable name in the **READ** statement and another specification in the **FØRMAT** statement. The statements

READ(5,93)JUG,INK,L,MM
93 FORMAT(I7,I13,I6,I8)

used to read the card of Fig. 5-7 would cause the integer numbers **328**, **15232**, **5464**, and

−208 to be stored in **JUG, INK, L,** and **MM** respectively. Figure 5-8 shows how these statements would interpret the card. There is no "control column" with input devices. All columns indicated by the **FØRMAT** specifications refer to actual columns on the card.

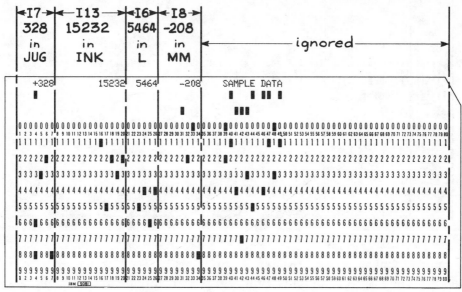

FIG. 5-8

The computer reads blank columns as zeros. The statements

```
        READ(5,97)JUG,INK,L,MM
     97 FORMAT(I8,I5,I6,I5)
```

used to read this same card would cause **3280, 0, 1523,** and **20054** to be stored in the indicated locations! The computer does not "look" at the card and say that there are obviously the numbers **+328, 15232, 5464,** and **−208** punched in this card; it examines the card column by column as indicated by the specifications. The **I8** specification tells the computer to examine the first eight columns, and these columns contain the characters bbb**+328**b where b represents a blank. Reading the blanks as though they were zeros, the computer stores **3280** in **JUG.** The next five columns (columns 9 through 13) contain blanks, and the computer stores zero in **INK.** The **I6** refers to columns 14 through 19, and these contain bb**1523** which is stored in **L** as **1523.** The final **I5** specification refers to columns 20 through 24, and the **2**bb**54** in these columns is stored in **MM** as **20054.** Figure 5-9 shows how the data card would be interpreted by these statements.

What numbers are stored is dependent on the **READ** statement, the **FØRMAT** statement, and the data card. If any one of these three things were changed the numbers stored would be different. Integer numbers to be read from a data card should therefore be completely within the field specified and should be right-justified in this field to prevent blanks being read as zeros in such a way that the magnitude of the number is misinterpreted.

The programmer should decide what columns on the data card he is going to use for punching each number and then make sure that the specifications refer to these columns.

An **X** specification may be used to tell the computer to ignore certain columns on a card. The statements

```
        READ(5,29)JILL,JACK
     29 FORMAT(4X,I5,6X,I4)
```

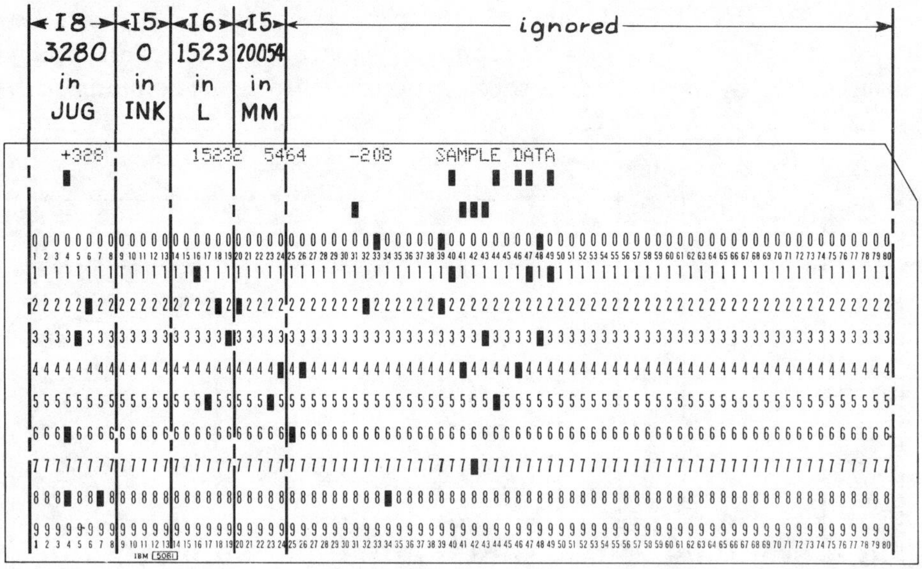

FIG. 5-9

tell the computer to take the next card, ignore anything punched in the first four columns, read an integer number from columns 5 through 9 and store it in **JILL**, ignore anything punched in columns 10 through 15, and read an integer number from columns 16 through 19 and store it in **JACK** (anything punched in columns 20 through 80 would also be ignored).

A real number may be read by the use of either an **F** or an **E FØRMAT** specification. The statements

```
      READ(5,627)X,P73,WIG
  627 FORMAT(F12.3,F10.5,F14.0)
```

tell the computer to take the next card, find a real number punched in the first twelve columns and store this number in location **X**, find a real number in the next ten columns (columns 13 through 22) and store this number in **P73**, and find a real number in the next fourteen columns (columns 23 through 36) and store this in **WIG**. Figure 5-10 shows how

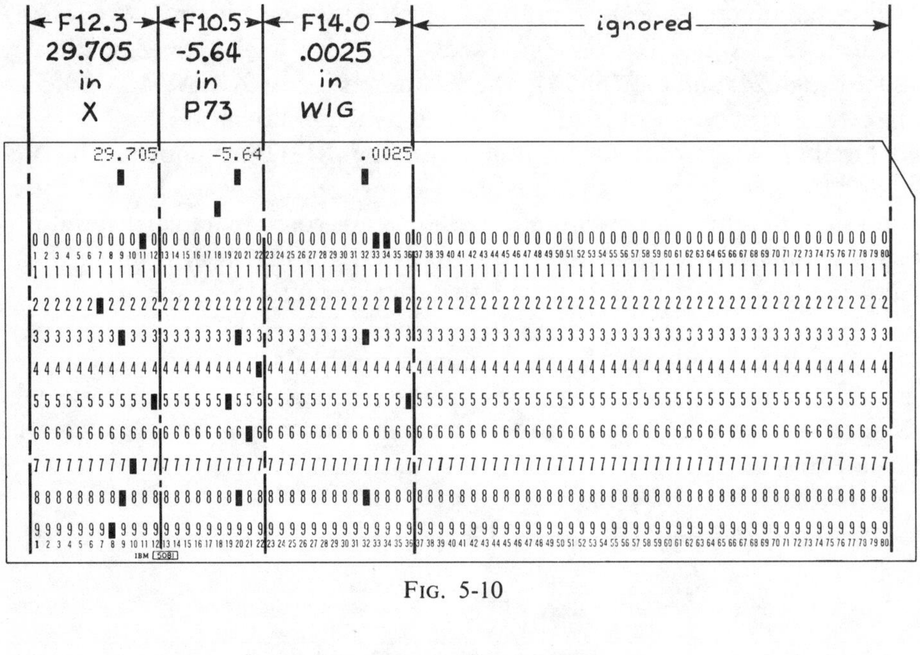

FIG. 5-10

these statements would read the numbers **29.705**, **−5.64**, and **0.0025** from the card shown and store them in **X**, **P73**, and **WIG**.   Remember that the clerk would convert these numbers

$$29.705 = 0.297050 \times 10^2$$
$$-5.64 = -0.564000 \times 10^1$$
$$.0025 = 0.250000 \times 10^{-2}$$

and write them in his table in the form **+297050+02**, **−564000+01**, and **+250000−02**. The computer will also convert the numbers but will store them in the equivalent binary form.

The integer numbers in the specifications between the letter **F** and the decimal point (the **12**, **10**, and **14** in the example) give a field width—tell the computer how many columns to examine in finding the number to be read. The integer numbers after the decimal point in the **F** specifications (the **3**, **5**, and **0** in the example) have a different meaning when the **FØRMAT** statement is used with a **READ** than it had when used with a **WRITE** statement. When the specification **F12.3** is used with a **READ** statement, the letter **F** tells the computer to find a real number, the **12** tells the computer to examine 12 columns in reading this real number, and the **3** tells the computer that *if there is no decimal point punched in these twelve columns* it is to read the number as though there were a decimal point in front of the right three of these twelve columns. If the statements

```
     READ(5,122)Q,RED,TWIT
 122 FORMAT(F12.3,F11.4,F13.4)
```

were used to read the card shown in Fig. 5-11 the numbers **54.306**, **65.97**, and **−27.542**

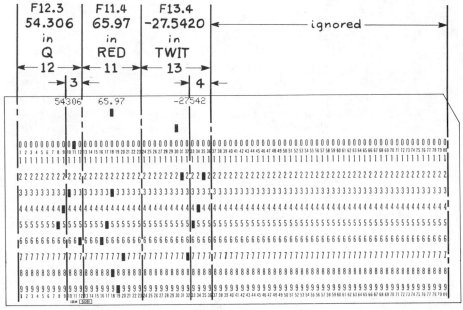

FIG. 5-11

would be stored in **Q**, **RED**, and **TWIT** respectively. After this card had been fed into the read station of the card reader the computer would examine the first 12 columns of the card. When the computer failed to find a decimal point in these twelve columns it would read the number **54306** it found as **54.306** since the **3** in the **F12.3** tells it to read the number as though there were a decimal point in front of the last three of these twelve columns—just in front of columns 10, 11, and 12. The number **54.306** would be stored in **Q**. The computer would then examine the next 11 columns and since it would find a decimal point punched in these eleven (13 through 23) columns it reads the number as **65.97** ignoring the **4** of the **F11.4** since this **4** tells the computer where to imagine the decimal point only if there is no actual decimal point punched in the columns examined. The computer would finally examine the next thirteen (24 through 36) columns. Failing to find a decimal point it would read the **−27542b** as **−27.5420** and store this number in **TWIT**. The **4** in the **F13.4** told the computer to imagine a decimal point in front of the last four columns examined in this field when it did not find a punched decimal point. It will read the blank in column 36 as a zero and place a decimal in front of the **542b**. Note that the fact that the **65.97** is not right-justified in its field does not change what number is read since reading the number as **−27.5420** instead of **−27.542** does not change its magnitude. The placement of a number in a field without a decimal does have an effect. If the **−27542** had been punched with the minus sign in column 31 instead of column 30 the number stored in **TWIT** by the **READ** statement would have been **−2.7542** instead of **−27.542**.

The statements

```
    READ(5,16)BIG,BAD,WOLF
 16 FORMAT(E12.3,E14.1,E15.4)
```

might be used to read the data card shown in Fig. 5-12. The first number after each letter

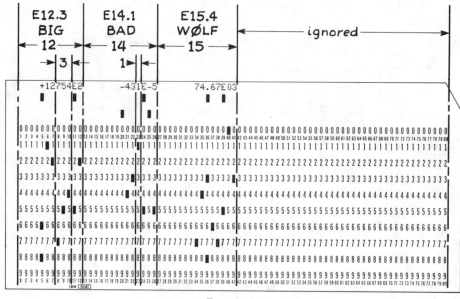

FIG. 5-12

E in the **FØRMAT** statement (the **12**, **14**, and **15** in the example) indicates a field width, and each second number, the number after the decimal point (the **3**, **1**, and **4** in the example), indicates the location of the decimal point in the number on the card if no decimal point is punched in the card field indicated. The **FØRMAT** statement therefore asks the computer to find a number punched in **E FØRMAT** in the first twelve columns of the card, assume a decimal point in front of three digits of the number in front of the **E** on the card since there is no decimal punched in this number on the card (read the number as **12.754**), and multiply this number by ten raised to the power given after the **E** on the card (multiply by 10^2). The **READ** statement tells the computer to store this number at a location **BIG** in memory. A real number equal to

$$12.754 \times 10^2 = 1275.4$$

would be stored at location **BIG**.

Similarly, a real number equal to

$$-43.1 \times 10^{-5} = -0.000431$$

would be stored at location **BAD**.

Since there is a decimal point punched in the third number on the card, **74.67**, the **4** in the specification **E15.4** would be ignored, and a real number equal to

$$74.67 \times 10^3 = 74670.$$

would be stored at location **WØLF**.

The exponent (the letter **E** and the following number on the card) may be punched in many different ways. Figure 5-13 shows eight different ways that the number read into **BIG** in the above example might be punched.

```
12754E+02
12754E+2
12754E 02
12754E 2
12754E02
12754E2
12754+02
12754+2
```

FIG. 5-13

The exponent may be punched as a one- or two-digit number (**02** or **2**). A space may be left in place of the plus sign of the exponent (**E+02, E+2, E 02, E 2**) or the one- or two-digit number may be punched next to the letter **E** without leaving room for the sign (**E02, E2**). The letter **E** is required in **E** constants used in arithmetic expressions, but the **FØRMAT** statement used with the **READ** statement has already given this information, so the letter **E** may be omitted on the card. If the letter **E** is omitted, the sign of the exponent must be punched (**12754 02** or **12754 2** are not valid). Each of the eight numbers given in Fig. 5-13 would result in the storage of a number equal to **1275.4** in location **BIG** when the card is read with the **READ** and **FØRMAT** statements given with Fig. 5-12. The number should be right-justified in its field regardless of which form is used.

A plus sign may be punched in front of a positive number regardless of the form

```
12754E 02
```

or

```
+12754E 02
```

The shortened forms are used when it is desirable to get the maximum number of numbers on a card.

Figure 5-14 shows four ways that a number with a negative exponent may be punched. The sign of the exponent must be punched if negative, since if no sign is given the computer will assume it to be positive.

In addition to this large number of ways a number with an exponent may be punched

```
                    -431E-05
                    -431E-5
                    -431-05
                    -431-5
```

FIG. 5-14

on a card, the computer will accept a number punched without any letter and any exponent. In other words, the computer will accept a number punched with the **F FØRMAT** on the card in a field that the **FØRMAT** statement designates as an **E** field. Numbers punched

```
                   +1275.4
                    1275.4
                   +1275400
                    1275400
```

right-justified in the first twelve columns of a data card used with the statements

```
        READ(5,16)BIG,BAD,WOLF
     16 FORMAT(E12.3,E14.1,E15.4)
```

would cause a number equal to **1275.4** to be stored in location **BIG**.

As with output, an integer number in front of a letter in the **FØRMAT** statement indicates the number of times this specification is to be repeated. The statement

```
     91 FORMAT(3I4,2E16.5,3F8.2)
```

is equivalent to the statement

```
     91 FORMAT(I4,I4,I4,E16.5,E16.5,F8.2,F8.2,F8.2)
```

The **READ** statements may have statement numbers and are written in the programs so that they will be executed when desired. The **FØRMAT** statements may be placed anywhere within the program before the **END** statement. One **FØRMAT** statement may be referred to by both **READ** and **WRITE** statements.

When a FORTRAN program is loaded into a computer the FORTRAN compiler produces a set of machine-language instructions that are intended to carry out the procedure the programmer had described by use of the FORTRAN statements. No FORTRAN instruction is "executed" before the entire program is compiled, and this cannot be completed until the **END** statement has been loaded into the computer. No **READ** statement is executed until after the entire FORTRAN program including the **END** statement has been fed into the computer. The *next card in the input hopper* that is read by the **READ** statement therefore cannot be before the **END** statement. The *next card* that is read is *not* the card immediately after the **READ** statement or immediately after the **FØRMAT** statement but is a card placed after the **END** statement (and after any monitor control cards that may be required after the **END** card).

When the computer executes a **READ** statement it moves the next card in the hopper of the card reader to the read station and consults the first specification in the **FØRMAT** statement to determine which columns of the data card are to be examined to find the number to be stored at the location indicated by the first variable name. The second specification is then used with the second variable name and this process continues through the specifications and variable names until either all of the specifications or all of the variable names have been used. If there are fewer variable names in the **READ** statement than there are specifications in the **FØRMAT** statement the process described above is terminated when all variable names have been handled. The statements

```
      READ(5,16)BIG,BAD
   16 FORMAT(E12.3,E14.1,E15.4)
```

would cause the computer to use the **E12.3** specification to read a number into location **BIG** and the **E14.1** specification to read a number into location **BAD**. The **E15.4** specification would never be used.

If there are more names in the **READ** statement list than there are specifications, the process proceeds until all of the specifications have been used. Then a new card is brought to the read station, and the process continues after a return to the preceding left parenthesis in the **FØRMAT** statement. If data cards were punched from the listing shown in

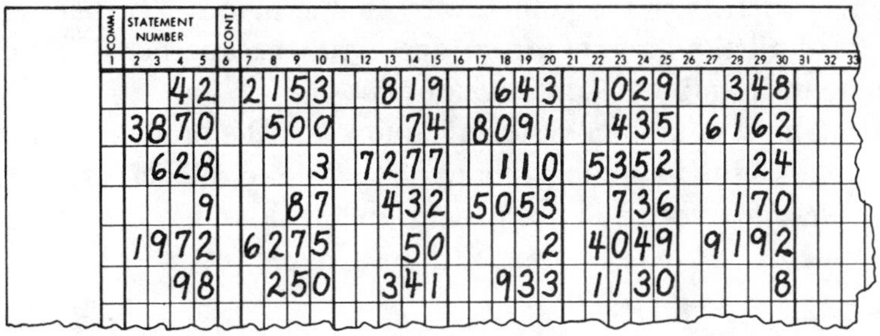

FIG. 5-15

Fig. 5-15 and these cards were the next cards in the hopper when the statements

```
      READ(5,7)X1,X2,X3,X4,X5
    7 FORMAT(F5.0,F5.1)
```

were executed, the first card shown would be taken and the **42** in the first five columns would be read as **42.** according to the specification **F5.0**, and this number would be stored in X1. The **2153** in the second five columns of this card would be read as **215.3** according to the **F5.1** specification, and this number would be stored in **X2**. Since the specifications would then all have been used without all of the variable names having been satisfied, the second card would be taken and the **3870** in the first five columns of this card would be read as **3870.** according to the **F5.0** and the **500** as **50.0** according to the **F5.1**. These numbers would be stored in **X3** and **X4**. Again the specifications would all have been used without satisfying all the variable names. The third card would be taken, and the **628** would be read as **628.** according to the **F5.0**, and **628.** would be stored in **X5**. This would complete the reading to be done by this **READ** statement since only one number will be read into each of the variables named. These statements would read five numbers from three cards, two from the first, two from the second, and one from the third. The remaining numbers on these three cards would be ignored, and the fourth card, the card starting with **9**, would now be the next card in the hopper and would be the card taken when the next **READ** statement in the program was executed.

If, on the other hand, the statements

```
      READ(5,130)J1,J2,J3,J4,J5
  130 FORMAT(6I5)
```

were the ones executed when the first card of Fig. 5-15 was the next card in the hopper, **42, 2153, 819, 643,** and **1029** would be read from the first card according to the first five

I5 specifications and would be stored in **J1**, **J2**, **J3**, **J4**, and **J5** respectively. Columns 26 through 80 of this card would be ignored, and the second card, the card starting **3870**, would be the next card to be read by the next **READ** statement.

The statements

```
      READ(5,22)Q1,Q2,Q3,Q4,Q5
   22 FORMAT(F4.1)
```

used to read these same cards would cause **0.4, 38.7, 6.2, 0.0,** and **19.7** to be stored in **Q1, Q2, Q3, Q4,** and **Q5.** The one specification permits one number to be read from the first four columns of each card.

One execution of a **READ** statement will result in the reading of as many numbers as there are variable names in the **READ** statement. These numbers will all be read from one card if the **FφRMAT** statement has enough specifications—if the number of specifications is equal to or greater than the number of variable names. If there are not enough specifications to read all the numbers from one card, the number of numbers read per card will be equal to the number of specifications.

As with output, most computer systems require that the mode of the specification be the same as the mode of the variable name to be read. No integer variable may be read with an **E** or an **F** specification, and no real variable with an **I** specification. A program including the statements

```
      READ(5,28)M,Z
   28 FORMAT(E14.6,F10.3)
```

would be compiled without any error comments on most computers and would start to run, but when the computer reached this **READ** statement it would "hang up" and quit calculating.

5-4. Sample Programs

Suppose we have a number of equations such as

$$2x^2 - 7.8x + 7.56 = 0$$
$$1.5x^2 - 4.215x - 5.6658 = 0$$
$$7.2x^2 + 395.496x - 138024.5 = 0$$
$$3.125x^2 + 1.2156x + 2.2517 = 0$$
$$1x^2 - 5.02x + 6.3001 = 0$$

and wish to write a FORTRAN program to find the real roots of the equations. (Real in this case means roots with no imaginary parts.) The equations are of the form

$$ax^2 + bx + c = 0$$

The roots of the equations may be found by the quadratic formula

$$x = \frac{-b \pm \sqrt{b^2 - 4ac}}{2a}$$

The two roots of the equation will be

$$x_1 = \frac{-b + \sqrt{b^2 - 4ac}}{2a}$$

and

$$x_2 = \frac{-b - \sqrt{b^2 - 4ac}}{2a}$$

The roots will be real if the quantity $(b^2 - 4ac)$ is nonnegative.

The program could be written introducing all the constants in arithmetic statements, but this would be involved, and the program would have to be rewritten if we wished to use it to find the roots of a different set of equations. It would be desirable to write the program to read the values of a, b, and c for each equation from one card. The solution of each equation is a problem in itself, in that the constants and roots of one equation are not required for finding the roots of another equation. There is no need to save any values pertaining to one equation after its roots have been found and printed.

One possible method of keeping track of when the job is done is to read an integer value such as N from the first card that tells how many equations are to be solved, subtracting one from N each time the work on an equation is finished, and ending the computation when N becomes zero (the value of N at any time will indicate how many equations have not been solved).

A decision must be made as to what is to be printed out in each possibility. If just the two roots are printed, someone looking at the results would find it difficult to determine which roots went with which equation. It would probably be best to print A, B, C, X1, and X2 for each equation that had real roots. It might be desirable to print A, B, and C for each equation that has no real roots so that there will be a record of which equations have been used in the calculation.

A flow chart for this problem is shown in Fig. 5-16. The blocks used for the reading operations on this chart are shaped like a punched card (which has one upper corner cut off) indicating that these operations involve punched cards. The block used for writing

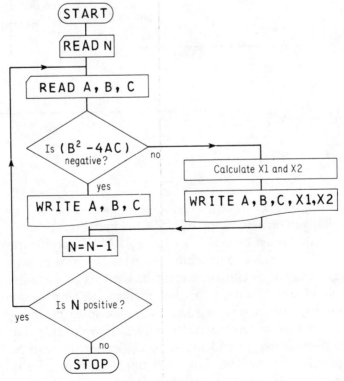

FIG. 5-16

the answer is shaped like a torn-off piece of paper indicating that the printer is involved. Input and output operations on a flow chart may use the trapezoids as used in Sec. 1-2, or they may use symbols that indicate which specific type of input or output device is to be used.

An examination of the flow chart of Fig. 5-16 will indicate which statements in the program will require statement numbers. The first statement in any block that may be reached by more than one path will require a statement number as will the first statement in any block that is reached by a path from a question block or other control statement. These are the only statements that will require statement numbers besides the **FØRMAT** statements, which always have statement numbers. It is helpful to add statement numbers at the required points in the flow chart as shown in Fig. 5-17 before the program is written.

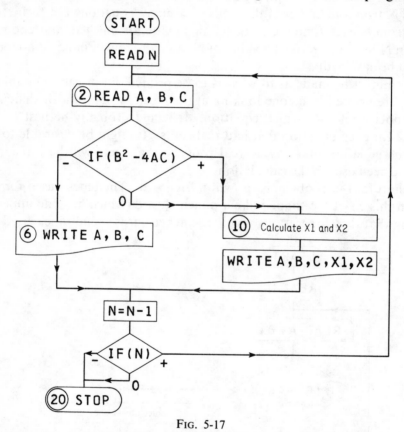

FIG. 5-17

The question blocks in Fig. 5-17 have been changed to a form that is closer to the arithmetic **IF** statement that will be used in the FORTRAN program.

The next decision that must be made is what **FØRMAT** specifications are to be used in reading the data. The first value to be read is **N**, the number of equations. This is to be an integer number and so an **I** specification must be used. There are five equations in the given problem and so **I1** could be used for this problem. The program is being written so that it may be used for other sets of equations. We must decide what is the largest number of equations that we will ever wish to solve. If we decide that the number will always be less than **1000** we may use **I3** for the specification to read **N**. The number of equations will be punched in the first data card right-justified in columns 1 to 3. The number **5** will be punched in column 3 for the problem given.

The values of **A, B,** and **C** contain decimals and therefore must be real numbers; an

E or an **F** specification must be used to read or write these values. There are a very large number of specifications that could be used, and we must examine the numbers that will be read as well as consider what numbers might appear in future problems that we would want the program to be capable of handling. We might reach the conclusion that no number would require more than seven significant digits. A number may require a space for a negative sign and will include a decimal point. Our conclusion is that a field width of nine is required to hold a number. A field width of ten would be easier to use, since it is easier to think of fields ending in columns 10, 20, and 30 than of fields ending in columns 9, 18, and 27. Leaving a space between the numbers on one card also eases the chore of proofreading. We might then decide to use an **F** specification with a field width of 10. It is usually better to punch the decimal point in each number instead of making use of the specification to imply the location of the decimal point, since we are less likely to be confused as to the location of the decimal point if it is actually punched. The implied location of the decimal point is used only when space on the card is limited and we do not wish to take the required space for the points. Because our problem will read only three numbers from each card, there is no space limitation, and we might decide to use a **3F10.2** specification for reading **A**, **B**, and **C**. Since we are going to punch a decimal point in the card for each number to be read, the **2** in the specification will not be used by the computer, and **3F10.3** or **3F10.0** would have done just as well, but the computer requires that there be a number and **3F10.** would not be accepted. The **3F10.2** specification would not do if **A**, **B**, or **C** had a value of such as **0.000000003546** or **45678200000**. If we suspect that we might want to run the problem when one of the constants has such a value we would use an **E** specification.

We might think that we could use this same specification for printing **A**, **B**, and **C**, but this would not work. The number **−5.6658** contains four digits after the decimal point and would be printed **−5.66** by this specification. The number **−139024.5** to be printed with four digits after the decimal would take more than ten spaces (**−139024.5000**) and could not be printed in ten spaces. Since the number of digits before and after the decimal points vary, we probably should use an **E** specification for this output. Seven significant digits of accuracy is about all we can count on in the calculation with many computers, so we have seven significant digits printed. The field width of an **E** specification must be at least seven spaces larger than the number of significant digits so we could use **E14.7**. This, however, would not leave any space between the numbers when printed, so we could use **3E16.7** to write **A**, **B**, and **C**.

Similarly, **5E16.7** could be used to write **A**, **B**, **C**, **X1**, and **X2**. We should check the number of spaces used to write these five numbers. Five numbers requiring 16 columns each would take a total of 80 columns, which is less than the number of columns available on the printer. A **1X** specification at the beginning of the **Fφrmat** is used to positively insure that a blank will be left in the carriage control column.

We are now ready to write the program using these **Fφrmat** specifications and consulting the flow chart of Fig. 5-17. Such a program is shown in Fig. 5-18.

The logic of this program is correct, but several improvements could be made. No decimal point was used with the **4** in the expression (**B∗B-4∗A∗C**), making it a mixed-mode expression. This will work on a few computers, but it would cause an error comment on many computers, and would take extra time for the computer that would accept the mixed mode to convert the integer number (**4**) to the real number (**4.**). This expression appears three places in the program, and when the compiler translates the FORTRAN program into a machine-language program, three identical sets of machine-language in-

```
PROGRAM  REAL ROOTS I
PROGRAMMER  R.A.M.                                    DATE

C     R.A.MAMM  REAL ROOTS I
      READ(5,1)N
   1  FØRMAT(I3)
   2  READ(5,4)A,B,C
   4  FØRMAT(3F10.2)
      IF(B*B-4*A*C)6,10,10
   6  WRITE(6,8)A,B,C
   8  FØRMAT(1X,3E16.7)
      GØ TØ 18
  10  X1=(-B+(B*B-4*A*C)**.5)/(2.*A)
      X2=(-B-(B*B-4*A*C)**.5)/(2.*A)
      WRITE(6,15)A,B,C,X1,X2
  15  FØRMAT(1X,5E16.7)
  18  W=N-1
      IF(N)20,20,2
  20  STØP
      END
  5

      2.           -7.8         7.56
      1.5          -4.215      -5.6658
      7.2         395.496   -138024.5
   3.125            1.2156      2.2517
      1.           -5.02        6.3001
```

FIG. 5-18

structions would be produced, each of which would be executed every time the roots of a quadratic equation were found. The memory space required to hold these duplicate instructions and computer time could be saved by giving this expression a variable name and having the program evaluate it only once per equation. The square root of this expression and **2.*A** each appear twice in the program. There is no need to ask the computer to make these calculations twice for each equation.

The same **FØRMAT** statement could be used for printing **A**, **B**, and **C** as is used for printing **A**, **B**, **C**, **X1**, and **X2**.

A revised program is shown in Fig. 5-19. We cannot say that the program given in Fig. 5-19 is correct and the program in Fig. 5-18 is wrong (if the computer being used accepts mixed-mode expressions or if we add the decimal points to the **4**s), since they would both give the same results. We can, however, say that the program of Fig. 5-19 is better than the other, since it would take less space in the memory and less computer time. Either of these programs would give the output shown in Fig. 5-20.

The results indicate that neither of the last two equations has real roots. This is correct for the fourth equation, but the last equation should have real roots. The equation

FIG. 5-19

```
0.2000000E 01  -0.7800000E 01   0.7560000E 01   0.2099997E 01   0.1800003E 01
0.1500000E 01  -0.4215000E 01  -0.5665800E 01   0.3803169E 01  -0.9931703E 00
0.7200000E 01   0.3954960E 03  -0.1380245E 06   0.1136886E 03  -0.1686186E 03
0.3125000E 01   0.1215600E 01   0.2251700E 01
0.1000000E 01  -0.5020000E 01   0.6300100E 01
```

FIG. 5-20

$$x^2 - 5.02x + 6.3001 = 0$$

may be factored

$$(x - 2.51)(x - 2.51) = 0$$
$$x_1 = x_2 = +2.51$$

The computer should have found

$$(b^2 - 4ac) = (-5.02)^2 - 4(1)(6.3001) = 25.2004 - 25.2004 = 0$$

but due to the conversion to binary numbers the calculation gave slightly different numbers for $(-5.02)^2$ and $4(1)(6.3001)$, and obtained a very small negative number for $(b^2 - 4ac)$. (Adding a printout of **Y** to the program of Fig. 5-19 showed that the computer obtained **−0.00000381** instead of zero for **Y** for this equation.) In order to be sure to obtain real roots when the roots are identical, the program could be modified to set $(b^2 - 4ac)$ equal to zero if it has a negative value that is small in comparison to b^2.

```
COMM | STATEMENT NUMBER | CONT |
C    |  R . A . M A N N      S U M
     |  S U M = 0 .
     |  J = 0
   1 |  R E A D ( 5 , 5 ) X
   5 |  F Ø R M A T ( F 6 . 1 )
     |  S U M = S U M + X
     |  J = J + 1
     |  I F ( J - 8 ) 1 , 7 , 7
   7 |  W R I T E ( 6 , 9 ) S U M
   9 |  F Ø R M A T ( 1 X , F 9 . 2 )
     |  S T Ø P
     |  E N D
 9 7 1 . 0
   3 6 . 2
   5 8 . 7
-6 3 2 . 4
   9 7 . 0
 - 3 4 . 8
 1 0 3 . 2
     7 . 8
```

FIG. 5-21

Figure 5-21 shows a program that will read eight numbers from cards, find the total of these numbers, and print the sum.

The first statement in the program

SUM=0.

is necessary, since most computers do not clear the memory before starting a computation. If this statement were not included, the program would obtain an answer for **SUM** that was equal to the sum of the eight numbers plus whatever number had been left in the location by a previous calculation.

Any variable used in a program should be "defined" before it is used. A number must be stored in the memory location assigned to this variable name before the computer may be asked to use a number stored in this location. A variable may be defined by having its name appear on the left-hand side of an equals sign in an arithmetic statement, or by having its name appear in the variable-name list in a **READ** statement. The program should be written so that a statement that defines a variable is executed before any arithmetic statement containing this variable name on the right-hand side of the equals sign, any **IF** statement containing this name, or any **WRITE** statement containing this name is executed.

PROBLEMS

5-1. If $J = 73$, $M = -693$, $L = 5328$, $X = 101.298$, $Y = -0.000792$, and $Z = 601000.$ what would the following statements cause to be printed?

   (a)   WRITE(6,7)J,X
       7 FORMAT(1X,I3,E12.4)

   (b)   WRITE(6,10)M,X,Y
      10 FORMAT(I4,2E10.3)

(c)   WRITE(6,13)X,Y,Z
   13 FORMAT(1X,3E12.4)

(d)   WRITE(6,28)J,X,L,Y
   28 FORMAT(I2,3X,E13.6,2X,I4,E12.4)

(e)   WRITE(6,52)X,Y
   52 FORMAT(E14.6,2X,E10.4)

5-2. If **X=5693.243** and **N=693**, what **FØRMAT** statement should be used with the statement

WRITE(6,74)X,N

to obtain the following printed output?

(a)		5	6	9	3	.	2	4			6	9	3		
(b)	5	6	9	3	.	2		6	9	3					
(c)		0	.	5	6	9	3	2	E		0	4		6	9	3
(d)	0	.	5	6	9	3	E		0	4		6	9	3	
(e)	5	6	9	3	.	2	4	3		6	9	3			

first column actually printed on page (not the control column)

5-3. Write **READ** and **FØRMAT** statements that would read the cards shown and store **329** in location **NUT** and **54.625** in location **X2Y**.

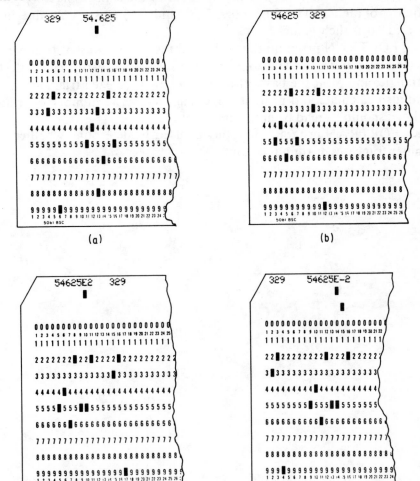

(a)   (b)

(c)   (d)

5-4. What numbers would be stored in **J, A, B, C, D, X,** and **Y** by the execution of the statements

```
      READ(5,28)J
   28 FORMAT(I7)
      READ(5,54)A,B,C,D
   54 FORMAT(F5.3,F5.0,F4.2)
      READ(5,54)X,Y
```

if the first **READ** statement starts reading with the first card punched from the listing shown in Fig. 5-15.

5-5. Modify the program of Fig. 5-19 to obtain the real roots when the roots are identical as explained at the end of the discussion of this program in the text. Assume that $(b^2 - 4ac)$ is small in comparison to b^2 if the absolute value of $(b^2 - 4ac)/b^2$ is less than 0.0001. (Watch your signs!)

5-6. Write a FORTRAN program that will read an income from a card, calculate the taxes according to the table given in Prob. 1-2, and print the income and tax on one line. The program should read the number of incomes to be computed from the first card and one income per card. Prepare the input data to calculate the tax on incomes of $5,450.00, $12,600.00, $2,945.00, $9,250.76, $14,211.50, and $8,925.67.

5-7. Write a FORTRAN program that will read x and y values from data cards and calculate and print one value of q that is equal to the sum of the x's plus the sum of the squares of the y's. Use 50.7, 60.9, 22.0, and -13.6 as the x values and 3.6, 4.8, -7.9, and 8.0 as the y values.

5-8. Write a FORTRAN program that will read the dimensions of triangles from data cards (the base and altitude of one triangle from each card), calculate the area of the triangle, and print the base, altitude, and area for each triangle. The program should also calculate and print the average area. The number of triangles to be calculated should be read from the first card.

5-9. Write a FORTRAN program that may be used to determine whether a particular computer truncates or rounds output.

CHAPTER 6

ARITHMETIC STATEMENTS (CONTINUED), SUBSCRIPTED VARIABLES

6-1. ARITHMETIC STATEMENTS (CONTINUED)

The rules about the order of evaluation of arithmetic expressions are really almost identical to the rules we are used to using in algebra. We expect exponentiation to take precedence over other functions. We would expect the algebraic expression

$$4 + 3^2$$

to be evaluated as

$$4 + 3^2 = 4 + (3^2) = 4 + 9 = 13$$

and not as

$$(4 + 3)^2 = 7^2 = 49$$

and the algebraic

$$5 \cdot 2^3$$

to be evaluated as

$$5 \cdot (2^3) = 5 \cdot 8 = 40$$

The two asterisks (**) used to indicate exponentiation thus refer only to the constant, variable name, or expression in parentheses immediately before the asterisks and to the constant, variable name, or expression in parentheses immediately after the asterisks. The FORTRAN statement

```
Q=3.*T**Z/W
```

is equivalent to the algebraic

$$q = \frac{3t^z}{w}$$

and

```
P=4.5-S**(A/B)
```

is equivalent to

$$p = 4.5 - s^{(a/b)}$$

We also expect multiplication to precede addition or subtraction. We would expect the algebraic expression

$$4 + 2 \cdot 3$$

to be evaluated as

$$4 + 2 \cdot 3 = 4 + (2 \cdot 3) = 4 + 6 = 10$$

and not as

$$(4 + 2) \cdot 3 = 6 \cdot 3 = 18$$

A difficulty arises with division because the FORTRAN expression must be written on one level and cannot represent a division as a dividend written above a horizontal line with a divisor written below the line. It is simple to see that the algebraic expressions

$$\frac{7 + 9}{3 - 1} \quad \text{and} \quad 7 + \frac{9}{3} - 1$$

should be evaluated as

$$\frac{7 + 9}{3 - 1} = \frac{16}{2} = 8 \quad \text{and} \quad 7 + \frac{9}{3} - 1 = 7 + 3 - 1 = 9$$

The slash (/) used in FORTRAN expressions without parentheses may be considered extending to the left under all elements until it is terminated by the first plus or minus sign it reaches or by the end of the expression. Its extension to the right over all elements will be terminated by any operation symbol other than the double asterisk indicating exponentiation. The FORTRAN expressions

$$\text{B+C/D-E,} \quad \text{X*Y/R**T-U} \quad \text{and} \quad \text{X*Y-Z*P/V*R}$$

are equivalent to the algebraic

$$b + \frac{c}{d} - e, \qquad \frac{x \cdot y}{r^t} - u, \qquad \text{and} \qquad xy - \frac{z \cdot p}{v} r$$

In expressions containing parentheses the extension of division indicated by the slash is not terminated by any operation symbol contained within a pair of parentheses on one side of the slash. The FORTRAN expressions

$$\text{(A+B)/C-D,} \quad \text{(A+B)/(C-D),} \quad \text{and} \quad \text{R+S*T*(B-C)/U**V}$$

are equivalent to the algebraic

$$\frac{a + b}{c} - d, \qquad \frac{a + b}{c - d}, \text{and} \qquad r + \frac{s \cdot t \cdot (b - c)}{u^v}$$

Even though it is desirable for a programmer to know the rules concerning the order of evaluation of FORTRAN expressions he should use a pair of parentheses at any time he is not absolutely certain that they are not necessary.

6-2. SUBSCRIPTED VARIABLES—THE DIMENSIØN STATEMENT

At times it is desirable to have the computer keep a table of values in its memory. The clerk might be told to make a list of six numbers:

$$567.04$$
$$356.91$$
$$-212.95$$
$$408.00$$
$$-120.19$$
$$725.33$$

If the problem were algebraic, we might give the table a name and specify which item in the list we wanted by a subscript. The first number (567.04) could be referred to as y_1, the third (-212.95) as y_3, and the nth as y_n.   The complete set of the quantities is called an *array*, and each individual quantity an *element* of the array.

An array used in FORTRAN is given a variable name.   This name must conform to all the rules used in naming any variable.   All the elements in one array must be the same mode—the numbers in the array must all be interger numbers if the name of the array starts with the letter **I**, **J**, **K**, **L**, **M**, or **N**; or must all be real numbers if the name does not start with one of these letters.   Since the printer, card punch, and keypunch do not permit writing a number below the line of printing as a subscript, subscripts in FORTRAN are written in parentheses.

The six numbers in the above list all contain decimal points and are therefore real numbers.   We could call this array "YAP".   The first number in the list would be referred to as **YAP(1)**, the fourth as **YAP(4)**, and the nth as **YAP(N)**.   The subscript must be a positive integer—there is no 2.5th number on the list.

The subscripted-variable name is used in FORTRAN statements just as an un-subscripted-variable name:

```
K=1
J(K)=6
L=J(2)-J(N)
X=(YAP(L)-Z2(L))/2.
IF(X-YAP(L))5,6,6
5 WRITE(6,8)X,YAP(L)
```

The subscripts may be integer constants or integer variables as shown in the above examples, or they may be certain integer arithmetic expressions.   The permitted expression forms are

Form	Example
Variable plus or minus a *constant*	**X(N+1)** or **X(N−1)**
Constant multiplied by a variable	**X(2∗N)**
Constant multiplied by a *variable* plus or minus a *constant*	**X(2∗N+4)** or **X(3∗N−2)**

All other forms of expressions will not be accepted by most FORTRAN compilers.   The following are *not* valid subscripted variables:

BUM(X−5)	**X** is not an integer variable.
NEXT(3+J)	For addition, the variable must precede the constant, **J+3** is correct.
X(−K)	The variable may not be signed.
EAT(MILK+MUSH)	Variable plus variable is not one of the permitted forms.
GIRL(KISS(LØVE))	Subscripts cannot themselves be subscripted.

The statement

```
X=EAT(MILK+MUSH)-GIRL(KISS(LOVE))
```

would be invalid because of the invalid subscripts.   The difficulty could be overcome by replacing the one statement with the three statements:

```
K1=MILK+MUSH
K2=KISS(LOVE)
X=EAT(K1)-GIRL(K2)
```

When subscripted variables are used in a program the FORTRAN compiler must reserve storage locations in memory for these values.   A **DIMENSIØN** statement at the beginning of the program tells the compiler which variables are subscripted and how many memory locations to reserve for each array. The statement

```
DIMENSION YAP(6),J(56),Z2(8)
```

tells the compiler to save space in memory for three arrays: an array called **YAP** containing six real numbers, an array **J** containing fifty-six integer numbers, and an array **Z2** containing eight real numbers.

As with all types of statements, the **DIMENSIØN** statement is written in columns 7 through 72 and must have exactly the form given. The compiler would not recognize the word **DIMENTIØN**, and any program containing this or any misspelling would give an error message.

More than one **DIMENSIØN** statement may be included in any one program. The statements

```
DIMENSION RED(8),X(4)
DIMENSION I(10),B(5)
DIMENSION WET(14)
```

would be treated by the computer exactly as if all the arrays had been dimensioned in the one statement

```
DIMENSION RED(8),X(4),I(10),B(5),WET(14)
```

All of the **DIMENSIØN** statements must come before any executable statement in the program. No array should be dimensioned more than once, and no name may be used as the name of both an unsubscripted variable and of an array in the same program.

6-3. SAMPLE PROGRAMS

Figure 6-1 shows a program that will read numbers from cards and compute the average of the numbers. Figure 6-2 shows the flow chart for this program. The number of cards to be read is not read from the first card as was done in the program of Fig. 5-19, but a different method of telling the computer that the last card has been read is illustrated. The variable **L** is read from the first column of each card, and the program is written so that the computer knows that it has the last card if **L** is not zero. A zero could be punched in the first column of every card except the last, or this column may be left blank, since the computer reads a blank field as zero. Any digit other than zero could be punched in the first column of the last card.

Note that the variable **N** has been used to count the cards as they are read so that the computer will know how many numbers there were so that the average may be calculated. The statement **XN=N** is used to obtain a real number equal to the integer number **N** used in counting so that the division does not involve the mixed-mode expression **TØTAL/N**.

Even though this program involves a number of different **X** values (as did the program of Fig. 5-21) it was not necessary to use an array to hold these numbers. The clerk could read a number from a card and write it on his blackboard in a rectangle labeled **X**. When he writes on the blackboard he must erase the number that was in that rectangle to make room for the new number. After he reads the desired number from a card he slides the card through a slot labeled "used cards" so that he is unable to go back

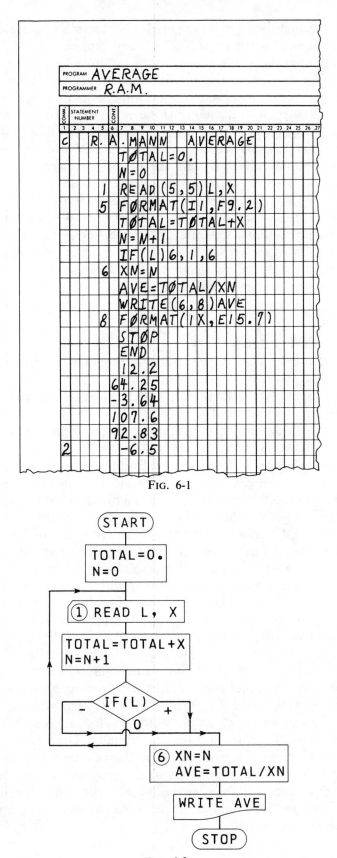

FIG. 6-1

FIG. 6-2

and look at a card a second time. After the clerk has stored a number in **X** he could add this number to the number in rectangle **TØTAL** and replace the old **TØTAL** with this new **TØTAL**. His erasing the old **X** would cause no more trouble than his erasing the old **TØTAL** since neither of these numbers will be needed at a later time in the calculation.

Suppose, however, the problem is to find the sum of six numbers and find what fraction each of the six numbers is of the sum. If the cards are read and the sum calculated by the method used in the program of Fig. 6-1, the clerk will find that after he has obtained the sum all of the cards have gone into the used card slot and he has only the last number recorded in rectangle **X**. He will not be able to carry out the divisions and obtain the fractions since all of the numbers are not available. He must have the six numbers written in six different rectangles on his blackboard after he has obtained the sum. This could be accomplished by using a different variable name for each of the numbers, but this would require a separate arithmetic statement in the program for the division of each of these variable names by the sum. The program could be greatly simplified by making the six numbers elements of an array so that the fractions could be calculated with one arithmetic statement

$$Y = X(J)/TOTAL$$

as **J** is made to progress from **1** to **6**.

Figures 6-3 and 6-4 show a flow chart and a program to solve this problem. The numbers could each be punched on a separate card, could be punched two or three on a card, or all on one card. The **READ** and **FØRMAT** statements in this program are written to read three numbers per card.

Remember that when an array is used space in memory for the subscripted variables must be reserved by a **DIMENSIØN** statement.

Figures 6-5 and 6-6 show a flow chart and a program to solve the same problem as solved by the program of Fig. 6-4 when the number of numbers involved is not predetermined. The program could be used to solve the problem with five numbers, 23 numbers, or any other number of numbers. The limiting factor on how many numbers could be handled would be the dimension of the array. The program of Fig. 6-6 assumes that there will be no more than 100 numbers in any one problem. The only change that would have to be made between different runs would be to supply different data cards.

The program could be shortened by combining the first two loops into one as shown in the flow chart of Fig. 6-7. The FORTRAN program for this shorter version is shown in Fig. 6-8. The programs of Figs. 6-6 and 6-8 would give the same results.

An array (a subscripted variable) must be used for the **X** values in the programs calculating the fractions since more than the last **X** value is used after the loop reading the **X** values has been executed the required number of times and the computation has proceeded beyond this loop. Any multiple-valued variable must be put into an array (subscripted) if any of the values other than the last is to be used after the computation has proceeded beyond the loop within which the multiple values are read or computed.

Any multiple-valued variable may be subscripted. The variables N, **TØTAL**, **L**, and **Y** in the program of Fig. 6-8 could each be dimensioned and used as subscripted variables as could N, **X**, **TØTAL**, **L**, and **NX** in the program for computing the average (Fig. 6-1). Using subscripted variables where the subscripts are not needed causes a very slight increase in computer time required to solve the problem, but requires more space in the computer memory.

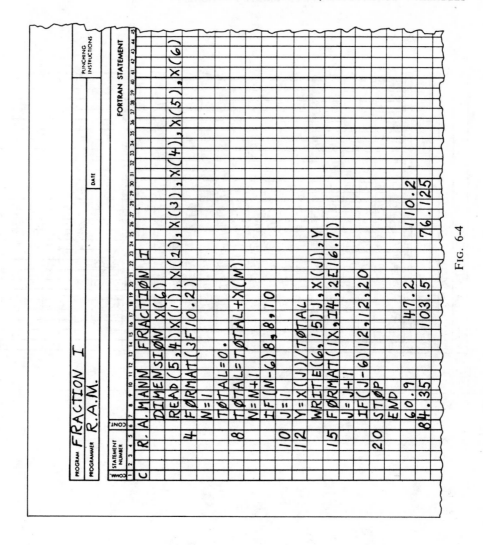

FIG. 6-4

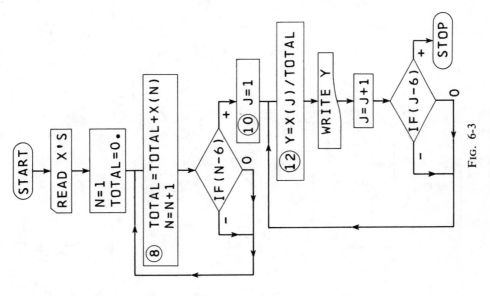

FIG. 6-3

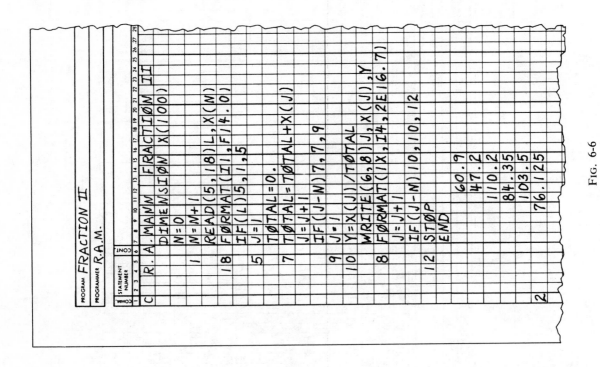

FIG. 6-6

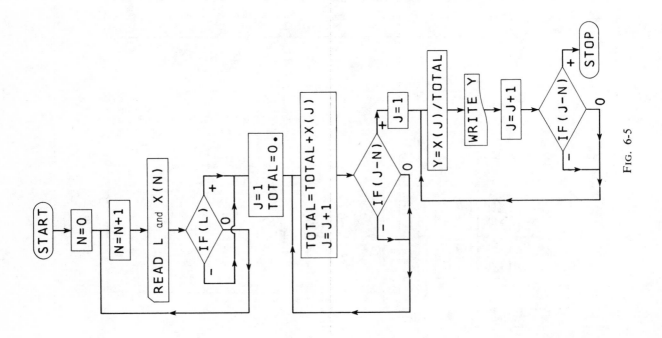

FIG. 6-5

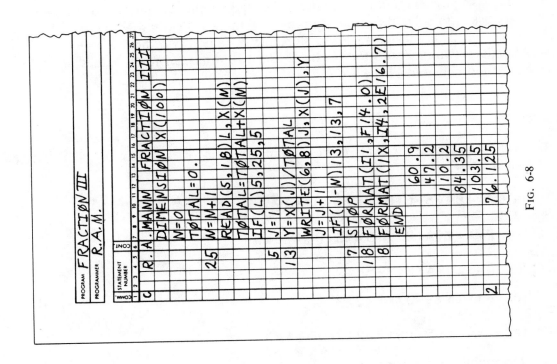

FIG. 6-8

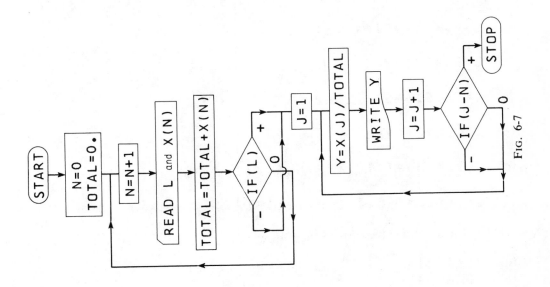

FIG. 6-7

None of the programs in this chapter would use anywhere near all of the storage available, but if a programmer does not try to get in the habit of minimizing the memory requirements in his short programs he will not know how to fit a program in which the core storage is a problem on the computer. The clerk might run out of blackboard space if he were asked to solve the fraction problem with two thousand **X** values if he were told to use two thousand rectangles to store the **N** values, two thousand rectangles for **TØTAL** values, two thousand for **L** values, and two thousand for **Y** values in addition to the two thousand used for the **X**'s.

PROBLEMS

6-1. Write algebraic statements corresponding to each of the following FORTRAN statements.

(a) `A=(B**5-C*C)/(2.*D**12)`

(b) `P=4.*(A+B)/(3.*C-D)**0.5`

(c) `Q=4.0*A/B**2*P`

(d) `M=4*N+3*J/K**2/3`

(e) `R=4.+(5.*S+7.2)/4.*T**3`

6-2. Determine the number that will be stored in **Q** as the result of each of the following arithmetic statements if **0.6** has been stored in **S**, **5.0** in **T**, **2** in **L**, and **−3** in **N**.

(a) `Q=4.+(5.*S)**L/2.*T`

(b) `Q=5.*S/T+7.5`

(c) `Q=T+(5.6-S)/2.5-2.0`

(d) `Q=N/L*2+L**2`

(e) `Q=5.+(3.*T-10.*(S+0.4)/T)/2.*S`

(f) `Q=(((2.*T+5.)*T-3.)*T)-12.`

6-3. Identify the invalid subscripts in the following list:

(a) `M(ITEM)`
(b) `XTRA(CASH)`
(c) `BOY(2*LAZY)`
(d) `FAT(OLD(MEN))`
(e) `W(2*K+L)`
(f) `YEAR(N-1921)`
(g) `X(N)`
(h) `G(-J)`
(i) `WET(K*4)`
(j) `Q(4*L-7)`
(k) `QUEER(+16)`
(l) `QUEEN(KING+3.)`

6-4. What values will be stored in array **Z** by the following program?

```
      DIMENSION Z(5)
      N=1
    2 READ (5,6)Z(N)
    6 FORMAT(E10.4)
      N=M+1
      IF(N-5)2,2,8
    8 STOP
      END
327E2
564.9E3
624-2
49.2E-02
52807+01
```

6-5. Write a FORTRAN program that will read n numbers punched one per card into $q_1, q_2, q_3, \ldots, q_n$, add all these numbers, add the squares of these numbers, calculate t which is equal to the sum of the numbers divided by the sum of the squares

$$t = \frac{q_1 + q_2 + q_3 + \cdots + q_n}{q_1^2 + q_2^2 + q_3^2 + \cdots + q_n^2}$$

and then calculate and print n values $a = q_i t$ for $i = 1, 2, 3, \ldots, n$ (calculate and print $q_1 t, q_2 t, q_3 t, \ldots, q_n t$. Do not use an array for a). Write the program so that it may be used for any value of n not larger than 20. Prepare input data using the numbers 29.35, 368.78, −63.57, 2.98, 85.0, and 0.02.

6-6. Write a FORTRAN program that will read numbers punched one per card into $v_1, v_2, v_3, \ldots, v_n$. Find the smallest of these numbers, subtract this value from each of the numbers, and print the differences. Write the program so that it may be used for any value of n not larger than 50. The program should work if any, all, or none of the numbers are negative or zero. Prepare input data using the numbers 673.8, −46.75, 57.48, 1.79, 573.98, −58.87, 430.8, 68.03, −8.90, and 45.76.

6-7. A number of students (less than 200) took an examination. The grades were from zero to one hundred. Write a FORTRAN program to determine how many of the students received a grade higher than the average. The input is to be a deck of cards with one grade punched in each card. Prepare input data using grades 73, 91, 82, 67, 84, 60, 32, 81, 43, 80, and 71.

CHAPTER 7

DØ, CØNTINUE,
LOGICAL IF STATEMENTS,
MORE ON INPUT

7-1. THE DØ STATEMENT

The use of an integer index and an **IF** statement to set up a loop to execute a group of statements a specified number of times was discussed in Sec. 4-2. A number of sample programs including those shown in Figs. 4-12, 5-18, 5-19, 6-4, 6-6, and 6-8 made use of such loops. Another example of this is shown in the partial program shown in Fig. 7-1.

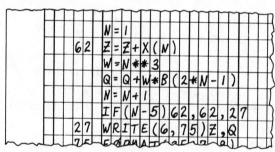

```
        N = 1
    62  Z = Z + X(N)
        W = N**3
        Q = Q + W*B(2*N-1)
        N = N+1
        IF(N-5) 62,62,27
    27  WRITE (6,75) Z,Q
    75  FORMAT (...)
```

FIG. 7-1

Three statements ($N=1$; $N=N+1$; and the **IF** statement) are required in this program to set up and control the index. The statements between the $N=1$ and $N=N+1$ statements would be executed five times (with values of N of **1, 2, 3, 4,** and **5**). Figure 7-2 shows the flow chart of this partial program.

FORTRAN contains a **DØ** statement of the form

        DO 93 N=1,5

that permits us to set up a loop using only one statement. The partial program shown in Fig. 7-3 would be executed in exactly the same manner as the program of Fig. 7-1.

The **DØ** statement in Fig. 7-3 causes the statements following the **DØ** statement, up to and including statement number **93**, to be executed repeatedly. N will be set equal to one for the first execution and will be increased by one after each successive execution. The execution will be repeated until the incrementing causes N to exceed **5**. The computer will then proceed to the statement following statement number **93**. Figure 7-4 shows that the **DØ** statement in Fig. 7-3 is equivalent to the three statements needed to set up the loop in Fig. 7-1. The instructions enclosed in the dashed hexagon will not actually appear

100

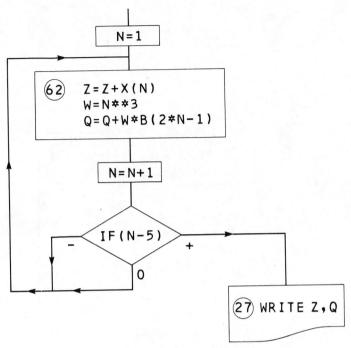

Fig. 7-2

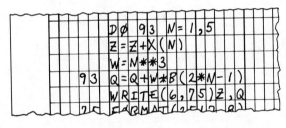

Fig. 7-3

in the FORTRAN program but represent the operation of the **DØ** statement. A beginning programmer might well use this representation of **DØ** statements on his flow charts until he has mastered their use. Fig. 7-5 illustrates one method that is used to represent **DØ** statements on flow charts.

A third integer constant in the **DØ** statement

        DO 76 N=1,15,3

causes the index **N** to be increased by a number equal to the third integer after each successive execution. The statements through number **76** would be executed with **N** equal to **1, 4, 7, 10,** and **13** (the next increase would give **N** a value **16** that exceeds **15**).

Note that any one of the three statements

        DO 76 N=1,13,3
        DO 76 N=1,14,3

or

        DO 76 N=1,15,3

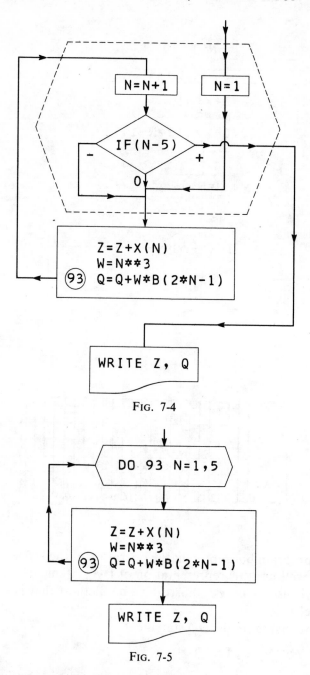

Fig. 7-4

Fig. 7-5

would cause the same computations. The statement

DO 35 K=7,24,5

would cause the statements through number **35** to be executed with **K** equal to **7, 12, 17,** and **22**.

The **DØ** statement may therefore have one of two different forms. It always starts with the word **DØ**, a statement number, an integer variable name used as an index, and an equals sign. The equals sign may be followed by two or three unsigned, positive, nonzero integer indexing parameters separated by a comma or commas.

DO 17 L=1620,1967

or

              DO 31 M=7,564,6

The indexing parameters may be either integer constants or unsubscripted-integer names that have been previously defined

              DO 685 J=7,N

is a valid **DØ** statement if **N** has been previously defined (assigned a value by being on the left of the equals sign in an arithmetic statement executed before the **DØ** statement or assigned a value by a READ statement). All of the indexing parameters should have *nonzero, positive* integer values. The statement

              DO 7 M=0,7

is invalid in most computer systems. A computation could be made with **M** having the values of zero to seven by starting the loop with the two statements

              DO 7 J=1,8
              M=J-1

The partial program shown in Fig. 7-6 is invalid since the parameters may not be zero or negative.

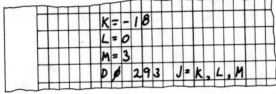

FIG. 7-6

The second parameter is normally larger than the first. It would be foolish to write a statement such as

              DO 43 M=7,4

but this is a valid statement and the statements through number **43** would be executed once with **M** equal to **7**, **M** would be increased to **8**, and the test would show that **8** is larger than **4**. This type of statement would probably not be written, but the programmer must be aware that a **DØ**-loop starting with the statement

              DO 6 J=7,K

or

              DO 6 J=7,K,2

would be executed once with **J** equal to **7** if **K** had a value of **7** or less. A **DØ**-loop starting with

              DO 35 M=K,L

or

              DO 35 M=K,L,J

would be executed once if **L** had a value equal to or smaller than **K**.

The index of the **DØ**-loop is often used only to count the number of times that the loop is to be executed. Figure 7-7 shows a program in which the index **J** is only used in this way.

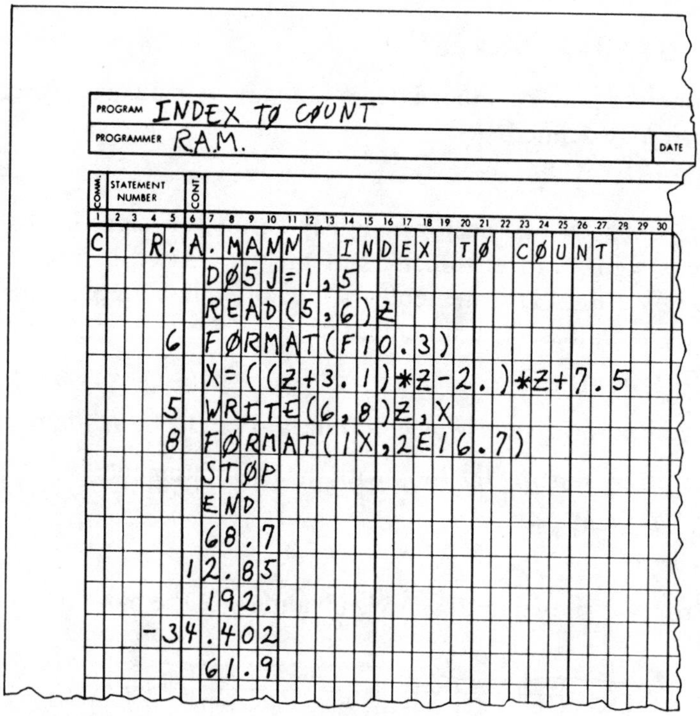
PROGRAM INDEX TØ CØUNT
PROGRAMMER R.A.M.
DATE

```
C   R.A.MANN    INDEX  TØ  CØUNT
      DØ5J=1,5
      READ(5,6)Z
    6 FØRMAT(F10.3)
      X=((Z+3.1)*Z-2.)*Z+7.5
    5 WRITE(6,8)Z,X
    8 FØRMAT(1X,2E16.7)
      STØP
      END
      68.7
     12.85
      192.
   -34.402
      61.9
```

FIG. 7-7

Figure 7-7 also shows that while spaces are usually left before and after the statement number in the **DØ** statement

```
DO 5 J=1,5
```

for the ease of reading, these spaces are not necessary, and the computer will recognize the statement if written as

```
DO5J=1,5
```

The index may be used within the loop as a subscript and/or as a factor in an arithmetic statement as shown in Fig. 7-3. It must be remembered that the index is an integer quantity, and it is necessary to convert it to a real number before it is used in an arithmetic statement that contains real quantities. The statements

```
DO 45 N=1,20
GAD=N*Q(N)
```

would include a mixed-mode expression. This is not permitted on most computers. The mixed-mode expression could be avoided by writing

```
DO 45 N=1,20
XN=N
GAD=XN*Q(N)
```

The index or indexing parameters should *not* be changed in the loop by appearing on the left-hand side of the equals sign of an arithmetic statement or in the variable list in a **READ** statement.

The last statement of a **DØ**-loop (the statement with the statement number that appears in the **DØ** statement) may not be an **IF**, **GØ TØ**, **STØP**, **PAUSE**, **FØRMAT**, **RETURN**, or **DØ** statement.

When a branching statement causes the computer to leave a **DØ**-loop before the cycling of the index has been completed, a "special exit" has been made. If the index completes its cycle in the normal manner and the computer proceeds to the statement immediately following the **DØ**-loop, a "normal exit" has been made. After a special exit has been made the value of the index at the time of the exit is available for use. Figure 7-8

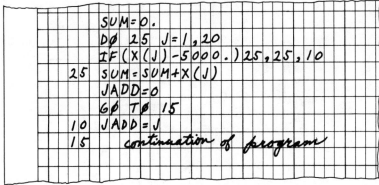

FIG. 7-8

shows a program that locates the first number in an array that is larger than **5000.** and calculates the sum of the numbers that precede this number in the array. If the computer finds such a number it will make a special exit and set **JADD** equal to **J** to indicate that the number is located in **X(JADD)**. If there is no number this large in the array, the computer will make a normal exit and set **JADD** equal to zero to indicate that there is no such number.

Transfers out of a **DØ**-loop may be made at any time, but transfers into a loop may only be made when returning to a loop after transfer out has first been made and the index and indexing parameters have not been changed.

7-2. THE **CØNTINUE** STATEMENT

A **DØ**-loop may contain one or more branching statements. Regardless of the number of branches in a loop all possible paths that do not cause special exits from the loop must end at the statement whose number is given in the **DØ** statement. For example if we wish to write a program that will examine each of the elements in an array **X** and set all negative elements equal to zero, we might start writing the program as

```
    DO 15 N=1,20
    IF(X(N))15, ? ,?
15  X(N)=0.
```

This will not work, since we have no statement number to use in the **IF** statement for zero or positive values. We might think that the **DØ** statement could be given a statement number:

```
10 DO 15 N=1,20
   IF(X(N))15,10,10
15 X(N)=0.
```

An examination of the flow diagram of Fig. 7-9 will show that this program would run but would not do the required job. When the computer found a zero or positive element, a special exit from the loop would be made, and the computer would restart the loop with

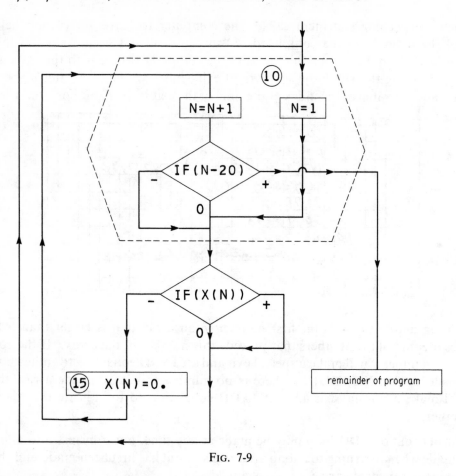

FIG. 7-9

N equal to one. We have created what is known as an *endless loop*. If there are any zero or positive elements in the array the computer would continue to restart the **DØ**-loop and would run without accomplishing our purpose until the operator intervened. What is needed is a statement that does nothing but may have a statement number. A **CØN-TINUE** statement is a dummy statement that causes no computation but furnishes the necessary end point for the **DØ**-loop:

```
     DO 25 N=1,20
     IF(X(N))15,25,25
  15 X(N)=0.
  25 CONTINUE
```

Figure 7-10 shows the flow diagram for these statements. Both Figs. 7-9 and 7-10 use the equivilant **IF** statement form for the **DØ** statement.

7-3. The Logical **IF** Statement

The arithmetic **IF** statement discussed in Sec. 4-2 uses the fact that the evaluation of an arithmetic expression could produce a negative, zero, or positive result to determine which of three possible branch directions the computation is to take. Most FORTRAN systems contain a logical **IF** statement in addition to the arithmetic **IF** statement. The logical **IF** statement uses the fact that a logical expression may be true or false to deter-

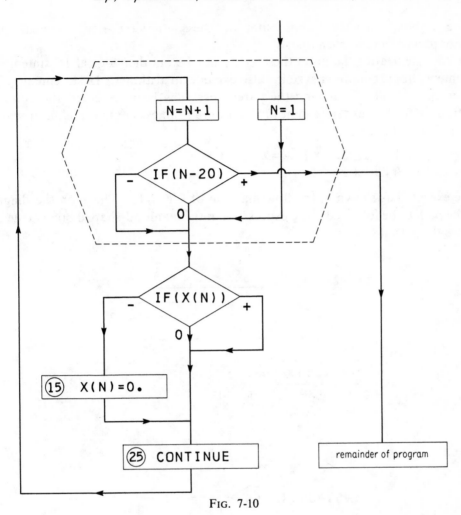

FIG. 7-10

mine which of two possible branch directions the computation is to take. The statement

IF(X .EQ. Y) W=X/2.5

tells the computer to execute the statement

W=X/2.5

if the logical expression "X is equal to Y." is true. If this expression is false the statement will not be executed and the computation will continue with the next statement in the program. The operation symbols shown in Fig. 7-11 are used in the logical expressions. The decimal points before and after the letters in the operation symbols are a necessary

Operation Symbol	Meaning	Mathematical Meaning
.EQ.	Equal to	=
.NE.	Not equal to	≠
.GT.	Greater than	>
.GE.	Greater than or equal to	≥
.LT.	Less than	<
.LE.	Less than or equal to	≤

FIG. 7-11

part of the symbols. They tell the computer that these letters represent a logical operation and are not parts of a variable name.

The statement after the parentheses may not be another logical **IF** statement or a **DØ** statement. Some computer systems also exclude an arithmetic **IF** statement.

After the statement following the parentheses has been executed the computation will continue with the next statement in the program unless control has been transferred elsewhere. The statements

```
IF(X .EQ. Y) W=X/2.5
P=4.5+X
```

would be executed as shown in the flow diagram of Fig. 7-12. The **T** on the diagram indicates the path to be followed if the expression in the diamond-shaped box is true and the **F** indicates the path if false.

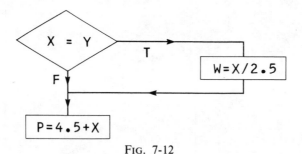

FIG. 7-12

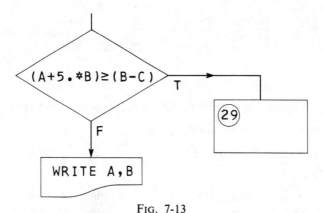

FIG. 7-13

Figure 7-13 shows the flow diagram for the statements

```
IF(A+5.*B .GE. B-C) GO TC 29
WRITE(6,57)A,B
```

The expressions before and after the operation symbol may be any valid arithmetic expressions of the same mode. The statement

```
IF(J .LT. G) G=X(J)
```

would be invalid in most computer systems since **J** is integer and **G** is real.

Figure 7-14 shows a program to solve the clerk's problem using a logical **IF** statement. Compare this program to the program shown in Fig. 4-18 that uses an arithmetic **IF** statement. The flow diagram of Fig. 1-2 is valid for either of these programs.

```
PROGRAM  CLERK'S PROBLEM WITH LOGICAL IF         PUNCHING
                                                 INSTRUCTIONS
PROGRAMMER  R.A.M.                      DATE
```

C		STATEMENT NUMBER		CONT.	FORTRAN STATEMENT
C		R.A.MAMM CLERK'S PRØBLEM WITH LØGICAL IF
					T=0.0
		2			X=(-2.*T+3.)*T+50.
					IF(X.LT.0.0)GØ TØ 10
					WRITE(6,11)T,X
					T=T+0.5
					GØ TØ 2
		10			STØP
		11			FØRMAT(1X,2F6.1)
					END

Fig. 7-14

7-4. More on Input

If we wished to read five numbers from cards into an array **X** we could use the statement

$$READ(5,56)X(1),X(2),X(3),X(4),X(5)$$

together with the necessary **FØRMAT** statement. These same numbers could be read by the use of a **DØ**-loop:

```
    DO 12 J=1,5
 12 READ(5,45)X(J)
```

The two methods are not exactly equivalent as the **DØ**-loop would require the numbers to be punched one to a card. The number of cards necessary with the earlier **READ** statement would depend on the **FØRMAT** statement used with it. If the **FØRMAT** were

```
 56 FORMAT(E10.3)
```

the numbers would have to be punched one to a card. If the **FØRMAT** were

```
 56 FORMAT(5E10.3)
```

the numbers would all be punched on one card.

```
 56 FORMAT(3E10.3)
```

would require three numbers being punched on the first card and two being punched on a second.

If we wished to read 50 numbers into the array **X** we could use the **DØ**-loop but this would require 50 data cards. Writing the statement

$$READ(5,83)X(1),X(2),X(3),\ldots,X(50)$$

would be impractical. Another widely used method is the *self-indexing list* technique, sometimes called an "implied **DØ**-loop." The statement

$$READ(5,83)(X(J),J=1,50)$$

is executed exactly as the statement

```
READ(5,83)X(1),X(2),X(3),...,X(50)
```

The index definition used in the input lists may be written in the same manner as in **DØ** statements. It may use the optional third quantity defining an increment other than one. The statement

```
READ(5,31)(X(J),J=4,15,3)
```

would cause values to be read into **X(4)**, **X(7)**, **X(10)**, and **X(13)**. An input list may contain other elements either before or after the self-indexing sequence. The statement

```
READ(5,6)B,NUT,(Z(L),L=1,4),WHY
```

would cause seven values to be read and assigned to **B**, **NUT**, **Z(1)**, **Z(2)**, **Z(3)**, **Z(4)**, and **WHY** respectively.

The input list may include more than one self-indexing sequence

```
READ(5,17)(MUG(J),J=1,3),(X(J),J=1,4),Q
```

would cause eight values to be read and assigned respectively to **MUG(1)**, **MUG(2)**, **MUG(3)**, **X(1)**, **X(2)**, **X(3)**, **X(4)**, and **Q**.

More than one variable may be included in one self-indexing sequence

```
READ(5,1)(X(I),Y(I),I=1,25)
```

This would cause 50 numbers to be read and assigned in the order **X(1)**, **Y(1)**, **X(2)**, **Y(2)**, **X(3)**, **Y(3)**, ..., **X(25)**, **Y(25)**. Be sure that you understand the difference between the two **READ** statements

```
READ(5,4)(X(I),I=1,5),(Y(I),I=1,5)
```

and

```
READ(5,4)(X(I),Y(I),I=1,5)
```

The index definition may use variables for the lower or upper limits and for the increment if used. The statement

```
READ(5,9)(R(K),K=J,M)
```

is valid if **J** and **M** have been previously defined by arithmetic or **READ** statements. This makes possible a very useful method of reading long lists of quantities:

```
READ(5,6)N,(X(I),I=1,N)
```

would read the integer quantity **N** from the first card and then read **N** numbers and store them in the **X** array.

As with almost every FORTRAN statement, the form used for the statement must agree exactly with that prescribed. The statement

```
READ(5,6)X(I),I=1,N
```

would be invalid because the index definition is not enclosed in parentheses. Both of the commas are also required.

Remember that the **READ** statement indicates how many numbers are to be read and at what locations in memory they are to be stored. The **FØRMAT** statement tells the maximum number of numbers that may be read from one card, what columns are used for each number, and in what form they are punched.

The character "/" (slash) is used in **FØRMAT** statements to separate groups of conversion codes if one **READ** statement is to read several cards all of which are not punched in the same **FØRMAT**. The statement

```
READ(5,7)X,Y,Z,GLUG
```

used with the **FØRMAT** statement

```
7 FORMAT(4F10.3)
```

will read numbers punched in columns 1 to 10, 11 to 20, 21 to 30, and 31 to 40 of one card. The same **READ** statement used with

```
7 FORMAT(2F10.3)
```

will read numbers punched in columns 1 to 10 and 11 to 20 of one card and in columns 1 to 10 and 11 to 20 of a second card. This same statement used with

```
7 FORMAT(2F10.3,2F5.0)
```

would read four numbers punched in columns 1 to 10, 11 to 20, 21 to 25, and 26 to 30 of one card. Used with

```
7 FORMAT(2F10.3/2F5.0)
```

it would read numbers from columns 1 to 10 and 11 to 20 of one card and columns 1 to 5 and 6 to 10 of the second card.

The statement

```
89 FORMAT(3I9/4I4)
```

tells the computer that the first card read with this **FØRMAT** will contain three integer numbers in fields of nine columns each and the second card read will contain four integer numbers in fields of four columns each. When a **READ** statement containing more than seven variables in the input list is used with the **FØRMAT** statement, the specifications would repeat from the *beginning* of the **FØRMAT**.

The statements

```
READ(5,19)(M(J),J=1,16)
19 FORMAT(3I9/4I4)
```

would read sixteen numbers, three from the first card, four from the second, three from the third, four from the fourth, and two from the fifth card. The statements

```
READ(5,5)X
5 FORMAT(6F12.4,6I5/4E15.0)
```

would read only one number from one card! The fact that reading stops when the input list is satisfied holds, no matter how complex the **FØRMAT** statement becomes.

The addition of an additional set of parentheses in a **FØRMAT** containing a "/" permit a very useful type of **READ** statement that was described above. When the end of the **FØRMAT** specifications is reached and the input list is not yet satisfied, the reading will continue repeating the specifications from the last open parentheses in the **FØRMAT** statement. The statements

```
READ(5,6)I,J,W,X,Y,Z
6 FORMAT(2I5/(2E10.0))
```

would read two **I5** numbers from the first card, two **E10.0** numbers from the second card, and two **E10.0** numbers from the third card. This feature is most often used in statements such as

```
      READ(5,17)N,(X(J),J=1,N)
   17 FORMAT(I4/(5F10.2))
```

This permits an integer number read from the first card to be used as the index limit for the self-indexed list. If N were **500** on the first card, a total of 101 cards would be read (the value of N from the first card and the 500 real numbers from 100 cards). This same reading could have been accomplished with two **READ** statements and two **FØRMAT** statements

```
      READ(5,13)N
   13 FORMAT(I4)
      READ(5,18)(X(J),J=1,N)
   18 FORMAT(5F10.2)
```

Another use of parentheses within a **FØRMAT** statement is to shorten the writing required if there are repeating patterns within a single card layout. The statement

```
   12 FORMAT(3(E5.1,I4))
```

will produce the same results as the statement

```
   12 FORMAT(E5.1,I4,E5.1,I4,E5.1,I4)
```

The statement

```
   35 FORMAT(E6.2,2(I3,F8.1),I4)
```

is equivalent to

```
   35 FORMAT(E6.2,I3,F8.1,I3,F8.1,I4)
```

A few computer systems permit repeated groups of specifications to be nested. With such a system the statement

```
    8 FORMAT(I5,2(7X,3(I2,I3),I4),I6)
```

would indicate the use of specifications **I5, 7X, I2, I3, I2, I3, I2, I3, I4, 7X, I2, I3, I2, I3, I2, I3, I4, I6**.

7-5. CARD LAYOUT

The statement number of any FORTRAN statement is written in the first five columns of the coding sheet and is punched in these columns on the cards. The statement itself is written and punched in columns 7 through 72. Columns 73 through 80 are not used by FORTRAN and so may be left blank or may be used for any identification desired. Some programmers use these identification columns to number consecutively the cards in a deck 1, 2, 3, etc., so that if the deck is dropped or otherwise disarranged it may be easily put back into the proper order. Other programmers put the same identification code in every card of a program so that they may quickly tell the card deck for one program from that for another. Sometimes these two functions are combined, and a programmer may punch the characters

```
PG  1
PG  2
PG  3
PG  4
```

etc., in the identification field of the cards of a program he calls **PG**.

Sometimes more than 66 columns are required for a long statement. If columns 7 through 72 of one card will not hold the statement, these same columns on the following card or cards may be used for the continuation of the statement. Column 6 of the coding sheet and of the card is used to indicate that one statement requires more than one card. Column 6 of the first card for the statement is either left blank or is punched with a zero. Any character other than blank or zero is punched in column 6 of the continuation cards for the statement.

The number of continuation cards permitted per statement depends on the computer system being used. Several small computers permit a maximum of five continuation cards, a maximum of six cards for each FORTRAN statement, while some of the larger computers have no limit on the number of cards that may be used for a statement.

Column 6, the continuation column, of the first card of a statement is usually left blank, but it may contain a zero. The character in column 6 of the additional cards is arbitrary, but many programmers use the integers 1, 2, 3, etc. to indicate the order of the cards. The computer treats the statements that include continuation cards as though the statement had been punched on one long card, with the information in columns 7 through 72 on the second card punched in columns 73 through 138 of the long card, immediately following column 72 of the first card.

Care should be taken to see that no character is punched in column 6 of most FORTRAN statements since most statements do not involve a continuation. This does not apply to comment cards or data cards. There is no continuation column on comment cards or data cards.

PROBLEMS

7-1.   Correct any FORTRAN language errors in the following statements.
   (a)   DO 5 I=1,N
   (b)   DO 56, I=1,3
   (c)   DO 376 X=1,17,3
   (d)   DO NEXT K=L,M
   (e)   DO 45 J(2)=1,K
   (f)   DO 65 LAT=MAT,NAT,PAT
   (g)   DO 3, J=0,N-1

7-2.   For what values of the index will the loops formed with the following statements be executed?
   (a)   DO 1 I=1,7
   (b)   DO 2 J=3,7
   (c)   DO 3 K=3,10,3
   (d)   DO 4 L=7,2,6
   (e)   DO 5 M=8,6
   (f)   DO 6 N=2,11,2

7-3. What value would be stored in **K** after each of the following programs had been executed?

(a)
```
    J=5
    K=4
    DO 5 M=1,J
  5 K=K+M
```

(b)
```
    J=3
    L=10
    K=2
    DO 6 M=J,L
    K=K+M
    IF(K-25)6,6,8
  6 CONTINUE
  8 K=K+18
```

(c)
```
    K=6
    M=10
    DO 7 N=3,10,2
    K=K+N+M
  7 M=M-1
```

7-4. Write a program to solve Prob. 5-7 using one **DØ**-loop. Two numbers, one x value and one y value, should be punched on each data card.

7-5. Write a FORTRAN program to calculate the first 20 values of r from the equation

$$r = 8s^5 - 4s^4 + 6s^3$$

for $s = 0.00$, $s = 0.01$, $s = 0.02$, $s = 0.03$ etc. The output desired is a table of values of s and r. Use a **DØ**-loop.

7-6. What value would be stored in **K** after each of the following programs had been executed?

(a)
```
    J=5
    K=4
    M=1
  7 K=K+M
    M=M+1
    IF(M.LE.J)GO TO 7
    J=J+1
```

(b)
```
    M=0
    J=4
    K=3
  5 IF(J.GT.K)K=K+2
    J=J+1
    M=M-1
    IF(K.LT.7)GO TO 5
    M=M+10
```

(c)
```
    K=5
    M=2
  3 IF(M.LT.K)M=M+2
    IF(M.GE.K)K=K+3
    IF(K.LT.10)GO TO 3
    K=K-2
```

7-7. Write a FORTRAN program that will add all the even integers from 2 to 50 using a logical **IF** statement and print the sum.

$$J = 2 + 4 + 6 + 8 + \cdots + 46 + 48 + 50$$

7-8. Solve Prob. 6-6 using **DØ**-loops. Use a logical **IF** statement when comparing the size of two numbers.

7-9. Solve Prob. 6-7 using **DØ**-loops. Use a logical **IF** statement to check whether a grade is above the average or not.

7-10. State what columns on what cards the data should be punched to be read by the statements

(a)
```
    READ(5,6)R,S,T,U,V,W,X
  6 FORMAT(F10.2,F5.0/2F8.2)
```

(b)
```
    READ(5,8)N,(Y(J),J=1,5)
  8 FORMAT(I5/(2F10.2))
```

(c)   ```
READ(5,9)I,J,U,V,W,X,Y,Z
9 FORMAT(2I5/2E16.4,F10.1/3F8.2)
```

**7-11.**  Write **READ** and **FØRMAT** statements that will read the following data from cards. The first number (**20**) is to be read into **N** and indicates that there are 20 additional numbers to be read into array **RUG**. The numbers are to have two digits after the decimal point: **45.32** should be stored in **RUG(1)**, **–05.61** in **RUG(2)**, **6.92** in **RUG(3)**, . . . ,**40.78** in **RUG(20)**.

```
20
4532  -561       692  7031  6000
-290  9028  -603       29    537
 424   129  7602  548  -429
6780  7091        3  -817  4078
```

7-12. What numbers will be stored in each element of arrays **PUT** and **TAKE** (what numbers in **PUT(1)**, **PUT(2)**, etc. and in **TAKE(1)**, **TAKE(2)**, etc.) if the data given in Prob. 7-11 is read with the following statements?

(a)   ```
READ(5,16)N,(PUT(J),J=1,10),(TAKE(K),K=1,10)
16 FORMAT(I3/5F5.0))
```

(b)   ```
READ(5,54)N,(PUT(J),TAKE(J),J=1,10)
54 FORMAT(I3/(3F5.1,2F5.2))
```

**7-13.**  Write a FORTRAN program that will read numbers into two arrays, calculate the sum of the squares of the elements of the first array, calculate the sum of the elements of the second array, divide the first of these sums by the second:

$$d = a_1^2 + a_2^2 + a_3^2 + \cdots + a_n^2$$
$$p = b_1 + b_2 + b_3 + \cdots + b_n$$
$$w = \frac{d}{p}$$

and then calculate and print $n$ values $x = (7.5a_i + 5.2b_i)w$ for $i = 1, 2, 3, \ldots, n$. Write the program so that it may be used for any value of $n$ not larger than 20. Prepare input data using the values

| $i$ | $a_i$ | $b_i$ |
|---|---|---|
| 1 | –20.7 | 54.6 |
| 2 | 62.8 | –37.0 |
| 3 | 42.9 | 26.8 |
| 4 | 71.0 | 13.7 |
| 5 | 34.4 | –70.0 |

**7-14.**  Write a FORTRAN program that will read numbers into three arrays, calculate and print

$x = $ (the 1st $a$)/(the 1st $b$) + (the last $c$)/(the 1st $a$)
$x = $ (the 2nd $a$)/(the 2nd $b$) + (the next to last $c$)/(the 2nd $a$)
$x = $ (the 3rd $a$)/(the 3rd $b$) + (the 2nd from last $c$)/(the 3rd $a$), etc

Read the numbers into the elements of the arrays in the order shown.  Write the
```

program so that the number of elements read into each array may be any number up to 25. Prepare input data using the following numbers:

m	a_m	b_m	c_m
1	16.9	120.0	15.6
2	9908.3	0.001	−9.0
3	−0.002	3472.0	499.5
4	128.0	−32.8	528.3
5	96.3	3.0	64.8
6	−50.7	−40.8	75.0

MULTIPLE SUBSCRIPTS, EXPLICIT SPECIFICATION, NESTED DØ-LOOPS

8-1. MULTIDIMENSIONAL ARRAYS

Subscripts, discussed in Sec. 6-1, are used to identify individual numbers in a group or list of numbers called an *array*. **PIG(3)** and **PIG(N)** refer to the third and Nth item in an array called **PIG**. Such arrays are known as *singly-subscripted arrays*.

FORTRAN also permits the use of arrays with more than one subscript. Figure 8-1 shows the grade made by each of five students on each of three examinations.

		Examination		
		1	2	3
	1	90.0	84.0	92.5
	2	65.0	59.0	52.5
Student	3	42.0	56.5	60.0
	4	74.0	79.0	63.0
	5	100.0	98.0	93.5

FIG. 8-1

This group of grades could be stored in the memory of the computer in a doubly subscripted array. The programmer must give the array a name following the same naming rules used for naming a variable and may arbitrarily decide which of the two subscripts refers to the examination. The array could be named **GR** since all the numbers are to be stored as real numbers. If it is decided that the first subscript is to refer to the student, memory location **GR(3,2)** would be used to store the grade made by the third student on the second examination and location **GR(J,K)** would store the grade made by the Jth student on the Kth examination.

Space for these numbers might be reserved in memory by the statement

        DIMENSION GR(5,3)

This statement will cause the computer to reserve space for fifteen real numbers divided into three blocks of five numbers each. These numbers will be stored in successive blocks in the memory as shown in Fig. 8-2.

Some other programmer might easily decide to have the grades stored in an array that he calls **SC** with the first subscript refering to the examination. His program would use the statement

        DIMENSION SC(3,5)

to reserve space for five blocks of three numbers each. The grade made on the second examination by the third student would be stored in location **SC(2,3)**. The grades would be stored in the memory in the order shown in Fig. 8-3. Note that they are stored in the

90.0	GR(1,1)
65.0	GR(2,1)
42.0	GR(3,1)
74.0	GR(4,1)
100.0	GR(5,1)
84.0	GR(1,2)
59.0	GR(2,2)
56.5	GR(3,2)
79.0	GR(4,2)
98.0	GR(5,2)
92.5	GR(1,3)
52.5	GR(2,3)
60.0	GR(3,3)
63.0	GR(4,3)
93.5	GR(5,3)

FIG. 8-2

90.0	SC(1,1)
84.0	SC(2,1)
92.5	SC(3,1)
65.0	SC(1,2)
59.0	SC(2,2)
52.5	SC(3,2)
42.0	SC(1,3)
56.5	SC(2,3)
60.0	SC(3,3)
74.0	SC(1,4)
79.0	SC(2,4)
63.0	SC(3,4)
100.0	SC(1,5)
98.0	SC(2,5)
93.5	SC(3,5)

FIG. 8-3

order produced by having the first subscript cycle fastest. The first three locations are used for **SC(1,1)**, **SC(2,1)**, and **SC(3,1)** and not **SC(1,1)**, **SC(1,2)**, and **SC(1,3)**.

Mathematicians refer to a rectangular array of numbers as a *matrix* and state that when numbers are arranged in a matrix the first subscript will refer to the row and the second to the column. The programmer should follow this convention when the problem being solved involves the mathematical concept of a matrix, but in many problems such as one involving the grades shown in Fig. 8-1 the first subscript may refer to either parameter at the programmer's discretion. Once the decision has been made, the designation of the meaning of the subscripts should not be changed within the program.

Figure 8-4 shows the grades made on the individual problems of the examinations.

Student	Exam 1				Exam 2				Exam 3			
	Prob. 1	Prob. 2	Prob. 3	Prob. 4	Prob. 1	Prob. 2	Prob. 3	Prob. 4	Prob. 1	Prob. 2	Prob. 3	Prob. 4
1	25.0	20.0	23.0	22.0	21.0	18.0	22.0	23.0	25.0	20.0	25.0	22.5
2	20.0	18.0	16.0	11.0	15.0	13.0	16.0	15.0	25.0	10.0	11.0	6.5
3	10.0	11.0	10.0	11.0	15.0	12.5	13.0	16.0	20.0	15.0	12.0	13.0
4	20.0	18.0	16.0	20.0	20.0	20.0	18.0	21.0	21.0	17.0	13.0	12.0
5	25.0	25.0	25.0	25.0	25.0	25.0	23.0	25.0	25.0	22.0	25.0	21.5

FIG. 8-4

This information could be most readily stored in the memory of the computer in a triply subscripted array. This array would use a subscript to refer to a particular student, a subscript to refer to a particular examination, and a subscript to refer to a particular problem on that examination. The programmer may arbitrarily decide which of the three subscripts refers to which of these parameters. He might decide that he will use the first subscript to refer to the student, the second subscript to refer to the examination, and the third to refer to the problem. He would then use the statement

```
DIMENSION PR(5,3,4)
```

to reserve space for these sixty grades. Location **PR(2,1,3)** would contain the grade made by the second student on the third problem of the first examination.

The FORTRAN compilers for most digital computers permit the use of singly, doubly, and triply subscripted arrays. Some of the larger computers permit arrays with more than three subscripts—several popular computers permit seven subscripts, and a few computers permit a larger number.

The subscripts used with these multidimensional arrays may have the same forms that are permitted in singly subscripted arrays. The subscripts must be in the integer mode and be in any one of the following forms:

a constant
a variable
a variable plus (or minus) a constant
a constant times a variable
a constant times a variable plus (or minus) a constant

The following are valid subscripted variables:

```
X(3,2)                BLOCK(I,J,K)
RATS(K,5)             NEXT(3,4,8)
NUTS(5*J,3*K+1)       Z3(2*K,5,4*K-3)
PAY(5,LAB+2)          PUG(LIKE,7*JAB,KAN-1)
X2Z(N-1,M-1)          WAR(M2Y,N,LAP)
Q(K,K)                WE2R(2*K-3,3*J+2,4*L-1)
```

Great care must be taken to make sure that the subscripts are within the proper range at all times. The statements

```
DIMENSION FUSS(10)
X=FUSS(21)
```

would cause a number taken from some unknown memory location not in array **FUSS** to be stored in location **X**. The statement

```
FUSS(21)=X
```

might cause even more trouble, since a number is stored in some unknown location. The number that had been stored in **X** would replace the value in the unknown location. The number replaced might be some other variable such as **BAD(4,1)** or might be an instruction. This type of error is obvious and therefore easily avoided, but it is not as readily apparent that the subscripts in the statements

```
X=GLUG(K)
```

and

```
B2=BAMB(4*J-3,L+5)
```

will always be within the proper range. Be sure that the subscripts in your programs will always be greater than zero and equal to or less than the maximum size as defined by the **DIMENSIØN** statement.

The same name must not be used in one program as both a subscripted and an unsubscripted variable name. If an array **J** is used in a program, this program may not use **J** as a single integer variable or as an index.

One **DIMENSIØN** statement may reserve space in memory for both singly and multiply subscripted variables. For example, the statement

```
DIMENSION J(5),R(5,2,3),ST(10,10),P2(8)
```

would reserve space for all of the arrays listed.

8-2. EXPLICIT VARIABLE NAME SPECIFICATION—INTEGER, REAL

Implicit specification of variable names was described in Sec. 3-2. Variable names that start with the letter **I**, **J**, **K**, **L**, **M**, or **N** are integer variables. Variable names that start with any other letter are real variables. At times the programmer may wish to use mnemonic names that do not agree with this system. For example, he might wish to use **BETA** as an integer-variable and **NEXT** as a real-variable name. One method that is often used is to use an additional letter at the beginning of the name. Thus **IBETA** and **XNEXT** could be used as names that would include the mnemonics and still implicitly specify the correct mode for the variable names.

The type statements **REAL** and **INTEGER** are specification statements that permit the explicit specification of the mode of variable names. Specification statements are nonexecutable statements that do not cause the compiler to generate any machine-language instructions, but provide information about the nature of the constants and variables used in the program. The **DIMENSIØN** and **FØRMAT** statements are specification statements.

The statements

```
INTEGER X,BETA,ZUGG,N2,ALPHA
REAL NEXT,SMALL,MAX,J23
```

tell the computer to treat the variables **X**, **BETA**, **ZUGG**, **N2** and **ALPHA** as integer variables and **NEXT**, **SMALL**, **MAX**, and **J23** as real variables, regardless of the initial letter of the variable name. Note that the variable name **N2** which would ordinarily indicate that this variable is integer is included in the list of names in the **INTEGER** statement and that **SMALL** which would ordinarily be a real variable name is included in the **REAL** statement. It is not necessary to include such names in the type statements, but their inclusion causes no harm.

Any variable whose name starts with one of the letters **I**, **J**, **K**, **L**, **M**, or **N** is treated as an integer variable by the compiler *unless* its name appears in a type statement other than an **INTEGER** statement, and any variable whose name does not start with one of these letters is treated as a real variable *unless* its name appears in a type statement other than a **REAL** statement.

Most FORTRAN compilers permit the array names that appear in a type statement to be dimensioned in the type statement. If **BETA** and **ALPHA** are to be used as integer variable names, **ZUGG** is to be an array of five integer elements, **NEXT** and **J23** are to be used as real-variable names, and **MAX** is to be an array of ten real elements, the type statements

```
INTEGER BETA,ZUGG(5),ALPHA
REAL NEXT,J23,MAX(10)
```

give this information to the compiler, and the names **ZUGG** and **MAX** *must not* appear in the **DIMENSIØN** statement.

Any array names that do not appear in a type statement must be dimensioned in a **DIMENSIØN** statement. The statements

```
INTEGER BETA,ZUGG(5),ALPHA
REAL NEXT,J23,MAX(10)
DIMENSION X(6),J(20)
```

tell the compiler that **BETA** and **ALPHA** are to be integer variables, **NEXT** and **J23** are to be real variables, **ZUGG** and **J** are to be arrays with integer elements, and **MAX** and **X** are to be arrays with real elements (the first letter of the variable names **X** and **J** in the **DIMENSIØN** statement implicitly specify the mode of these arrays). The variable names used in the program that do not appear in these statements will have the mode specified by the first letter of their names.

In some FORTRAN compilers array names without dimensions are included in the type statements and the dimensioning is done in the **DIMENSIØN** statement. With such compilers the example above would require the statements

```
INTEGER BETA,ZUGG,ALPHA
REAL NEXT,J23,MAX
DIMENSION X(6),J(20),ZUGG(5),MAX(10)
```

An array should never be dimensioned in more than one statement.

Some FORTRAN systems permit the type statements to appear anywhere in the program prior to the first use of the variable concerned. Other compilers require that the type statements appear prior to the first executable statement and before the **DIMENSIØN** statement if there is one. Either the **REAL** or the **INTEGER** statement may come first. If the programmer places his statements in the order

```
INTEGER
REAL
DIMENSION
```

or

```
REAL
INTEGER
DIMENSION
```

immediately after the required control cards and before the first executable statement of his program the program will run on any FORTRAN system. A program may of course contain no **REAL**, **INTEGER**, or **DIMENSIØN** statements or may contain any one, any two, or all three of these statements.

Even though this explicit method of specification of mode is available, beginning programmers are less likely to make errors if they use the implicit method of specification by using names such as **IBATA**, **JZUGG**, **KALPH**, **XNXT**, **XJ23**, and **QMAX** where they wish to use mnemonic names that would not agree with the implicit mode.

The **REAL** and **INTEGER** statements are most often used to correct errors in mode in a program. For example, if a programmer finds that he has used **MAX** as the name of a variable that should have been real, it would probably be easier for him to place a **REAL** statement at the beginning of his program than to try to find and change every statement in the program that includes the name **MAX**.

8-3. NESTED DØ-LOOPS

The **DØ** statement and **DØ**-loops were discussed in Sec. 7-1. The statements within a **DØ**-loop are executed a number of times as the index is cycled. A loop might be used to set each of the elements of an array equal to zero:

```
DO 10 N=1,100
10 X(N)=0.
```

If we wished to set **X(1)** equal to **5.0** and **X(23)** equal to **4.7** and the rest of the elements equal to zero, we might write

```
     DO 10 N=1,100
  10 X(N)=0.
     X(1)=5.0
     X(23)=4.7
```

This would cause all 100 elements to be set equal to zero and then would set **X(1)** and **X(23)** to the desired values. Of course we could have written

```
     X(1)=5.0
     X(2)=0.
     X(3)=0.
     • • • • • • •
     • • • • • • •
     • • • • • • •
     X(22)=0.
     X(23)=4.7
     X(24)=0.
     X(25)=0.
```

but the **DØ**-loop method is much simpler if there are a large number of elements in the array and most of the elements are set equal to the same value.

If one loop is completely inclosed in another loop they are called *nested loops*. The program shown in Fig. 8-5 uses **IF**-statements to set up nested loops to set each element of the doubly subscripted array **Z** equal to zero.

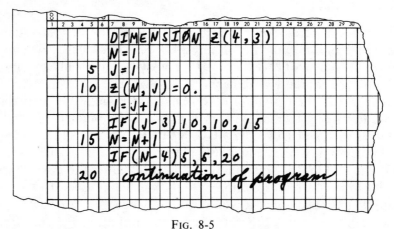

FIG. 8-5

This program would set the elements equal to zero in the order **Z(1,1)**, **Z(1,2)**, **Z(1,3)**, **Z(2,1)**, **Z(2,2)**, **Z(2,3)**, **Z(3,1)**, **Z(3,2)**, **Z(3,3)**, **Z(4,1)**, **Z(4,2)**, **Z(4,3)**.

Figure 8-6 shows a program that will set the elements equal to zero in the same order making use of nested **DØ**-loops.

We could think of these nested loops as being equivalent to our driving around the county fair grounds four times. Each time we reached the racetrack we drive around it three times. We have two counters of the type on which punching a button increases the number on the counter by one. When we first start around the grounds we set the counter we have labeled **N** to one. Each time we enter the race track we set the counter labeled **J** to one. Each time we complete a circuit of the grounds we push the button on the **N** counter, and each time we complete a circuit of the racetrack we push the button on

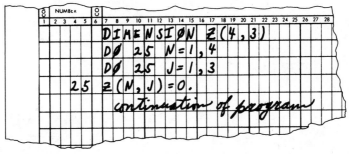

FIG. 8-6

the **J** counter. When the **J** counter shows a number larger than three we leave the race-track and continue our trip around the grounds. When the **N** counter shows a number larger than four we drive away from the fair grounds.

Note that we need two counters. If we tried to use one counter we would set it to one when we entered the racetrack and lose count of how many times we had gone around the grounds. The index of a **DØ**-loop inside another **DØ**-loop must be a different integer-variable name than the index of the outer loop. We couldn't use **N** for the index of both the loops of Fig. 8-6. If we did make the indices both **N**, the program would not make the computations we wished, and we might find that we had created an endless loop. We might find that the counter **N** never reached a value larger than four, and we would continue to drive around the fair grounds until we ran out of gas.

Both of the **DØ** statements of Fig. 8-6 contain the same statement number. This is equivalent to having the exit from the racetrack at the same point as the exit from the grounds.

```
      DIMENSION GR(5,3)
      DØ 6 K=1,5
      READ(5,2)(GR(K,J),J=1,3)
    2 FØRMAT(3F6.1)
      SUM=0.
      DØ 4 I=1,3
    4 SUM=SUM+GR(K,I)
      AVE=SUM/3.
    6 WRITE(6,8)K,AVE
    8 FØRMAT(I3,F8.2)
      DØ 12 J=1,3
      SUM=0.
      DØ 10 K=1,5
   10 SUM=SUM+GR(K,J)
      EXAV=SUM/5.
   12 WRITE(6,14)J,EXAV
   14 FØRMAT(I6,F8.2)
      STØP
      END
   90.0    84.0    92.5
   65.0    59.0    52.5
   42.0    56.5    60.0
   74.0    79.0    63.0
  100.0    98.0    93.5
```

FIG. 8-7

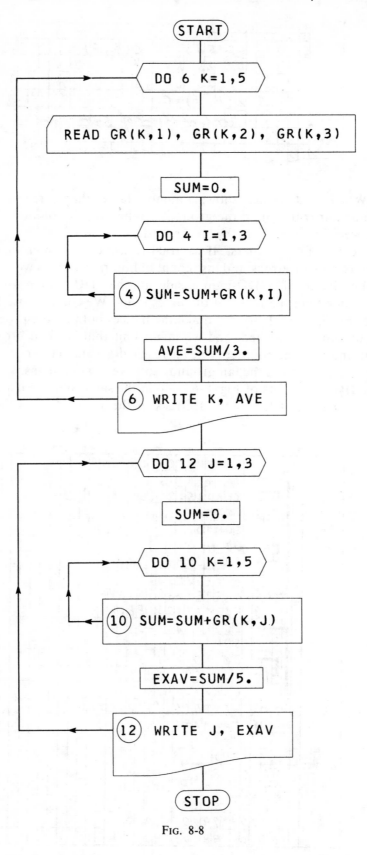

FIG. 8-8

Figure 8-7 shows a program that reads the grades shown in Fig. 8-1, computes and prints each student's average for the three examinations and the class average for each of the three examinations.

The marks

on Fig. 8-7 indicate the range of the **DØ**-loops. Such marks are used on many programs in this book.

The presence of one or more executable statements between the **DØ** statements in the nests as in Fig. 8-7 is equivalent to the entrance to the racetrack not being at the entrance to the fair grounds.

Figure 8-8 shows the flow chart for this program. Follow the computations step by step as they will be made by the computer and see what order the grades are added and how the averages are made.

When nested **DØ**-loops are used the inner loop must be entirely within the outer loop. A set of two nested loops may have the forms shown in Figs. 8-9 or 8-10 but may never have the form shown in Fig. 8-11.

```
 ┌──── DØ 6 K=1,10
 │┌─── DØ 6 L=3,7
 ││
 └┴─ 6 ────
   FIG. 8-9
```

```
 ┌──── DØ 6 K=1,10
 │┌─── DØ 8 L=3,7
 ││
 │└─ 8 ────
 └── 6 ────
   FIG. 8-10
```

```
 ┌──── DØ 6 K=1,10
 │┌─── DØ 8 L=3,7
 ││
 │└─ 6 ────
 └── 8 ────
   FIG. 8-11
```

A third loop may be nested inside the two as shown in Fig. 8-12. In fact most FORTRAN systems permit nesting to much greater depth than is ever required.

```
 ┌───── DØ 21 K=1,8
 │┌──── DØ 17 N=5,19,2
 ││┌─── DØ 7  L=4,288
 │││
 ││└─ 7 ────
 │└── 17 ────
 └─── 21 ────
   FIG. 8-12.
```

DØ-loops may be nested in many ways. Figure 8-13 shows one of the infinite number of possible arrangements of nested loops.

There are several rules that must be remembered concerning the nesting of **DØ**-loops. While more than one loop may terminate at the same statement number, none of the lines that indicate the range of the loops may cross. All of the loops that mutually include any segment of the program must each use a different integer variable name for its index (the three loops whose ranges cross the dotted line in Fig. 8-13 must have different indices).

The index of a **DØ**-loop may be used as an indexing parameter of a **DØ**-loop nested within it. Suppose, for example, we wished to set the shaded elements in the 6 × 6 array *A* shown in Fig. 8-14 equal to zero. In other words, we wish to set the first element in the first column, the first two elements in column 2, and the first *n* elements in column *n*

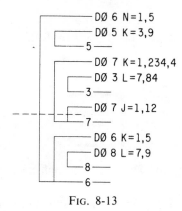

FIG. 8-13

equal to zero. The statements

```
       DO 8 K=1,6
       DO 8 L=1,K
     8 A(L,K)=0.
```

would set the required elements equal to zero in the order indicated by the numbers in the rectangle of Fig. 8-14.

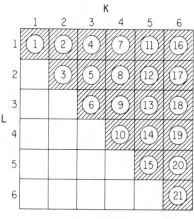

FIG. 8-14

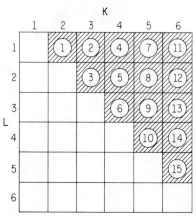

FIG. 8-15

The index of the **DØ**-loop may be used to calculate one or more of the index parameters of a **DØ**-loop nested within it. The elements of array *A* shown shaded in Fig. 8-15 would be set to zero in the order indicated by the statements

```
      DO 4 K=2,6
      J=K-1
      DO 4 L=1,J
    4 A(L,K)=0.
```

Transfers by the use of **IF** or **GØ TØ** statements that cause a special exit from any **DØ**-loop in a nest are valid if they do not cause entry into any loop. The transfer from point **A** to point **B** in Fig. 8-16 is valid, since transfer is made from a point within

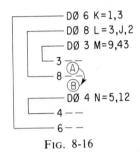

FIG. 8-16

the **DØ 6 K=1,3** and **DØ 8 L=3,J,2** loops to a point within the **DØ 6 K=1,3** loop only. No loop is entered by this transfer.

Transfers that enter a **DØ**-loop are permissible only in very special cases. It is often desirable to have a program transfer out of a **DØ**-loop, execute a portion of the program outside of the loop, and then return to the loop. Transfers that enter a **DØ**-loop are permissible only when the entrance is a return to the range of the same **DØ**-loop from which transfer was originally made. The execution of the program between the transfer out and the return must not change any index or indexing parameters of the **DØ**-loop or nest of **DØ**-loops.

PROBLEMS

8-1. Identify each of the following subscripted variables as valid integer, valid real, or invalid.
  (a) BAD(GOOD,IDEAL)
  (b) J2(J-4,6*K+7)
  (c) FUZZ(7L,5*M)
  (d) X(H,I,J)
  (e) JAM(K+L,K-7,L+5)
  (f) J(K-8,4*K-3,J)
  (g) RUT(K,KD(3),MEN)

8-2. The following statements appear at the beginning of FORTRAN programs. List all of the unsubscripted integer variables, unsubscripted real variables, integer arrays, and real arrays that you can identify in each program. Indicate any errors which occur in the specification statements.

```
(a)  INTEGER GIT,BAG(4,5),JOKE
     REAL MUD,X(6),Y
     DIMENSION Q(5,5),L2(10,10,10)

(b)  REAL LOVE,J7K,W
     INTEGER R,Q(90),M
     DIMENSION XX(7)
     Z=29.
     N3=46.7

(c)  REAL LM(45),IDEAL(6,4)
     DIMENSION XC(10),LM(45)
     W=25.4

(d)  DIMENSION X(25)
     REAL I(3,3,2),LP33
```

8-3. What integer number would be stored in each element of the **M** array by the following program (what number would be stored in **M(1,1)**, **M(1,2)**, etc.)?

```
     DIMENSION M(3,3)
     K=1
     DO 10 J=1,3
     DO 10 N=1,3
     M(N,J)=K
  10 K=K+1
```

8-4. What integer number would be stored in each element of the **M** array by the following program?

```
     DIMENSION M(2,2,3)
     K=2
     DO 6 J=1,2
     DO 6 L=1,3
     DO 6 N=1,2
     M(J,N,L)=K
   6 K=K+2
```

8-5. Write a program that will read the data punched on cards from the data listing shown into a two-dimensional array. The program should find and print the sum of each line and then find and print the sum of each column.

Data

7.8	64.	18.2	192.	2.87	
25.3	-6.7	1.0	-9.7	80.	
289.	3.02	-54.	7.91	1.92	

8-6. Write a program that will set all of the elements of the array shown equal to zero and then using loops set the shaded elements equal to one. Have the program print out the matrix line by line. Do not use data cards to provide the information; use a relationship involving **J** and **M** to determine whether or not an element should be set equal to one.

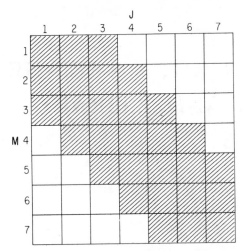

8-7. A professor gives two to five examinations during a school term (one term he may give two examinations, another term he may give four, etc.). Write a FORTRAN program that he may use every term to obtain a table giving the four-digit student identification number and the examination average for each student. The program should also print the class average for each of the examinations. No class will have more than 75 students. Use the data given in Fig. 1-7 for this term.

8-8. Write a FORTRAN program that reads the x and y coordinates of points in a plane and finds and prints the greatest distance between any two of the points.

n	x	y
1	-1.00	-2.54
2	-3.68	7.90
3	4.89	3.68
4	-0.20	8.75
5	6.75	-7.06

8-9. Write a FORTRAN program that will read the information given from cards and print the identification number, the girl's bust measurement minus the average bust measurement, the girl's waist measurement minus the average waist measurement, and the girl's hip measurement minus the average hip measurement for each girl. All the information for one girl is to be read from one card. One line of printing is to be used for each girl. Use a singly subscripted array to hold the identification numbers and a doubly subscripted array to hold the measurements.

Girl Identification Number	Bust Measurement (inches)	Waist Measurement (inches)	Hip Measurement (inches)
1026	36.	24.	36.
1232	35.5	23.	37.
2129	37.	24.25	36.
3328	37.25	24.5	36.75
3417	39.	25.	37.25
5390	42.	27.	40.

LITERAL OUTPUT, CARRIAGE CONTROL, AND LIBRARY FUNCTIONS

9-1. LITERAL OUTPUT

Output statements may be used to print alphabetic information. This feature is very useful in labeling answers, putting titles on output, or column headings on tables. Literal information which is to be printed may be written verbatim making use of a *Hollerith specification*. The portion of the output thus obtained is known as a *Hollerith field* or **H** *field*. This type of field and specification is named for Herman Hollerith, who originated the idea of tabulating data with the aid of punched cards while working for the United States Census Bureau. He developed electromechanical equipment for punching, sorting, and collating cards that was used for tabulating the 1890 census.

The statements

```
      WRITE(6,19)
   19 FORMAT(1X,21HWHAT IS TO BE PRINTED)
```

would cause the printer to print

```
      WHAT IS TO BE PRINTED
```

with the **W** of **WHAT** in the first column. The specification **21H** tells the computer that the next twenty-one characters in the **FØRMAT** statement following the letter **H** are to be printed. Blanks in Hollerith fields are considered characters and must be counted. This count must be accurate and either

```
   19 FORMAT(1X,20HWHAT IS TO BE PRINTED)
```

or

```
   19 FORMAT(1X,22HWHAT IS TO BE PRINTED)
```

would cause an error since there are twenty-one characters including blanks after the **H**.

Remember that the first column described is used for carriage control and will not be printed. The statements

```
      WRITE(6,53)
   53 FORMAT(17HWHATISTOBEPRINTED)
```

would cause the printer to print

```
      HATISTOBEPRINTED
```

The blank in the carriage control column to cause normal single spacing may be furnished by leaving at least one blank after the **H**

```
      WRITE(6,54)
   54 FORMAT(22H WHAT IS TC BE PRINTED)
```

The literal information may include numerals and special characters:

```
      WRITE(6,27)
   27 FORMAT(25H RESULTS (FCR $12.00/HR.))
```

would print

RESULTS (FOR $12.00/HR.)

with the **R** of **RESULTS** in the first column of the page.

When the programs are written on FORTRAN coding forms blanks may be easily indicated as shown in Fig. 9-1. A programmer writing this program on ordinary paper

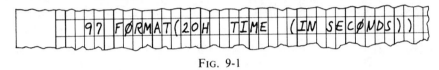

FIG. 9-1

usually indicates the position of blanks in the literal field by the use of the lowercase letter "b" or with a small triangle as shown in Fig. 9-2.

97 FØRMAT(20HbbbTIMEbb(INbSECØNDS))

97 FØRMAT(20HΔΔTIMEΔΔ(INΔSECØNDS))

FIG. 9-2

When the number of blank spaces to be left is not obvious, the printed statements in this book will use a lowercase letter "b" to indicate that a blank column is to be left by pushing the space key on the card punch.

A large number of blanks may be indicated by the use of the **X** specification. The statements shown in Fig. 9-3 and in Fig. 9-4 would each cause the printer to print

AGE   WEIGHT

with the **A** in column **5** and the **W** in column **15**.

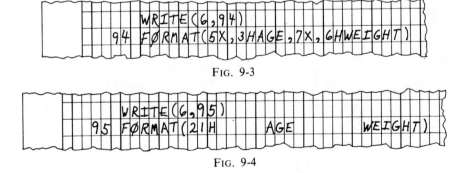

FIG. 9-3

FIG. 9-4

Literal and numerical fields may be combined in one line of printing by including a list of variable names in the **WRITE** statement and including the **I**, **E**, and **F** specifications with the literal information in the **FØRMAT** statement. The statements

```
      WRITE(6,5)V
    5 FORMAT(12H VELOCITY = ,E12.5)
```

would cause the printing of the line

```
     VELOCITY = -0.50923E 03
```

if the variable **V** had the value **−509.23** at the time the **WRITE** statement was executed. The statements

```
        WRITE(6,33)J,Q(J)
    33 FORMAT(5X,2HQ(,I2,4H) = ,F5.2)
```

would cause

```
          Q(16) =   5.25
```

to be printed if **J** and **Q(16)** had the values of **16** and **5.25**. The **5X** indicates five spaces (one space for the carriage control and four blank spaces on the page), the **2HQ(** is a Hollerith specification that asks for the printing of the **Q(**, the **I2** asks for the printing of the first variable named in the list of the **WRITE** statement, **4H)b=b** is another Hollerith specification, and the **F5.2** is the real specification for the second variable named in the list. Care must be taken to leave enough room for the variables. If **J** and **Q(128)** had the values **128** and **765.37** the above **FØRMAT** would not permit the correct numbers to be printed since these numbers would require more than the two and five spaces allotted by the specifications.

    The use of the slash "/" in an output **FØRMAT** has the same basic meaning it did for the input **FØRMAT**. If specifies the end of one line specification and the beginning of the next. The statements

```
        WRITE(6,45)
    45 FORMAT(9H THE TIME/9H HAS COME)
```

would cause the printer to print

```
          THE TIME
          HAS COME
```

just as would the statements

```
        WRITE(6,46)
    46 FORMAT(9H THE TIME)
        WRITE(6,47)
    47 FORMAT(9H HAS COME)
```

The slash "/" causes the printer to advance to a new line. The use of extra slashes will leave blank lines on the printed page. The statements

```
        WRITE(6,75)
    75 FORMAT(4H THE/5H TIME//4H HAS///5H COME/)
```

would cause the printing of

```
          THE
          TIME
```
                                (one blank line)
```
          HAS
```
                                (two blank lines)
```
          COME
```

The final slash after the "**CØME**" in the **FØRMAT** will cause the printer to space. The next **WRITE** statement would start printing after a blank line had been left. The statements

```
      WRITE(6,82)
   82 FORMAT(9H THE TIME/)
      WRITE(6,83)
   83 FORMAT(9H HAS COME)
```

or the statements

```
      WRITE(6,84)
   84 FORMAT(9H THE TIME)
      WRITE(6,85)
   85 FORMAT(/9H HAS COME)
```

would cause the lines

```
      THE TIME
                    (one blank line)
      HAS COME
```

to be printed. The start of the execution of a **WRITE** statement normally causes the printer to advance to a new line. A slash at the beginning or end of a **FØRMAT** statement causes the printer to advance another line.

All the examples of **FØRMAT** statements given above have shown the specifications within the **FØRMAT** as separated by commas or slashes. One permissible exception to this rule is that the comma following a Hollerith field is optional and may be omitted. The **FØRMAT** statements

```
   38 FORMAT(11H WHEN K IS ,I2,6H W IS ,F6.2)
```

and

```
   38 FORMAT(11H WHEN K IS I2,6H W IS F6.2)
```

would be equivalent.

We might decide to give the output on the clerk's problem (program shown in Fig. 4-18) the form shown in Fig. 9-5. This could be accomplished by the program shown in Fig. 9-6. The output of this program is shown in Fig. 9-7.

The use of a Hollerith field requires the programmer to count the spaces used in this field. A miscount normally results in an error. Some of the more recent FORTRAN systems have introduced an alternative method of designating literal fields that does not

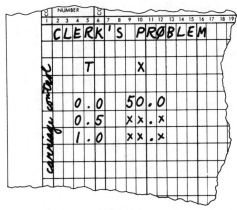

FIG. 9-5

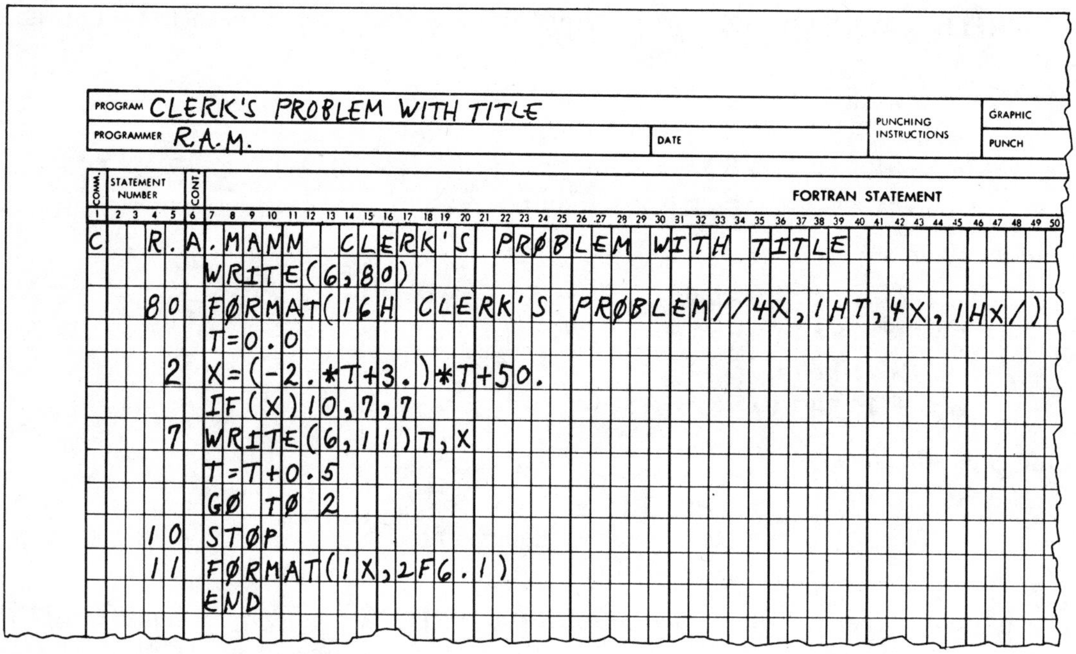
PROGRAM CLERK'S PROBLEM WITH TITLE
PROGRAMMER R.A.M.
DATE
PUNCHING INSTRUCTIONS
GRAPHIC
PUNCH
COMM.
STATEMENT NUMBER
CONT.
FORTRAN STATEMENT
C   R.A.MAMM CLERK'S PROBLEM WITH TITLE
      WRITE(6,80)
   80 FØRMAT(16H CLERK'S PRØBLEM//4X,1HT,4X,1HX/)
      T=0.0
    2 X=(-2.*T+3.)*T+50.
      IF(X)10,7,7
    7 WRITE(6,11)T,X
      T=T+0.5
      GØ TØ 2
   10 STØP
   11 FØRMAT(1X,2F6.1)
      END

FIG. 9-6

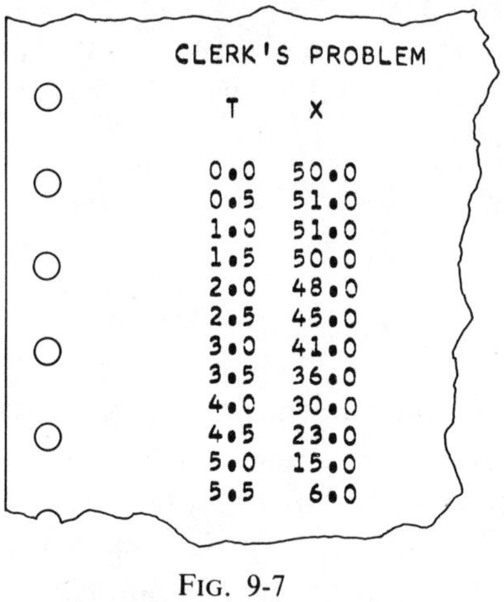
CLERK'S PROBLEM
T X
0.0 50.0
0.5 51.0
1.0 51.0
1.5 50.0
2.0 48.0
2.5 45.0
3.0 41.0
3.5 36.0
4.0 30.0
4.5 23.0
5.0 15.0
5.5 6.0

FIG. 9-7

require the counting of spaces. This method uses a special character, usually an apostrophe, to enclose the literal information. The statement

```
71 FORMAT(' X = ',F8.2,' AND Z = ',E12.4)
```

would be equivalent to

```
71 FORMAT(5H X = ,F8.2,9H AND Z = ,E12.4)
```

Literal fields that include apostrophes in the material to be printed must be handled in a special manner. If we wished to have the printer print

```
HOUSEMAID'S KNEE
```

we might think that we could use the statements

```
   WRITE(6,66)
66 FORMAT(' HOUSEMAID'S KNEE')
```

This would not work. The compiler would examine the F**Ø**RMAT, find the first two apostrophes, and conclude that we intended

```
' HOUSEMAID'
```

to be a literal field. The computer would print an error message telling us that we had made a syntax error in the F**Ø**RMAT statement since the remainder of the F**Ø**RMAT

```
S KNEE'
```

is not a recognizable field specification. Printing literal material that contains an apostrophe causes no trouble when an integer number and the letter **H** are used to indicate the Hollerith field. When apostrophes are used to set off the literal field, doubling an apostrophe indicates that the apostrophe is to be printed and does not indicate the end of a literal field. The statements

```
    WRITE(6,67)
 67 FORMAT(' HOUSEMAID''S KNEE')
```

would cause the printer to print

```
HOUSEMAID'S KNEE
```

with the **H** in the first column.

Some computers use a different character in place of the apostrophe to identify the literal field, and some computers, including some of the largest, do not permit the entry of literal data except in a Hollerith field indicated by the letter **H**.

9-2. CARRIAGE CONTROL

The character specified for the first column by a F**Ø**RMAT statement is not printed when the F**Ø**RMAT statement is used with a **WRITE** statement specifying the printer. This character, and all characters, are typed when used with a **WRITE** statement that specifies the console printer (typewriter) and is punched when the card punch is specified.

When the first character is specified to be blank and the **WRITE** statement calls for the printer, the printer advances one line and then prints the specified information. A series of **WRITE** statements using F**Ø**RMAT statements making the first character of each line blank will cause single-spaced printing unless slashes provide for multiple spacing.

The first character may be made blank by use of a Hollerith field, a literal field, an **X** field, or by providing more room than necessary to hold the number in an **I**, **E**, or **F** field.

If the first character for a line of printing is specified to be a zero, the printer will double-space and then print the line (the zero is not printed). The statements

```
    WRITE(6,40)X
 40 FORMAT(F7.2)
    WRITE(6,41)Y
 41 FORMAT(1H0,F6.2)
```

would cause the printer to print

```
25.25
```
                         (one blank line)
```
51.03
```

if **X** and **Y** had the values **25.25** and **51.03** respectively.

The statements

```
      J=0
      WRITE(6,42)J,Y
   42 FORMAT(I1,F6.2)
```

would print

(one blank line)

51.03

The character one (1) causes the printer to skip to the top of the next page. The statements

```
      WRITE(6,72)Z
   72 FORMAT(1H1,F6.2)
```

or

```
      K=1
      WRITE(6,80)K,Z
   80 FORMAT(I1,F6.2)
```

would cause the sheet at the printing position to be ejected and the value of Z to be printed at the top of the next sheet. The value of K would not be printed.

A plus sign (+) in the control column suppresses spacing before printing. The statements

```
      WRITE(6,67)
   67 FORMAT(18H THE VALUE OF X IS)
      WRITE(6,68)X
   68 FORMAT(18X,F6.2)
```

would cause

THE VALUE OF X IS

25.25

to be printed with regular single-spacing. The statements

```
      WRITE(6,67)
   67 FORMAT(18H THE VALUE OF X IS)
      WRITE(6,69)X
   69 FORMAT(1H+,17X,F6.2)
```

would cause

THE VALUE OF X IS 25.25

to be printed on one line. The first **WRITE** statement would print

THE VALUE OF X IS

The **1H+** in the second **FØRMAT** statement would suppress spacing, and the numerical value **25.25** would be printed on the same line.

A program that does not allow for the control character in the **FØRMAT** statements may lose the first character in some lines of printing and may have erratic spacing in the output.

The control characters and their effects are

Blank	Single-space before printing
0	Double-space before printing
1	Skip to top of next page before printing
+	Suppress space before printing

It should be emphasized that a control column is only used with the printer. There is *no* control column on any other output device or on any input device.

9-3. Library Functions

Problems to be solved often involve functions such as the trigonometic functions, logarithms, and roots. Many such functions can be calculated by the expansion of a series, and computer programs may be written to evaluate them. If every programmer wrote a program to do this, a great amount of needless duplicated effort would be expended. Most FORTRAN systems provide a package of previously written programs to compute these common functions for your program. Such a package of prewritten programs is known as a *library*.

One such function provided in the libraries of all FORTRAN systems is a program which calculates the trigonometic sine. The variable **Q** could be set equal to the sine of **X** by the arithmetic statement

```
Q=SIN(X)
```

All that is necessary to use one of the library functions is to write its name (in this case **SIN**) followed by the *argument* (the quantity for which this function is to be evaluated, **X**) enclosed in parentheses. The argument of the **SIN** function should be real and in radians.

The argument may be a real-variable name as above or it may be a real constant or expression. The statement

```
W=SIN(30.)
```

would set **W** equal to the sine of **30** radians (not **30** degrees). If a program contained the statement

```
R2=SIN(3.*X-7.5*Z/D)
```

the argument in the parentheses would be evaluated and the sine of that many radians would be found.

The statement

```
Q7=SIN(0.01745329*X)
```

could be used to determine the sine of **X** degrees since one degree is equal to **0.01745329** radians.

The usual rules concerning variable names apply to the names of the library functions. **SIN** begins with the letter **S**, and therefore the **SIN** function is real.

The argument of a function may be another function.

```
PHAW=SIN(SQRT(X))
```

would set **PHAW** equal to the sine of the square root of **X**.

The functions may be used in expressions just as though they were variable names.

PLOP=7.34*X-Z*SIN(X-0.2)

The functions may appear more than once in one expression, with the same arguments

C45G=SIN(X)+(Y-3.4)/SIN(X)

or with different arguments

CL=Y/SIN(Y)-Z/SIN(X)

or

CM=SIN(X)*SIN(Y)-SIN(Y)

The function may be used in an **IF** statement:

IF(SIN(X))23,24,53

or

IF(X-SIN(X))3,54,8

Some functions available with most FORTRAN systems are given in Fig. 9-8.

Name	Description	Definition	Mode of Function	Mode of Argument	Comments	Examples
SIN (X)	Trigonometric sine	$\sin(x)$	real	real	arg. in radians	W=SIN(X+Y)
CØS(X)	Trigonometric cosine	$\cos(x)$	real	real	arg. in radians	P=T+CØS(Z)
SQRT(X)	Square root	$\sqrt{x}$	real	real	argument $\geqslant 0$	TY=SQRT(P)
ALØG(X)	Natural logarithm	$\log_e x$	real	real	argument > 0	G=ALØG(D-C)
ALØG10(X)	Logarithm to base 10	$\log_{10} x$	real	real	argument > 0	W=ALØG10(A)
EXP(X)	Exponential	e^x	real	real		R2=EXP(C+P)
TANH(X)	Hyperbolic tangent	$\tanh(x)$	real	real	arg. in radians	V=TANH(YZ)
ATAN(X)	Arc tangent	$\tan^{-1} x$	real	real		S=G*ATAN(B)

Fig. 9-8

The mode of the argument must be the one given in the table. All of the functions shown in Fig. 9-8 require real arguments, and the use of integer arguments for any of these functions will give the wrong answer. The statements

Y=SQRT(4)

or

N=4
Y=SQRT(N)

will give incorrect answers.

The argument of the **SQRT** function must not be negative since the computer is unable to store an imaginary number in a location specified as real. An **IF** statement is often used in programs to check the argument before the **SQRT** function is used with a procedure being provided for the computer to follow if the argument is negative (perhaps print a literal message and the value of the argument and stop). The use of the **SQRT** is more efficient for computing square roots than using the notation ****0.5**. Incidentally, raising a negative number to the **0.5** power also gives an incorrect answer.

The argument of the **ALØG** and **ALØG10** functions must not be zero or negative.

All trigonometric functions other than the sine and cosine may be determined from these two functions, for example

TANX=SIN(X)/COS(X)

would store a real number in **TANX** equal to tan x. This statement should probably be preceded by a test to make sure that **CØS(X)** is not zero.

Some additional library functions available with most FORTRAN systems are shown in Fig. 9-9.

Additional Library Functions

Name	Description	Mode of Function	Mode of Argument	Example
ABS	Absolute value	real	real	W=7.*ABS(X+Y)
IABS	Absolute value	integar	integer	L=IABS(J−N)
FLØAT	Mode conversion	real	integer	T=SQRT(FLØAT(V))
IFIX	Mode conversion	integer	real	M=K+IFIX(W)

FIG. 9-9

The absolute-value functions provide the absolute value of the argument. The function **ABS** must be used with real arguments, and **IABS** must be used with integer arguments. The statement

Y = ABS (X)

would store **+5.678** in **Y** if **X** had the value **−5.678**, and the statement

Q = ABS (R)

would store **+67.89** in **Q** if **R** had the value **+67.89**. Similarly, the statements

J = IABS (K)

and

L = IABS (M)

would store **+56** in **J** and **L** if **K** and **M** had the values **−56** and **+56** respectively.

The mode-conversion functions **FLØAT** and **IFIX** as the names imply are used to convert integer values to real values and real values to integer values. The statement

Y = FLOAT (K)

would store the real number **50.** in **Y** if **K** had the value **50**, and the statement

J = IFIX (T)

would store the integer number **56** in **J** if **T** had the value **56.79**. In other words, these two statements do exactly the same as the statements

Y = K

and

J = T

The functions have no advantage over the single-variable name in such statements, but one statement may take the place of two where a variable's mode must be changed so that it may be used as an argument of another function. The statement

Y = SIN (N)

would give the wrong answer, since the **SIN** function requires a real argument. The correct result could be obtained by the use of the two statements

XN = N
Y = SIN (XN)

or by the use of a single statement

Y = SIN (FLOAT (N))

These mode-conversion functions may also be used to avoid mixed-mode expressions which are not acceptable on most computers. The statements

$$J = K + 7*W$$

and

$$R = S/L$$

contain mixed-mode expressions, but the statements

$$J = K + 7*IFIX(W)$$

and

$$R = S/FLOAT(L)$$

do not.

All of the library functions may be used alone or combined with variable names and/or constants as arguments of other functions, in the **IF** statements, and on the right-hand side of arithmetic statements.

The use of these function names as variable names should be avoided. Some computer systems permit a program that does not call for the **SIN** function to use **SIN** as a subscripted- or unsubscripted-variable name, but with such systems a program that calls for the **SIN** function *and* uses **SIN** as a subscripted- or unsubscripted-variable name will not compile and will give error messages. It is a good idea to avoid using variable names which are function names or which are other common words used in FORTRAN such as **IF**, **DØ**, **WRITE**, or **GØ**. Some FORTRAN systems have a list of "reserved words" that may not be used as variable names. In any case it is best to avoid such words, since their inclusion in a program might confuse someone studying a listing of the program.

The library functions shown in Figs. 9-8 and 9-9 are available with most FORTRAN systems. Some systems have a longer list of library functions available, and the names given to the functions may be different with a few systems.

Problems

9-1. Write a program that sets **X** and **Y** equal to **593.5** and **−64.75** respectively and prints the following (use **F** format specifications for the printing of the numbers):

```
RESULTS
             (one blank line)
X = 593.50
Y = -64.75
```

9-2. Write a program that sets **X** and **Y** equal to **94.0** and **76.28** respectively, and prints the following using **F** format specifications to print the numbers.

$$Xb = b94.0bANDbYb = 76.28$$

9-3. Write a program that will print the following.
(a) Using slashes to produce the spacing.
(b) Using carriage control to produce the spacing.

```
WE ALL
TRY
            (one blank line)
TO DO
            (one blank line)
OUR
BEST
```

9-4. Write a program that uses **R** as an integer array, sets each element of this array equal to

$$R(j,k) = 2j^2 - k^2$$

and prints the resulting matrix in the following form using **I** format specifications for printing the matrix elements.

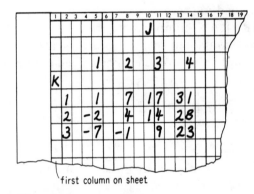

first column on sheet

9-5. Indicate whether each of the following FORTRAN statements is valid or invalid.
  (a) K=SIN(X−COS(Y))
  (b) T=SIN(10.7/X)
  (c) RT=SQRT(−X)
  (d) J=SQRT(2.*3.14159−8.9*ABS(SIN(X)/COS(X)))
  (e) XTRA=TANH(IABS(SQRT(X)−COS(Y)))
  (f) LB2=SQRT(IABS(IFIX(Y)))
  (g) L=IABS(IFIX(FLOAT(N)))

9-6. Write a program to calculate and print a table of angles and the tangents of the angles for 0°, 10°, 20°, 30°,...,120°. Have the computer print column titles and print the word **INFINITY** in place of a number when the tangent is infinite.

9-7. Write a program that will print out the last two paragraphs of Sec. 9-2 on the printer as they appear in the text.

9-8. Write a program to compute and print a table of the number, square, cube, and square root for the whole numbers 1 to 50. Align the columns with headings over each. Double space between the heading and first row of numbers and single space between the remaining rows of numbers. Put 25 numbers per page with column headings on each page.

ARITHMETIC STATEMENT FUNCTIONS, THE COMPUTED GØ TØ, INPUT AND OUTPUT (CONTINUED)

10-1. ARITHMETIC STATEMENT FUNCTIONS

The library functions described in the proceding chapter are programs that were written and supplied with the FORTRAN compiler program. Occasionally a programmer will find that some function not contained in the library is used a number of times in his program. Suppose, for example, the problem to be solved contained the three formulas

$$q = 7t^5 - 4t^3 + 3t$$
$$d = 7y^5 - 4y^3 + 3y - 42$$

and

$$s = 8v^2(7w^5 - 4w^3 + 3w)$$

Noting that there are three terms in each of these formulas that are identical except for the variable, we might define a function as

$$f_1(x) = 7x^5 - 4x^3 + 3x$$

and then, using this definition, write the three formulas

$$q = f_1(t)$$
$$d = f_1(y) - 42$$

and

$$s = 8v^2 f_1(w)$$

The variable x used in the function definition is a "dummy" argument in that the x does not actually appear in the problem but is used to show that certain constants and powers of a variable are to be combined in a particular manner. The function could have been defined as

$$f_1(t) = 7t^5 - 4t^3 + 3t$$

or

$$f_1(z) = 7z^5 - 4z^3 + 3z$$

or using any other letter to represent the variable involved.

The above discussion describes a mathematical handling of the problem. The FORTRAN procedure would be very similar. A "function defining statement" is written using any valid variable name *of the correct mode* as a dummy argument. The function must be given a name, and the usual rules apply: the name must be one to six alphameric characters (the maximum number of characters may be different than six with other computers), the first of which must be alphabetic, and the first letter indicates the mode

142

of the function. We could define the function with the function defining statement

$$F1(X)=7.*X**5-4.*X**3+3.*X$$

or we could save computer time by defining the function using nesting as described in Sec. 1-1.

$$F1(X)=((7.*X**2-4.)*X**2+3.)*X$$

and use this function in arithmetic or **IF** statements exactly as we used the library functions:

```
Q=F1(T)
D=F1(Y)-42.
S=8.*V**2*F1(W)
```

Care must be taken writing the defining function since the name of the function and the dummy argument *must* have the correct mode. The statement using the function *must* use arguments of the same mode as the dummy arguments. The arguments of the functions in the arithmetic and **IF** statements may be expressions, variable names, constants, or other functions (either functions defined in other function defining statements or library functions). In other words, the defined functions may be used in exactly the same manner as the library functions.

The function defining statements are placed before any executable statements in the FORTRAN program. This type of statement is not executed in the same sense that an ordinary arithmetic statement is; it appears only once in the program but its indicated operations are executed under the control of the statement which called upon the functions each time the function name appears in an expression. The order of the program might be

> Type statements (**INTEGER** and **REAL**)
> **DIMENSIØN** statement
> Function defining statements
> Executable program statements (including a **STØP**)
> **END**
> Data cards if any

The **FØRMAT** statements may come anywhere between the **DIMENSIØN** and **END** statements.

The FORTRAN compiler is able to distinguish functions from array names, since the function name is not dimensioned in a specification statement.

The expression to the right of the equals sign in the function defining statement may contain other function names, *unsubscripted* variable names, and constants:

```
DUMB(X)=SIN(X)-7.5*CØS(X)
DN74(X)=8.23*DUMB(X)-ABS(X)
```

If the expression contains a variable name that does not appear as a dummy argument, each time the function is called for it will be evaluated using the value this variable has at the time the function is called. If the defining statement were

```
DRAB(G)=S-G**5
```

the statement

```
Q=DRAB(W)
```

would be evaluated as though it had been written

```
Q=S-W**5
```

and

```
TYPE=RED*DRAB(T)
```

as

```
TYPE=RED*(S-T**5)
```

The function defining statement may have more than one dummy argument. If the function **QUACK** were defined as

```
QUACK(X,Y,Z)=X-X*Y+7.98/Z
```

the statement

```
GILL=QUACK(A,B,C)
```

would be executed as though it had been written

```
GILL=A-A*B+7.98/C
```

Subscripted variable names may *not* be used in the defining statement:

```
CAR(X,N)=X(N)-Y(N)+56.0
```

would be invalid, but subscripted variables may be used in the statements making use of the defined functions.

```
QUACK(X,Y,Z)=X-X*Y+7.5/Z
R=QUACK(W(1)-82.3,W(5)**3,W(N)-W(2))
```

Once an arithmetic statement function has been defined by a function defining statement, it may be used repeatedly throughout a program by referring to its name and giving the desired arguments. There would be no point in writing a defining statement for a function that is used only once. In this case it would be better to write out the expression at the point where it was used instead of writing a function defining statement.

10-2. The Computed GØ TØ Statement

An arithmetic **IF** statement has *three* possible branch directions. Several **IF** statements may be combined when a branching is required that has more than three possible branch directions. Figure 10-1 shows a flow chart and Fig. 10-2 part of a program that illustrates

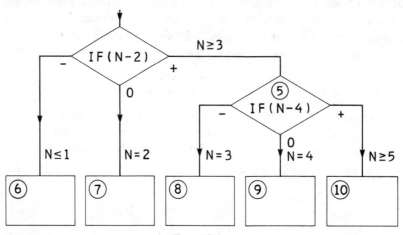

Fig. 10-1

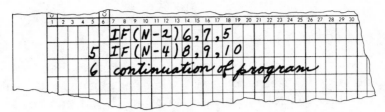

FIG. 10-2

the use of two **IF** statements to provide a five-way branch. More **IF** statements could be added to provide more branch directions.

There is another control statement, a special form of the **GØ TØ** statement called the "computed **GØ TØ**" statement, that is used for multiple branching. It begins with the words "**GØ TØ**" followed by any desired amount of statement numbers separated by commas and enclosed in a pair of parentheses. The close-parenthesis is followed by a comma and a nonsubscripted *integer*-variable name.

When a computed **GØ TØ** statement is executed the computer will go next to the statement whose statement number appears in the list in the parentheses in the position indicated by the value of the integer variable. The statement

$$\text{GO TO (29,46,2,16),N}$$

would send the computer to statement number **29** (the first statement number in the list) if N had the value of **1**, to statement number **46** (the second in the list) if N had the value **2**, to statement **2** if N had the value **3**, and to **16** if the value of N was **4**. Note that the computer does *not* go to the statement number equal to the value of the integer variable but to the statement number in the position in the list indicated by this value; when **N** has the value **2** the computer goes to the second statement number (**46**) not to statement number **2**.

The list of statement numbers may be as long as desired and the same statement number may appear more than once in the list:

$$\text{GO TO (5,8,8,2,5),J}$$

would send the computer to statement number **5** if **J** had the value of **1** or **5**, to statement number **8** if the value of **J** was **2** or **3**, and to statement number **2** if the value of **J** was **4**.

Statement numbers must appear in the list for every integer value from one to the maximum possible, even though some of these values may never be met in the program; for example, a program containing the statements

$$\text{DO 50 K=3,9,2}$$
$$\text{GO TO (5,5,5,8,8,3,3,5,16),K}$$

would reach the computed **GØ TØ** with values of **K** of **3**, **5**, **7**, and **9**—but the list must contain nine statement numbers. **K** will never have values of **1**, **2**, **4**, **6**, or **8** but statement numbers must appear in the positions in the list corresponding to these values. These statement numbers may be the number of any executable statement in the program. The statements could be

$$\text{DO 50 K=3,9,2}$$
$$\text{GO TO (10,10,5,10,8,10,3,10,16),K}$$

if there is an executable statement number **10** anywhere in the program.

The results are unpredictable if the value of the integer variable is not within the proper range. There is no way of predicting where the computer would go after reaching the statement

```
        GO TO (6,17,3,192),M
```

if **M** had a value less than one (negative or zero) or a value larger than four.

The computed **GØ TØ** statement may itself have a statement number that is re-ferred to by some other control statement such as an **IF** statement or another **GØ TØ** statement. The statement number of a computed **GØ TØ** statement may *not* appear in its own statement number list. The statement

```
    56 GO TO (34,16,56,4),L
```

would be invalid, since the statement number of the **GØ TØ** statement (**56**) appears in the statement list creating an endless loop when **L** has the value **3**.

The statement number of any control statement, including a computed **GØ TØ** statement, may *not* be the statement ending a **DØ**-loop:

```
    DO 4 N=1,30
    ....
    ....
    ....
    4 GO TO (5,7,13,2),M
```

would be invalid.

10-3. Input and Output (continued)

Input and output statements are very similar in appearance. They consist of the word **READ** or **WRITE** followed by two integer numbers enclosed in parentheses. The first of these integer numbers refers to the input or output unit that is to be used, and the second refers to the statement number of a **FØRMAT** statement that describes the form and location of the information on the printed sheet or punched card. The **WRITE** state-ment has no variable-name list if only literal information is to be printed or punched, but both the **READ** and **WRITE** statements usually have a list of variable names following the parentheses. The names in this list are separated by commas.

A slash (/) in the **FØRMAT** statement indicates an advance to a new line of printing or to a new card.

The variable-name list of the **READ** or **WRITE** statement and the **FØRMAT** specifications are inspected by the computer from left to right. The statements

```
    WRITE(6,5)X,Y
    5 FORMAT(3H X=,F5.1,3H Y=,F5.2)
```

would cause the computer to use output unit **6**. The first item in the **FØRMAT** statement is a Hollerith specification that would place a blank in the carriage-control character which would cause the printer to advance to a new line. The remainder of this Hollerith specification would cause **X**= to be printed in the first two columns of this line. The next item in the **FØRMAT** statement is **F5.1**, and the computer would print the value of the first item in the variable-name list (**X**) right-justified in the next five columns of this same line with one digit after the decimal point. The next literal field would cause b**Y**= to be printed in the next three columns. Finally, the **F5.2** specification would cause the value of the next item in the list (**Y**) to be printed right-justified in a five-column field with two digits after the decimal point. Both the variable-name list and the

FØRMAT specifications would be satisfied and the computer would go on to the next statement. If **X** and **Y** had the values **46.5** and **50.0** respectively, these statements would cause the printer to print

X= 46.5 Y=50.00

Remember that the mode of the variable name to be printed must be the same as the mode of the **FØRMAT** specified. An integer variable name in the list must be printed with an **I** specification, and a real-variable name in the list must have an **E** or **F** specification in the corresponding place in the **FØRMAT** statement.

If there are more **FØRMAT** specifications in the statement than there are variable names in the list the computer will print until it reaches an **I**, **F**, or **E** specification for which there is no unused name in the list. Anything in the **FØRMAT** statement beyond what has been printed will be ignored and the computer will go on to the next statement to be executed. The statements

```
    WRITE(6,5)X
  5 FORMAT(3H X=,F5.1,3H Y=,F5.2)
```

would cause the printing of

X= 46.5 Y=

The printing in this case would continue just as described above until the computer reached the **F5.2** specification and found no unsatisfied variable names in the list to use for this specification.

If there are more variable names in the list that there are **I**, **F**, and **E** specifications, the computer works through the variable list and the **FØRMAT** specifications in the usual manner until it has used all of the specifications and then advances the sheet one space (or starts a new card if the output unit specified is the card punch) and goes back to the right-most open parentheses in the **FØRMAT** statement and continues as before. The statements

```
    WRITE(6,5)X1,Y1,X2,Y2,X3
  5 FORMAT(3H X=,F5.1,3H Y=,F5.2)
```

would cause the printing of

```
          X= 46.5 Y=50.00
          X= 39.3 Y= 4.75
          X=  4.5 Y=
```

if **X1, Y1, X2, Y2,** and **X3** had the values **46.5, 50.0, 39.3, 4.75,** and **4.5** respectively.

A simpler example would be the use of the statement

```
 62 FORMAT(I4,F5.1)
```

The statement

```
    WRITE(6,62)J
```

used with this **FØRMAT** statement would cause the printing of

349

The statement

```
    WRITE(6,62)J,X
```

would print

$$349 \quad 59.2$$

and

```
WRITE(6,62)J,X,K
```

would cause the printing of

$$349 \quad 59.2$$
$$67$$

and

```
WRITE(6,62)J,X,K,Y,L,Z,M
```

would print

$$349 \quad 59.2$$
$$67 \quad 6.6$$
$$104 \quad -5.0$$
$$19$$

assuming of course that the variables had the values shown.

The statements

```
WRITE(6,702)V,W,X,Y,Z
702 FORMAT(F5.1/(E14.5,F6.3))
```

would cause the output to have the form

$$53.6$$
$$0.82039E-01 \quad 1.218$$
$$-0.71308E \quad 12 \quad 5.096$$

The implied **DØ**-loop discussed in Sec. 7-4 may be used for output as well as for input. The statement

```
WRITE(6,34)(Q(J),J=1,6)
```

has the same meaning as

```
WRITE(6,34)Q(1),Q(2),Q(3),Q(4),Q(5),Q(6)
```

and the statement

```
WRITE(6,16)(R(K),T(K),K=1,3)
```

has the same meaning as

```
WRITE(6,16)R(1),T(1),R(2),T(2),R(3),T(3)
```

Other variable names may be included in the list of variables with the implied **DØ**-loop. The statement

```
WRITE(6,9)N,J,(W(M),M=1,4),Q
```

has the meaning

```
WRITE(6,9)N,J,W(1),W(2),W(3),W(4),Q
```

Doubly subscripted arrays may be read or written in several different ways. The statements

```
      DO 8 J=1,3
      DO 8 K=1,4
    8 READ(5,87)A(J,K)
```

would be equivalent to the statements

```
      READ(5,87)A(1,1)
      READ(5,87)A(1,2)
      READ(5,87)A(1,3)
      READ(5,87)A(1,4)
      READ(5,87)A(2,1)
      READ(5,87)A(2,2)
      READ(5,87)A(2,3)
      READ(5,87)A(2,4)
      READ(5,87)A(3,1)
      READ(5,87)A(3,2)
      READ(5,87)A(3,3)
      READ(5,87)A(3,4)
```

These statements would require that one number be read from each data card, since a new card is moved to the read station each time a **READ** statement is executed. A **READ** statement containing only one variable name can never read more than one number per card no matter what **FØRMAT** is used. The statements

```
      DO 9 J=1,3
      DO 9 K=1,4
    9 WRITE(6,88)A(J,K)
```

would print the elements of the array one per line no matter how many specifications are given in **FØRMAT** statement number **88**.

The implied **DØ**-loop (sometimes called a self-indexed list) may also be used to read or write the doubly subscripted array. The statements

```
      DO 7 J=1,3
    7 READ(5,93)(A(J,K),K=1,4)
```

would be equivalent to the statements

```
      DO 7 J=1,3
    7 READ(5,93)A(J,1),A(J,2),A(J,3),A(J,4)
```

and would also be equivalent to the statements

```
      READ(5,93)A(1,1),A(1,2),A(1,3),A(1,4)
      READ(5,93)A(2,1),A(2,2),A(2,3),A(2,4)
      READ(5,93)A(3,1),A(3,2),A(3,3),A(3,4)
```

These statements used with a **FØRMAT** statement such as

```
   93 FORMAT(F10.2)
```

would also read one number from each data card. Used with the statement

```
   93 FORMAT(4F10.2)
```

they would read four numbers from each card. Note that more than four numbers may not be read from each data card with these statements since each **READ** statement contains the equivalent of four variable names—the names of four elements of the array **A**.

If they were used with the statement

```
93 FORMAT(7F10.2)
```

the input list of the **READ** statement would be satisfied by the first four specifications and another execution of the **READ** statement would bring another data card to the read station, and these same four specifications would be used in connection with the new card.

The above example used an implied **DØ**-loop to cycle the second subscript **K**, and an actual **DØ**-loop to cycle the first subscript **J**. These functions could be reversed. The statements

```
CO 8 K=1,4
8 READ(5,94)(A(J,K),J=1,3)
```

would be equivalent to the statements

```
DO 8 K=1,4
8 READ(5,94)A(1,K),A(2,K),A(3,K)
```

and would also be equivalent to the statements

```
READ(5,94)A(1,1),A(2,1),A(3,1)
READ(5,94)A(1,2),A(2,2),A(3,2)
READ(5,94)A(1,3),A(2,3),A(3,3)
READ(5,94)A(1,4),A(2,4),A(3,4)
```

The numbers would be read one from each card if the **FØRMAT** statement contained one specification, two from each card if the **FØRMAT** statement contained two specifications, and three from each card if the **FØRMAT** statement contained three or more specifications. The numbers to be read would have to appear in a different order on the data cards than that used with the preceding example.

Similar instructions may be used for output:

```
DO 32 J=1,3
32 WRITE(6,95)(A(J,K),K=1,4)
```

or

```
DO 33 K=1,4
33 WRITE(6,96)(A(J,K),J=1,3)
```

The number of numbers printed on one line would be determined by the **FØRMAT** statement used but would be limited to the number of subscripted variables specified in the **WRITE** statement. A program using any of these statements would of course have to include a correct **FØRMAT** statement and a **DIMENSIØN** statement that reserves space for an array **A** that is 3 × 4 or larger.

A statement of the form

```
READ(5,97)((A(J,K),J=1,3),K=1,4)
```

uses implied **DØ**-loops to cycle both of the subscripts. As with all FORTRAN statements, the form of the statement must be exactly that given. If any one of the *six* commas in this statement is left out, the FORTRAN compiler will not accept the statement and will give an error message. The placement of the parentheses in this statement indicates that the implied **DØ**-loop $(A(J,K),J=1,3)$ is itself cycled within another implied **DØ**-loop using **K** for an index. The inner index, **J** in the example, will be completely cycled for each value of the second index **K**. This statement acts as a set of nested **DØ**-loops and its variable name list is equivalent to the list **A(1,1), A(2,1), A(3,1), A(1,2), A(2,2), A(3,2),** **A(1,3), A(2,3), A(3,3), A(1,4), A(2,4), A(3,4).** The statement using two implied **D∅**-loops permits the widest latitude in the choice of **F∅RMAT**s. All of the numbers to be read could be punched on one data card if the **F∅RMAT** statement contained twelve specifications.

The statement

```
READ(5,97)((A(J,K),K=1,4),J=1,3)
```

uses the index of the inner loop **K** as the second subscript. The variable name list of this statement would be equivalent to the list **A(1,1), A(1,2), A(1,3), A(1,4), A(2,1), A(2,2)** **A(2,3), A(2,4), A(3,1), A(3,2), A(3,3), A(3,4).** This statement would require the numbers to be punched in a different order on the data cards—the second number read would be stored in **A(1,2)** by this statement; the second number read by the statement

```
READ(5,97)((A(J,K),J=1,3),K=1,4)
```

would be stored in **A(2,1)**.

Care must be taken to insure that the **READ** statement will store each of the numbers in the desired array element and that the **F∅RMAT** statement agrees with the **READ** statement and the position of the numbers on the data cards.

This form may also be used to write the elements of an array:

```
WRITE(6,108)((A(J,K),J=1,3),K=1,4)
```

A similar form may be used to read or write triply subscripted arrays. The statement

```
READ(5,54)(((B(J,K,L),J=1,6),K=1,5),L=1,4)
```

would cause the computer to read 120 numbers into array **B**. The order in which the indices are cycled depends on the order in which the index loops are specified. The statement

```
WRITE(6,21)(((N(M,KX,L3),KX=1,4),L3=1,3),M=1,2)
```

would cause the numbers stored in the array to be written in the order

N(1,1,1), N(1,2,1), N(1,3,1), N(1,4,1),
N(1,1,2), N(1,2,2), N(1,3,2), N(1,4,2),
N(1,1,3), N(1,2,3), N(1,3,3), N(1,4,3),
N(2,1,1), N(2,2,1), N(2,3,1), N(2,4,1),
N(2,1,2), N(2,2,2), N(2,3,2), N(2,4,2),
N(2,1,3), N(2,2,3), N(2,3,3), N(2,4,3),

The index in the innermost specification (the **KX** index) is cycled the fastest, the index in the second specification (the **L3** index) is cycled more slowly, and the index in the outer specification (the **M** index) is cycled the slowest.

All the elements of an array may be written or read by including the name of the array without any subscript in the variable-name list. If the statement

```
DIMENSION W(8)
```

appears at the beginning of a program, the statement

```
READ(5,30)W
```

would be equivalent to the statement

```
READ(5,30)(W(J),J=1,8)
```

or to the statement

```
READ(5,30)W(1),W(2),W(3),W(4),W(5),W(6),W(7),W(8)
```

The statement

```
READ(5,30)W
```

will read all of the elements of the array. This type of statement may not be used to read or write part of the array. If only the first six elements of an eight-element array are to be read or written, one of the forms

```
READ(5,30)(W(J),J=1,6)
```

or

```
READ(5,30)W(1),W(2),W(3),W(4),W(5),W(6)
```

must be used. The first N elements of the array may be read by the statement

```
READ(5,30)(W(J),J=1,N)
```

Doubly or triply subscripted arrays may be read or written using this type of statement in which the array name without a subscript appears in the variable-name list. The statements

```
DIMENSION GR(5,3)
READ(5,31)GR
```

are equivalent to the statements

```
DIMENSION GR(5,3)
READ(5,31)((GR(M,N),M=1,5),N=1,3)
```

Either of these two sets of statements would result in the numbers on the data cards being read into the memory locations in the order shown in Fig. 8-2. The statements

```
DIMENSION GR(5,3)
READ(5,31)((GR(M,N),N=1,3),M=1,5)
```

would *not* be equivalent to the above sets of statements, since the order in which the memory locations were used would be different.

The unsubscripted array name may not be used in the variable-name list no matter whether the array is singly, doubly, or triply subscripted if only part of the elements are to be read or written. The statement

```
READ(5,31)GR
```

would always attempt to read fifteen numbers if the array had been dimensioned as **GR(5,3)**.

All of the methods described may be combined in one variable-name list. The statements

```
DIMENSION X(5),A(3,3),J(5,6)
READ(5,7)M,(X(K),K=1,3),((A(K,L),K=1,2),L=1,3),J
```

would be valid.

An integer-variable name may be used to designate the input or output unit number in **READ** and **WRITE** statements. This is particularly useful when a program is to be run at several computer installations. Statements could be used at the beginning of the program to define the unit numbers to be used for printing, reading cards, and punching cards:

```
       JP=3
       JCR=2
       JCP=2
```

These variable names could then be used in the **READ** and **WRITE** statements throughout the program:

```
       READ(JCR,17)X,J,W
       WRITE(JP,203)Q,T
       WRITE(JCP,57)(A(K),K=1,8)
```

The program could then be made usable for a different computer installation by replacing the defining statements given above by others using the unit numbers required by the second installation:

```
       JP=5
       JCR=8
       JCP=2
```

This would be much easier than changing unit numbers in each of the **READ** and **WRITE** statements in a long program.

PROBLEMS

10-1. Write a FORTRAN program using an arithmetic statement function to compute and print the values of **R** and **T** for **X = 6.0, Y = 3.0, Z = 4.0**.

$$r = \frac{\sqrt{x^2 + y}}{x} \qquad t = 5y\sqrt{y^2 + z}$$

10-2. Write a program to calculate values of b, x, and y where

$$b = a^3 - 6.5, \qquad x = \frac{\sqrt{a^2 + 7}}{\sqrt{b^2 + 7}}, \qquad y = b\sqrt{(a + b)^2 + 7}$$

for $a = 2.0, a = 4.0, a = 6.0, a = 8.0, \dots, a = 20.0$. Use an arithmetic statement function in the program. Have the computer print a table of values of a, b, x, and y. Use a loop to produce the values of a; do not have a **READ** statement in the program.

10-3. Write a program that uses a **DØ**-loop which on each circuit reads values of j and x from one card, calculates y such that

$$\begin{aligned} y &= 4x^2 & \text{if } j = -2 \text{ or } +1 \\ y &= 3\sqrt{x} & \text{if } j = -1 \text{ or } 0 \\ y &= 7x & \text{if } j = +2 \text{ or } -3 \end{aligned}$$

and prints j, x, and y. The **DØ**-loop should be executed six times. (*Hint:* Set $k = j + 4$ and use **K** as the indexing parameter of a computed **GØ TØ** statement.) Use the following pairs of input numbers:

j	x
0	25.0
−3	35.6
−1	144.0
2	14.7
1	15.4
−3	236.3

10-4. Complete the statements of the FORTRAN program shown. The program is to read six real numbers from the first card into a singly subscripted array **U** and six real numbers from the second card into array **V**, and compute and print six values of *w* such that

$$w = 5u_n^4 - 3v_n^2 \qquad \text{for } n = 1, 2, \text{ and } 5$$

and

$$w = 5v_n^4 - 3u_n^2 \qquad \text{for } n = 3, 4, \text{ and } 6$$

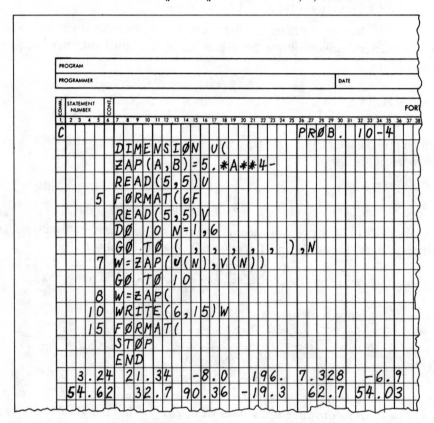

```
C                                              PRØB. 10-4
      DIMENSIØN U(
      ZAP(A,B)=5.*A**4-
      READ(5,5)U
    5 FØRMAT(6F
      READ(5,5)V
      DØ 10 N=1,6
      GØ TØ (  ,  ,  ,  ,  ,  ),N
    7 W=ZAP(U(N),V(N)))
      GØ TØ 10
    8 W=ZAP(
   10 WRITE(6,15)W
   15 FØRMAT(
      STØP
      END
      3.24  21.34  -8.0  196.  7.328  -6.9
     54.62  32.7  90.36  -19.3  62.7  54.03
```

10-5. Write a program that starts with the statements

```
      DIMENSION L(5,5)
      DO 50 J=1,5
      DO 50 K=1,5
      M=K-J+5
      GO TO (1,----------),M
    1 L(J,K)=8
```

This program is to store numbers in the matrix **L** as shown and then print the matrix (hint; **M** is used to indicate which diagonal the element being filled is on).

		K			
	1	2	3	4	5
1	0	7	0	8	7
2	8	0	7	0	8
J 3	7	8	0	7	0
4	0	7	8	0	7
5	8	0	7	8	0

10-6. What numbers will be stored in which elements of the array by each of the following sets of statements? Each of the **READ** statements will start reading with the first card punched from the listing shown.

1 2 3 4 5 6	7 8 9 10 11 12	13 14 15 16 17 18 19	20 21 22 23 24 25 26	27 28 29 30 31	32 33 34 35 36	37 38 39
29.37	14.56	-29.7	9.0	-8.15	17.94	
17.1	-6.82	54.3	84.9	96.7	-8.90	
-86.3	14.09	80.75	-7.	829.3	84.6	
4.28	29.3	29.1	54.7	7.05	-10.5	
50.6	-86.2	11.12	50.	-23.6	101.2	

(a)
```
    DIMENSION A(6)
    READ(5,6)A
  6 FORMAT(4F6.2)
```

(b)
```
    DIMENSION B(8)
    READ(5,7)(B(J),J=1,5)
  7 FORMAT(F6.2)
```

(c)
```
    DIMENSION C(3,3)
    READ(5,8)C
  8 FORMAT(3F6.2)
```

(d)
```
    DIMENSION D(3,3)
    READ(5,9)((D(L,M),M=1,2),L=1,3)
  9 FORMAT(6F6.2)
```

10-7. What output would be produced by each of the following programs? Write your answer on a coding sheet or other ruled paper so that you may indicate what columns are used.

(a)
```
    DIMENSION K(20),M(20)
    DO 5 J=1,20
    K(J)=2000+J
  5 M(J)=111*J
    WRITE(6,7)(K(N),N=1,8),(M(I),I=1,5)
  7 FORMAT(3I4)
    STOP
    END
```

(b)
```
    DIMENSION R(4,4)
    DO 8 J=1,4
    CO 8 K=1,4
  8 R(J,K)=1000*J+100*K
    WRITE(6,9)R
  9 FORMAT(1X,3F10.1)
    STOP
    END
```

```
(c)      DIMENSION P(5),Q(5)
         DO 10 N=1,5
         P(N)=128*N
     10  Q(N)=P(N)+150.
         WRITE(6,12)(P(M),Q(M),M=1,4)
     12  FORMAT(F10.1/(F8.0,F10.1,F9.1))
         STOP
         END
```

FUNCTIØN Subprograms, Reading Literal Data, the EQUIVALENCE Statement

11-1. FUNCTIØN Subprograms

Arithmetic statement functions discussed in Sec. 10-1 often may be used to reduce the length of programs since they permit the programmer to call for the function by writing its name and arguments instead of writing a long expression each time this function is required. Even though these functions are very useful they have several limitations; an arithmetic statement function definition is limited to one statement and it can compute only one value. A **FUNCTIØN** subprogram removes the first of these restrictions.

If, for example, during a computation we wish to set the value of w such that

$$w = q \qquad \text{if } q < 0$$
$$w = 0 \qquad \text{if } q = 0$$
$$w = \sqrt{q} \qquad \text{if } q > 0$$

This could be accomplished by the statements shown in Fig. 11-1. Later in the same computation we might wish to set the value of v such that

$$v = r \qquad \text{if } r < 0$$
$$v = 0 \qquad \text{if } r = 0$$
$$v = \sqrt{r} \qquad \text{if } r > 0$$

This could be accomplished by a series of statements similar to those of Fig. 11-1 sub-

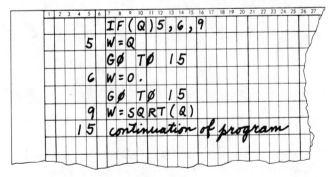

Fig. 11-1

stituting the variable names **V** and **R** for the variable names **W** and **Q**. If one of these sets of statements could be made into a function, the duplicate set could be eliminated shortening the program. An arithmetic statement function could not be used for this function, since there is no way of writing the required steps in one statement. FORTRAN provides a **FUNCTIØN** subprogram for use in a situation of this type.

A **FUNCTIØN** subprogram is a separate FORTRAN program that defines a function and provides the statements necessary to evaluate this function using dummy arguments. It may be called for in other programs in the same manner as is used to call for library functions or arithmetic statement functions.

The **FUNCTIØN** subprogram is distinguished from other types of programs by the first statement in the program. This first statement consists of the word **FUNCTIØN** followed by a function name and the dummy argument or dummy arguments enclosed in parentheses, as

```
FUNCTION THIS(X)
```

could be the first statement of a **FUNCTIØN** subprogram to evaluate the function **THIS,** using the real dummy argument **X.** The usual rules for naming the function apply. Figure 11-2 shows a **FUNCTIØN** subprogram to evaluate the function given at the

```
     FUNCTION THIS(X)
     IF(X)5,6,9
  5  THIS=X
     RETURN
  6  THIS=0.
     RETURN
  9  THIS=SQRT(X)
     RETURN
     END
```

FIG. 11-2

beginning of this section. This is a complete FORTRAN program in itself and includes an **END** statement. The **FUNCTIØN** subprogram is never used alone but is always called for by another program. The program that makes use of the subprogram is called the *main* or *main-line* program and uses the function name, together with arguments enclosed in parentheses, in the same way that it uses library functions or arithmetic statement functions. The main-line program that makes the computations described earlier could include the statements

```
W=THIS(Q)
```
and
```
V=THIS(R)
```

When the computer reached one of these statements in the main-line program it would transfer control to the **FUNCTIØN** subprogram, which would make the indicated calculations using the argument given in the calling statement in place of the dummy argument and would return control to the main-line program when it reached a **RETURN** statement in the subprogram. The computation in the subprogram always terminates with a **RETURN** statement instead of with a **STØP** statement as in any independent or main-line program. The function name without the parentheses or arguments (**THIS** in the example) must appear on the left-hand side of at least one arithmetic statement in the **FUNCTIØN** subprogram. A dummy argument may not be redefined in a **FUNCTIØN** subprogram. If a statement such as

```
X=X+1
```

were included in the subprogram of Fig. 11-3 it would redefine the dummy argument **X** and would be invalid.

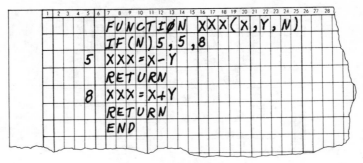

FIG. 11-3

More than one dummy argument may be used in a **FUNCTIØN** subprogram. Figure 11-3 shows a **FUNCTIØN** subprogram that uses three dummy arguments. This **FUNCTIØN** could be used in the main-line program with orders such as

```
W=XXX(Q,Z,M)
T=8.97*XXX(R,S,L)-56.4
```

or

```
V=7.61*D*XXX(D,H-6.5,3*J+4)
```

The **FUNCTIØN** may be used in an arithmetic expression together with constants, or other variable names, and operation symbols. The arguments *used in the main-line program* may be expressions.

When more than one argument is used the computer treats the arguments in the main-line program in the same order as they appear in the first statement of the **FUNCTIØN** subprogram. The statement

```
W=XXX(Q,Z,M)
```

in the main-line program would cause the computer to evaluate the function using **Q** in place of **X**, **Z** in place of **Y**, and **M** in place of **N** in the subprogram shown in Fig. 11-3. The statement

```
V=7.61*D*XXX(D,H-6.5,3*J+4)
```

would include the evaluation of the **FUNCTIØN** using **D** in place of **X**, the value of the expression **H–6.5** in place of **Y**, and the value of the expression **3*J+4** in place of **N** in the subprogram.

The corresponding arguments in the two programs *must* be of the same mode. The statement

```
GUM=XXX(R,NEXT,L)
```

would give an incorrect result unless a **REAL** statement were used to make the variable **NEXT** real. The second dummy argument **Y** in the subprogram is real, and the second argument in the call for this **FUNCTIØN** in the main-line program must be real to give the correct result.

One or more of the dummy arguments may be the name of a singly subscripted array. The subprogram shown in Fig. 11-4 uses the array **X** as one of its arguments. The array name **X** appears in the list of dymmy arguments without any parentheses or subscripts, and the second dummy argument **N** gives the number of the elements of the array to be used.

Every program that uses any array must contain a **DIMENSIØN** statement to reserve memory space for the array. The **FUNCTIØN** subprogram is a separate program and so must include a **DIMENSIØN** statement of its own if it uses arrays.

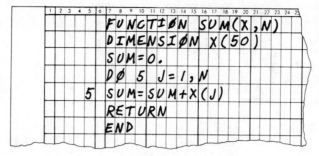

Fig. 11-4

The program shown in Fig. 11-4 puts the **FUNCTIØN SUM** equal to the sum of the first **N** elements of the array **X**. The main-line program using this **FUNCTIØN** might include the statements shown in Fig. 11-5.

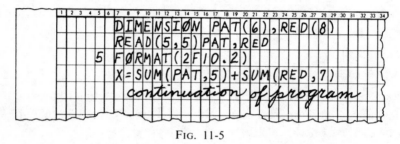

Fig. 11-5

This main-line program must also include a **DIMENSIØN** statement defining all of the arrays used.

The arguments in the main-line statement that include the **FUNCTIØN** name may be constants of the correct mode;

$$X = SUM(PAT, 5) + SUM(RED, 7)$$

The same result could have been obtained using the three statements

$$N = 5$$
$$M = 7$$
$$X = SUM(PAT, N) + SUM(RED, M)$$

The subprogram and the main-line program are completely separate programs and so may use the same statement numbers in each program. The subprogram of Fig. 11-4 and the main-line program of Fig. 11-5 each use a statement number **5**. The dummy arguments in the subprogram are just that—dummy arguments—so the variable names used as dummy arguments in the subprogram may be used as names for the same variables or for other completely unrelated variables in the main-line program.

On most computer systems the relationships between the dimensions of the arrays in the main program and the dimensions of the arrays in the subprogram may be handled in two different ways. With singly subscripted arrays, the simplest method is to make the dimension of the array in the subprogram at least as large as any array in the main-line program to be used in this function. For example, the **DIMENSIØN X(50)** in **FUNCTIØN SUM** of Fig. 11-4 would be acceptable if this function were never called on to operate on an array with more than fifty elements. If a main-line program contained the statement

$$DIMENSION \ GL(100)$$

and called for the function of Fig. 11-4 with the statement

$$TAINT=SUM(GL,100)$$

incorrect results would be obtained. The dimension in the function subprogram would have to be increased to at least **X(100)**.

This can result in very inefficient usage of memory space since we might decide to use

$$DIMENSION \ X(5000)$$

to be sure that we would never be caught with an array larger than permitted and waste 4980 memory locations when the largest array actually used has only twenty elements. Many computer systems permit the use of *adjustable dimensions* in subprograms. The use of adjustable dimensions is illustrated in Figs. 11-6 and 11-7.   Note that the

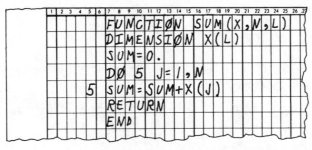

FIG. 11-6

DIMENSIØN statement in the subprogram of Fig. 11-6 uses an integer-variable name instead of an integer constant to indicate the size of the array.   This variable name **L** then appears as an additional dummy argument in the **FUNCTIØN** statement

$$FUNCTION \ SUM(X,N,L)$$

and the value of **L** is specified in the calling statement

$$X=SUM(PAT,5,6)+SUM(RED,7,8)$$

in Fig. 11-7. The **SUM(PAT,5,6)** then tells the computer to find the sum of the first

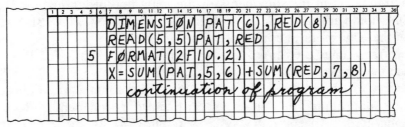

FIG. 11-7

five elements of the array **PAT**, the array **PAT** having a total of six elements. Note that the dimension of an array in a subprogram may be given by an integer-variable name, but *the dimension of an array in a main-line program must always be an integer constant.*

Doubly subscripted array names may be used as dummy arguments of subprograms, but incorrect results will be obtained if the first dimension of the array in the main-line program is different from the first dimension of the array in the subprogram or if the second dimension of the main-line program is greater than the second dimension of the subprogram. When triply subscripted arrays are used, the first two subscripts must be the same in the **DIMENSIØN** statements of the two programs and the third subscript not greater in the main-line program.

Adjustable dimensions may be used with the doubly and triply subscripted arrays. All of the subscripts may appear as integer-variable names in the **DIMENSIØN** statement of the subprogram if these names appear as dummy arguments in the **FUNCTIØN** statement and the sizes of the main-line arrays appear as integer constant arguments in the calling statements.

The mode of a function is usually implicitly specified by the first letter of the name, but a programmer may make a function a real function regardless of the name by using the words **REAL FUNCTIØN** instead of just the word **FUNCTIØN** in the first statement of the subprogram. A program beginning with the statement

```
REAL FUNCTION NAVY(BOATS,MEN)
```

would be treated by the computer as a real function. Any program that called for this function would have to be told that **NAVY** was a real function by the use of the type statement

```
REAL NAVY
```

in the calling program. Similarly a function **WEST** could be made integer by beginning the subprogram with the statement

```
INTEGER FUNCTION WEST(NILL,LAMB)
```

and using the type statement

```
INTEGER WEST
```

in any program that made use of this function.

Summarizing the main points about **FUNCTIØN** subprograms:
1. The **FUNCTIØN** subprogram must include **FUNCTIØN**, **RETURN**, and **END** statements.
2. The **FUNCTIØN** name must appear on the left-hand side of the equals sign of at least one arithmetic statement in the subprogram.
3. The dummy arguments must not be redefined in the subprogram. The names of the dummy arguments must *not* appear on the left-hand side of any arithmetic statements in the subprogram.
4. The arguments in the statements in the main-line program that use the **FUNCTIØN** should appear in the same order as in the **FUNCTIØN** statement and *must* be of the same mode in both programs.
5. The array names used in any program must be dimensioned in the program in which they appear.

The order in which cards must be loaded into the computer when the problem being solved requires subprograms as well as a main-line program depends on which computer system is being used. All computer systems require the use of one or more monitor control cards as discussed in Sec. 4-5. With most FORTRAN systems the subprograms are compiled first and the machine language instructions for the subprograms are stored on a mass storage unit such as a disk or magnetic tape unit until a main-line program that calls for the subprogram is compiled.

11-2. READING LITERAL DATA

Section 9-1 explained the use of Hollerith fields and literal fields enclosed in apostrophes for the printing of literal information that may include letters, numerals, blanks, and special characters. These fields may also be used to read literal information from cards.

The statement

```
19 FORMAT(17H 1ST RUN 02/02/72)
```

might be used with the statement

```
WRITE(6,19)
```

to print the heading

```
1ST RUN 02/02/72
```

on the top of a sheet of output. If the programmer later wished to make another run with the same program, he could just change the **FØRMAT** statement in the program before running, or he could use a **READ** statement to read the literal data from a data card.

The statements

```
READ(5,19)
19 FORMAT(17HXXXXXXXXXXXXXXXXX)
```

would cause the computer to read alphameric information from the first 17 columns of a card and store it in memory in the locations where it is keeping the information required for **FØRMAT** number **19**. If the card read by this statement had

b2ND RUN 03/04/72

punched in these 17 columns, the statement

```
WRITE(6,19)
```

would cause the printing of

2ND RUN 03/04/72

The programmer would probably include the three statements

```
READ(5,19)
19 FORMAT(17HXXXXXXXXXXXXXXXXX)
WRITE(6,19)
```

The first run would then be made having

b1ST RUN 02/02/72

punched in the first 17 columns of the card to be read by the **READ** statement. This data card would be replaced with one in which

b2ND RUN 03/04/72

was punched for the second run. A new card could be inserted for any later run to be made.

Any 17 characters could be used in this **FØRMAT** statement, and the programmer might wish to identify the **FØRMAT** statement by using the statements

```
READ(5,19)
19 FORMAT(17H RUN NO. AND DATE)
WRITE(6,19)
```

Numeric data may be read and printed along with the literal information. The statements

```
READ(5,4)K
4 FORMAT(5H TIME,2X,I4)
```

would cause the computer to store the literal data punched in the first five columns of the card at the read station of the card reader to be read into the literal field of **FØRMAT** statement **4** and the integer number punched in columns 8 through 11 of this card to be stored in location **K** of the memory. If

b**WHAT**bbb**367**

were punched in the first eleven columns of the card, the statements

```
READ(5,4)K
4 FORMAT(5H TIME,2X,I4)
WRITE(6,4)K
```

would cause the printing of

WHAT   367

while the statements

```
READ(5,4)K
4 FORMAT(5H TIME,2X,I4)
WRITE(6,4)J
```

would cause the printing of

WHAT   49

if the value **49** were stored in **J**.

If the computer system being used permits literal fields to be indicated by apostrophes these fields may be used in the same manner to read literal information. The statements

```
READ(5,62)
62 FORMAT(' RUN NO. AND DATE')
WRITE(6,62)
```

would cause the computer to read a card and print

1ST RUN 02/02/72

if

b**1STbRUNb02/02/72**

were punched in the correct columns of the card.

The program shown in Fig. 11-8 reads a student's name and three examination grades for the student, computes the examination average for the student, and prints the student's name and average. This method of reading and printing literal data requires that the same **FØRMAT** statement be used for reading and printing. A more compact **FØRMAT** specification such as **3F4.0** could be used to read the examination grades, but this would not permit the printing of a decimal part of the average. Column 1 of the data card may be read, but with this program it is necessary to leave this column blank on all of the cards since any character punched there would have been placed in the control column and so not printed. Figure 11-9 shows the output of this program.

PROGRAM EXAM AVE.
PROGRAMMER R.A.M.
DATE
PUNCHING INSTRUCTIONS

```
C  R.A.MANN  EXAM AVE.
      READ(5,3)J
    3 FØRMAT(I3)
      N=0
    4 READ(5,6)G1,G2,G3
    6 FØRMAT(21H STUDENT NAME XXXXXXX,3F8.2)
      AVE=(G1+G2+G3)/3.
      WRITE(6,6)AVE
      N=N+1
      IF(N-J)4,8,8
    8 STØP
      END
 10
 ALLEN, RØBERT J.           80.     85.     83.
 BEAM, DAVID R.             73.     82.     70.
 FØX, ADØLF W.              69.     75.     73.
 HØØVER, GARY G.            90.     82.     95.
 JØNES, SUSAN B.           100.     95.     97.
 MARTIN, WILLIAM P.         76.     80.     72.
 MC NEAL, EDWARD E.         95.     98.    100.
 SCØTT, CARL D.             67.     75.     82.
 TAYLØR, JANET R.           57.     60.     42.
 WILSØN, RICHARD F.         85.     90.     88.
```

FIG. 11-8

```
ALLEN, ROBERT J.          82.66
BEAM, DAVID R.            75.00
FOX, ADOLF W.             72.33
HOOVER, GARY G.           89.00
JONES, SUSAN B.           97.33
MARTIN, WILLIAM P.        76.00
MC NEAL, EDWARD E.        97.66
SCOTT, CARL D.            74.66
TAYLOR, JANET R.          53.00
WILSON, RICHARD F.        87.66
```

FIG. 11-9

11-3. The **EQUIVALENCE** Statement

Two or more different variable names may be made to refer to the same location in memory. If the statement

```
EQUIVALENCE (X,Y)
```

is placed at the beginning of a program (after the type and **DIMENSIØN** statements if there are any), the computer will use the same location in memory for the two variables **X** and **Y**. The statement

```
X=5.
```

in this program would leave the real number **5.0** stored in the location shared by **X** and **Y**. The statement

```
W=3.*Y
```

would then store **15.0** in location **W** since it would take the number stored by the statement **X = 5.** as the value of **Y**.

More than two variable names may be given the same memory location.

```
EQUIVALENCE (X,Y,Z)
```

would cause the computer to go to the same location to store or find the value of any one of the three variables **X**, **Y**, or **Z**.

Several sets of variable names may be made equivalent in the same **EQUIVALENCE** statement. The statement

```
EQUIVALENCE (X,Y,Z),(M,N)
```

would cause the computer to use one memory location for the three variables **X**, **Y**, and **Z** and a different single location for the two variables **M** and **N**.

An integer variable name should not be made equivalent to a real variable name. The statement

```
EQUIVALENCE (N,X)
```

would cause errors. Since integer and real numbers are stored in different manners, a number stored in one mode would be misread when read in the other mode. All the variable names within one set of parentheses in an **EQUIVALENCE** statement should be of the same mode.

More than one **EQUIVALENCE** statement may be used in one program. The two statements

```
EQUIVALENCE (X,Y,Z),(A,B)
EQUIVALENCE (J,K)
```

would be treated just as though they had been written in the one statement

```
EQUIVALENCE (X,Y,Z),(A,B),(J,K)
```

The variables listed in an **EQUIVALENCE** statement may be subscripted, if the subscript is an integer constant and the arrays involved have been previously dimensioned. When two subscripted variable names are made equivalent, the remainder of the arrays are made to share the same locations. The statements

```
DIMENSIØN A(5),B(3)
EQUIVALENCE (A(1),B(1))
```

would establish the equivalences

> **A(1)** and **B(1)** share the same location
> **A(2)** and **B(2)** share the same location
> **A(3)** and **B(3)** share the same location
> **A(4)**
> **A(5)**

The statements

```
DIMENSION X(6),Y(3)
EQUIVALENCE (Y(1),X(3))
```

would establish the equivalences

> **X(1)**
> **X(2)**
> **X(3)** and **Y(1)** share the same location
> **X(4)** and **Y(2)** share the same location
> **X(5)** and **Y(3)** share the same location
> **X(6)**

The subscript in the **EQUIVALENCE** statement must be an integer constant. The statement

```
EQUIVALENCE (A(1),D(K))
```

would be invalid, since **K** is not an integer constant.

The equivalence of a set of variable names should not be overspecified. The statement

```
EQUIVALENCE (X,Y),(Y,Z)
```

would cause the variables **X**, **Y**, and **Z** to share the same memory location. The statement

```
EQUIVALENCE (X,Y),(Y,Z),(X,Z)
```

should not be used since it overspecifies the equivalence.

The **EQUIVALENCE** statement is used when the programmer has written a large program and discovers that his program requires more memory locations than are available. If the program uses an array **Q** in the early part of the program and then uses an array **R** later on after the numbers stored in the **Q** array are no longer needed, memory locations may be saved by using an **EQUIVALENCE** statement to make the two arrays share memory locations.

A correction may be made with an **EQUIVALENCE** statement if it is discovered that two different variable names have been used in a program for the same variable. If the programmer finds that he has used **X1Y** for the name of a variable in one part of his program and inadvertently used **XY** for the name of the same variable in another part of the same program, it would probably be easier for him to use an **EQUIVALENCE** statement to make the two names equivalent than to try to change one of the two names each time it appears.

Some FORTRAN systems permit great flexability in the order in which specification statements including **EQUIVALENCE** statements may appear. Other systems require that the statements appear in a certain order. The following order will always be acceptable:

Type statements (**INTEGER, REAL**, etc.)
EXTERNAL statement
DIMENSIØN statement
CØMMØN statement
EQUIVALENCE statement
NAMELIST statement
DATA statement
Arithmetic statement function
Executable statements and **FØRMAT** statements
END statement

Several of the specification statements listed above are discussed in the appendixes. An array must be dimensioned in the first statement in which its name appears, and it must not be dimensioned twice.

Problems

11-1. Write a **FUNCTIØN** subprogram that evaluates the **FUNCTIØN** $q(a,b)$ such that:

$$q(a,b) = 5 \sin(a) + 3 \cos(b) \qquad \text{if } a \geq b$$

and

$$q(a,b) = 3 \sin(a) - 5 \cos(b) \qquad \text{if } a < b$$

Write a main-line program that uses this **FUNCTIØN** subprogram. The main-line program is to read the three numbers 0.5, 1.0, and 0.75 from one card, store these numbers in X, Y, and W, compute g and h such that

$$g = q(x,y) - 28.3$$
$$h = \frac{q(y,w)}{q(w,y)}$$

and print the values of g and h.

11-2. Write a **FUNCTIØN** subprogram that evaluates the **FUNCTIØN** curve (x) according to the graphical description shown. Write a main-line program that uses this **FUNCTIØN** subprogram. The main-line program is to read six numbers into an array, find the largest and smallest numbers in the array, compute

$$\text{Ratio} = \frac{\text{curve (big)}}{\text{curve (small)}}$$

(where *big* and *small* are the largest and smallest numbers in the array), and print

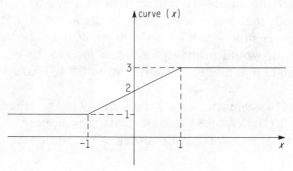

the value of Ratio. Use the numbers 59.87, 7.09, 28.72, 0.50, 197.03, and 0.75 for the first run.

11-3. Write a **FUNCTIØN** subprogram that will find the average of the absolute values of the first **N** elements of an array. Write a main-line program that reads the numbers 28.92, 11.64, −3.27, 196.85, −963.50, 68.72, −8.95, 921.00, 54.7, −63.18, 964.17, and 2.90 into an array, uses the subprogram to find the average of the absolute values of the first ten elements, and prints this average.

11-4. The cosine of an angle may be obtained from the series

$$\cos x = 1 - \frac{x^2}{2!} + \frac{x^4}{4!} - \frac{x^6}{6!} + \cdots$$

where x is measured in radians. Write a **FUNCTIØN** subprogram to compute the cosine of x using as many terms of this series as necessary to insure that the absolute value of the quantity obtained by dividing the last term used by the sum of all terms used is less than 0.000001. Give your **FUNCTIØN** some other name than **CØS**. Check your subprogram by writing a main-line program that produces a three column table giving x, cosine x as calculated by your subprogram, and cosine x as calculated by the library function **CØS(X)** for $x = 0.2$, $x = 0.4$, $x = 0.6$, $x = 0.8, \ldots, x = 2.0$.

11-5. Write statements to read the literal information bentNØW IS THE TIME from a card and print this information (a) using a Hollerith field and (b) using apostrophes to designate the literal field.

11-6. Write **DIMENSIØN** and **EQUIVALENCE** statements that set up the equivalences as shown.

		C(1)
A(1)		C(2)
A(2)		C(3)
A(3)	B(1)	C(4)
A(4)	B(2)	C(5)
A(5)	B(3)	
	B(4)	

11-7. What numbers will be printed by the following program?

```
      DIMENSION L(10),M(10)
      EQUIVALENCE (L(3),M(9))
      DO 2 J=1,10
    2 L(J)=J
      DO 4 K=1,10
    4 M(K)=K*K
      WRITE(6,8)L
    8 FORMAT(1X,I5)
      STOP
      END
```

11-8. The baseball lineup shown below includes the following information for each player: name, position he plays, number of times he came to bat in the game played yesterday (the item under *ab* in the table), and number of hits he made in this game (the item under *h* in the table). Write a program that will read all of this information from cards (one card for each player), compute his batting average, and print his name, position, and batting average. The batting average is considered to be zero if the player has zero times at bat and is equal to the number of hits divided by the times at bat if his times at bat is not zero. Have the program print three digits after the decimal point.

	ab	h
Allen, lf	4	2
Moore, cf	5	1
Anderson, rf	5	0
Johnson, 3b	4	1
Chance, ss	3	1
Crane, 1b	5	2
Brown, 2b	0	0
Henry, c	4	1
Little, p	3	1

THE **SUBRØUTINE**, THE **A FØRMAT**, OVERFLOW, THE **PAUSE** STATEMENT

12-1. THE **SUBRØUTINE**

The arithmetic statement functions discussed in Sec. 10-1 are easily written and simple to use, but their application is limited since the function definition is limited to one statement, and this function can compute only one value. The **FUNCTIØN** subprograms discussed in Sec. 11-1 are somewhat more difficult to write and are called for in the main program in exactly the same manner as are the arithmetic statement functions. The **FUNCTIØN** subprograms are not limited to one statement, but the limitation that they may compute only one value remains. The **SUBRØUTINE** is a subprogram that is slightly more difficult to use in the main program but is not limited to computing a single value. The **SUBRØUTONE** may perform any of the operations including reading and writing that may be performed in the main program.

The **SUBRØUTINE** subprogram is a complete program in itself and must contain a **DIMENSIØN** statement if any arrays are used in it, must contain at least one **RETURN** statement, and must have **END** as its last statement.

As with the **FUNCTIØN** subprogram, the **SUBRØUTINE** subprogram must begin with a special statement. This statement consists of the world **SUBRØUTINE** followed by the subprogram name and a list of dummy argument names enclosed in parentheses:

```
SUBROUTINE FUD(X,Y,N)
```

The program name must contain one to six alphameric characters, the first of which must be alphabetic. Unlike most FORTRAN names, the **SUBRØUTINE** names are not associated with any numerical value and thus have no mode. Any letter may be used as the first character in any **SUBRØUTINE** name.

The names of the library functions, the arithmetic statement functions, and the **FUNCTIØN** subprograms were all used in arithmetic statements or **IF** statements to return the value computed to the main program:

```
Y=5.3*COS(X)-RED(W,Z,N)
```

This method may not be used with a **SUBRØUTINE**, since the **SUBRØUTINE** may have to return more than one value to the main program. The **SUBRØUTINE** is called into action by a **CALL** statement in the main program. This statement consists of the word **CALL** followed by the name of the **SUBRØUTINE** subprogram and its parenthesized list of arguments:

```
CALL FUD(A,B,K)
```

171

When a program reaches a **CALL** statement, the control of the computation is given to the **SUBRØUTINE** which makes the indicated computations, using the variable names in the name list of the **CALL** statement in place of the corresponding names of the dummy arguments in the first statement in the **SUBRØUTINE**. When the **SUBRØUTINE** reaches a **RETURN** statement, control is returned to the first executable statement after the **CALL** statement in the main program.

Unlike the **FUNCTIØN** subprogram, the dummy argument names may appear on the left-hand side of the equals sign in an arithmetic statement in the **SUBRØUTINE**. In fact, at least one of the dummy arguments must thus appear if the **SUBRØUTINE** is to return any computation results to the main program.

Figure 12-1 shows a **SUBRØUTINE** that finds the sum and difference of two numbers. Figure 12-2 shows a main program that uses this **SUBRØUTINE**.

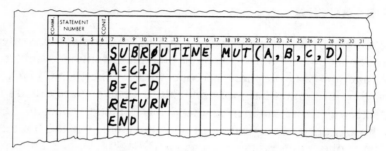

FIG. 12-1

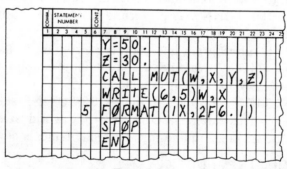

FIG. 12-2

The main program would first store **50.** and **30.** in locations **Y** and **Z**. The **CALL** statement would transfer control to the **SUBRØUTINE MUT**, which would be executed using the memory location **W**, **X**, **Y**, or **Z** whenever **A**, **B**, **C**, or **D** appeared in one of its statements. We may think of the clerk being told that while he is carrying out the instructions of **SUBRØUTINE MUT** this time he should think of the number written in rectangle **052** on his blackboard as being the value of **A** if he had been using this rectangle for the value of **W** when he was executing instructions of the main program. When the computer reached the **RETURN** statement the control would be returned to the **WRITE** statement of the main program. The execution of the subroutine would leave **80.0** and **20.0** stored in locations **W** and **X**, and these values would be printed by the **WRITE** statement.

This is a trivial example, and the problem could of course be more easily solved by putting all the required statements in one program without using a **SUBRØUTINE**. A **SUBRØUTINE** is normally not used unless it is called for more than once either in one program or in several different programs. If the sums and differences of a number of pairs of variables were required, the **SUBRØUTINE** shown in Fig. 12-1 could be called

```
                Y=50.
                Z=30.
                CALL MUT(W,X,Y,Z)
                WRITE(6,5)W,X
        5       FØRMAT(IX,2F6.1)
                T=7.0
                U=2.5
                CALL MUT(R,S,T,U)
                WRITE(6,5)R,S
                E=8.0
                F=6.5
                CALL MUT(C,D,E,F)
                WRITE(6,5)C,D
                STØP
                END
```

FIG. 12-3

for a number of times, as in the main-line program shown in Fig. 12-3. The output of this program is shown in Fig. 12-4.

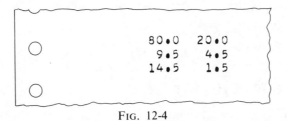

```
        80.0      20.0
         9.5       4.5
        14.5       1.5
```

FIG. 12-4

The **SUBRØUTINE** and main program could be modified as shown in Fig. 12-5 and 12-6 to make use of the fact that a **SUBRØUTINE** may include **WRITE** statements.

```
                SUBRØUTINE MUP(C,D)
                A=C+D
                B=C-D
                WRITE(6,5)A,B
        5       FØRMAT(IX,2F6.1)
                RETURN
                END
```

FIG. 12-5

The two programs shown in Figs. 12-5 and 12-6 contain only one **WRITE** statement, while the two programs shown in Figs. 12-1 and 12-3, which accomplish the same result, require three **WRITE** statements. **READ** statements may also be included in **SUBRØUTINE** subprograms.

There is one other difference in these two combinations. The latter pair of programs use only two variable names in the **SUBRØUTINE** statement and in each calling statement, while the former requires four variable names in each of these statements. The

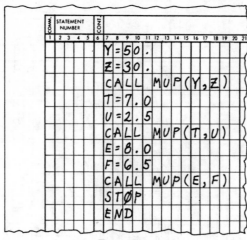

Fig. 12-6

difference is due to the fact that the program in Fig. 12-5 does not have to make the results of any computations available to the main program. If an additional computation were added at the end of the program in Fig. 12-6 that required the values of **A** and **B**, the first statement of the subprogram could be made

```
SUBROUTINE MUP(A,B,C,D)
```

and the calling statements in the main program could become

```
CALL MUP(W,X,Y,Z)
CALL MUP(R,S,T,U)
```

and

```
CALL MUP(C,D,E,F)
```

Any number that is to be transmitted from the calling program to the **SUB-RØUTINE** or from the **SUBRØUTINE** to the calling program must be represented by a dummy argument in the list of variable names in the **SUBRØUTINE** defining statement and by a corresponding variable name *of the same mode* in the list of the **CALL** statement (or may occur in **CØMMØN** as described in Appendix D). The name of a variable whose value is returned to the calling program must appear on the left of the equals sign of an arithmetic statement or in the variable name list of a **READ** statement in the **SUB-RØUTINE**.

COMM.	STATEMENT NUMBER	CONT.	
			SUBRØUTINE X2Y(X,Y)
			IF(X-Y)5,5,6
	5		X=X**3
			Y=Y**4
			RETURN
	6		X=X**4
			Y=Y**3
			RETURN
			END

Fig. 12-7

The **SUBRØUTINE** subprogram shown in Fig. 12-7 illustrates the fact that a **SUBRØUTINE** may be used to make computations that change the number stored in one or more of the locations that supply the input for the **SUBRØUTINE**.

If **4.0** and **3.0** were initially stored at locations **A** and **B**, the statement

```
CALL X2Y(A,B)
```

would leave **256.0** and **27.0** stored at these two locations.

As with a **FUNCTIØN** subprogram, one or more of the dummy arguments used in a **SUBRØUTINE** subprogram may be the name of an array. Again the array must be dimensioned in both the **SUBRØUTINE** and the program that calls the **SUBRØUTINE**. The rules concerning the dimensioning of arrays with **SUBRØUTINE**s are the same as those given in Sec. 11-1 for **FUNCTIØN** subprograms. Figure 12-8 shows a subprogram

```
      SUBRØUTINE SQ(K,L,J)
      DIMENSIØN K(50),L(50)
      DØ 3 M=1,J
    3 L(M)=K(M)**2
      RETURN
      END
```

FIG. 12-8.

that stores the square of each element of an array **K** in an element of the array **L**. The dummy argument **J** is used to indicate the number of elements of the array to be operated upon.

The calling statement

```
CALL SQ(JB,LB,10)
```

would cause the squares of each of the first ten numbers in the array **JB** to be stored in the corresponding elements of the array **LB**. The program that included this calling statement would have to include a **DIMENSIØN** statement.

When a dummy argument in the **SUBRØUTINE** statement is an array name, the corresponding argument in the **CALL** statement must be an array name. The dummy arguments in the **SUBRØUTINE** must be either *unsubscripted*-variable names or array names. An argument in the calling statement that is not an array name but returns a single value to the calling program must be a subscripted- or unsubscripted-variable name. An argument in the **CALL** statement that is not an array name and does not return a value to the calling program may be a subscripted- or a nonsubscripted-variable name, a constant, or an arithmetic expression.

If **12.5** were stored in **GRAPE(7)**, the statement

```
CALL MUT(XT(6),XT(4),GRAPE(7),3.5)
```

used with the **SUBRØUTINE** in Fig. 12-1 would store **16.0** and **9.00** in **XT(6)** and **XT(4)**. The statement

```
CALL MUT(XT(5),G10,BG**2-2.*GRAPE(7),3.75)
```

would store **−5.25** and **−12.75** in **XT(5)** and **G10** if **12.5** and **4.0** had previously been stored in **GRAPE(7)** and **BG**.

The dummy arguments in the **SUBRØUTINE** should agree in mode with the corresponding arguments in the **CALL** statement. If they do not, the program as executed will give incorrect results.

Both the **FUNCTIØN** subprogram and the **SUBRØUTINE** subprogram are complete and separate programs. Either must include a defining statement, a **DIMENSIØN** statement if arrays are used, and a **RETURN** statement. As with all programs, they must have **END** as the last statement.

Either of these subprograms may use arithmetic statement functions and may call for other **FUNCTIØN** or **SUBRØUTINE** subprograms but may not call themselves.

The four types of subprograms are listed below in the order of ease of writing and calling.

> Library functions
> Arithmetic statement functions
> **FUNCTIØN** subprograms
> **SUBRØUTINE** subprograms

The type highest on this list that is able to handle the task required should be used for each job.

A subprogram is normally used when it is to be called a number of times. If a subprogram is called only once, it is easier to include all the operations within one program and not to write a subprogram. The same subprogram may be used with several different programs which call for it without rewriting or repunching. It may be worth while to write a subprogram that is called for only once by any one program if several programs are to be written that may call for it.

There are a large number of library subprograms available that perform common computational tasks. A great amount of effort would be needlessly expended if, for example, every programmer who wished to compute statistical correlations wrote his own program. Every computer installation keeps manuals on hand that describe the use and method of calling for the subprograms available in its library.

12-2. The **A FØRMAT**

Section 9-1 described the use of Hollerith fields and literal fields enclosed in apostrophes to specify alphanumeric information to be printed. The use of these types of specifications to read alphanumeric information from data cards was described in Sec. 11-2. The term *alphanumeric* in this sense includes special characters such as parentheses, commas, and decimal points as well as alphabetic characters and the numerical digits. The fields are useful in many instances, but the fact that the characters involved are stored in locations in the memory that are not assigned variable names prevents the programmer from moving these characters from one storage location to another by the use of arithmetic statements. The only way in which a character stored in one of these fields may be changed is by reading a new character from a card.

FORTRAN includes another type of literal specification, and **A FØRMAT** specification which permits characters to be stored in memory locations that have been given variable names. This permits characters to be moved from one memory location to another by the use of arithmetic statements of the form

$$XEG = Q2$$

The statements

```
      READ(5,16)N1,N2,N3
   16 FORMAT(3A1)
```

tell the computer to read the three characters punched in the first three columns of a data card and to store the first character in location **N1**, store the second character in location **N2**, and the third in location **N3**. Remember that the specification **3A1** has the same meaning as the specification **A1,A1,A1**. The digit **1** after the letter **A** tells the computer to store one character in each memory location. If the characters **X**, **Y**, and **Z** had been punched in the first three columns of the data card read by these statements, a special sequence of binary digits that the computer would later recognize as specifying the character **X** would be stored in location **N1**. Sequences specifying **Y** and **Z** would be stored in locations **N2** and **N3**.

After these characters had been stored, the statements

```
      WRITE(6,19)N2,N1,N3
   19 FORMAT(5X,A1,2X,2A1)
```

would cause

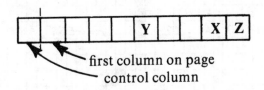

first column on page
control column

to be printed.

The statement
```
      J=N2
```

would cause the sequence of bits specifying the character **Y** that had been stored in location **N2** to be also stored in location **J**. The statements

```
      WRITE(6,24)J
   24 FORMAT(4X,A1)
```

would then print the character **Y** in the fourth column.

The program shown in Fig. 12-9 finds the largest of three numbers and prints a statement that includes a character that is the name of the largest variable. Figure 12-10 shows the output of this program.

The **1X** specification in **FØRMAT** statement number **105** in Fig. 12-9 provides a blank space for the carriage control. This statement shows that literal or Hollerith specifications may be included in a **FØRMAT** statement that contains an **A** specification.

Location **NL** will contain the code representing a character and so should be printed with an **A** specification and not with an **I**, **F**, or **E** specification. This restriction holds even if the character stored is a digit (for example 7). Location **BIG** in this program will contain a number and must be printed by an **E** or **F** specification. The statements

```
      N2=3
      WRITE(6,64)N2
   64 FORMAT(1X,A1)
```

would not print the digit **3**, since the integer number three will be stored in location **N2** and not the code for the character **3**. The statement

```
      MK=0
```

will store the integer number zero in location **MK**. The integer zero is *not* the same as the

COMM.	STATEMENT NUMBER	CONT.	FORTRAN STATEMENT
			READ(5,5)MX,NY,NZ
	5		FØRMAT(3A1)
			READ(5,8)X,Y,Z
	8		FØRMAT(3F5.0)
			IF(X-Y)65,60,60
	60		IF(X-Z)90,70,70
	65		IF(Y-Z)90,80,80
	70		ML=MX
			BIG=X
			GØ TØ 100
	80		ML=NY
			BIG=Y
			GØ TØ 100
	90		ML=NZ
			BIG=Z
	100		WRITE(6,105)NL,BIG
	105		FØRMAT(1X,A1,22H IS LARGEST AND EQUALS,F6.2)
			STØP
			END
XYZ			
50.0	75.5	12.3	

Fig. 12-9

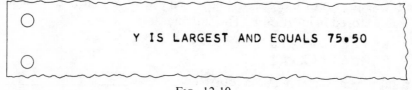

Fig. 12-10

A code for either the character **0** or the character "blank." Incidently, a blank is a legitimate character in an **A** specification and may be read with an **A FØRMAT** specification.

The **A** code for a character may be stored in a location identified by either an integer-variable name or by a real-variable name in most computers. The statements

```
    READ(5,17)KL
 17 FORMAT(1X,A1)
    WRITE(6,17)KL
```

would print the character (in the first column on the page if (had been punched in the second column of the data card. The same character would be printed by the statements

```
    READ(5,18)ZAP
 18 FORMAT(1X,A1)
    WRITE(6,18)ZAP
```

if they were used with this same data card.

More than one character may be stored in one location. The statements

```
    READ(5,7)WAB
  7 FORMAT(A2)
```

would store codes for the two characters punched in the first two columns of the data card in location **WAB**. The statements

```
        WRITE(6,82)WAB
 82 FORMAT(5X,A2)
```

would print these two characters in the fifth and sixth columns of the page. The statements

```
        T6G=WAB
        WRITE(6,82)T6G
 82 FORMAT(5X,A2)
```

would print the same two characters in the same columns.

```
PROGRAM  GRADE                                    PUNCHING INSTRUCTIONS
PROGRAMMER  R.A.M.            DATE

C      R. A. MANN   GRADE
          DIMENSIØN X(5),L(10),E(6)
          WRITE(6,2)
       2  FØRMAT(7X,4HNAME,11X,13HAVERAGE GRADE/)
          READ(5,4)(L(J),J=1,10)
       4  FØRMAT(10A1)
       6  READ(5,8)M,(X(J),J=1,5),(E(K),K=1,6)
       8  FØRMAT(I1,5A4,6F4.0)
          T=0.
          DØ 9 J=1,5
       9  T=T+E(J)
          AVE=.15*T+.25*E(6)
          M=AVE/10.
          IF(M)11,10,11
      10  M=1
      11  WRITE(6,12)(X(J),J=1,5),AVE,L(M)
      12  FØRMAT(1X,5A4,F7.1,4X,A1)
          IF(N)14,6,14
      14  STØP
          END
FFFFFDCBAA
ALLEN, RØBERT J.          82  85  79  90  84  80
BEAM, DAVID R.            80  69  72  76  78  82
FØX, ADØLF W.             72  76  64  74  80  72
JØNES, SUSAN B.           95 100  89  98  96  95
MARTIN, WILLIAM P.        40  55  48  60  32  38
MC MEAL, EDWARD E.       100  95  98 100 100  98
SCØTT, CARL D.            74  70  65  50  62  60
TAYLØR, JANET R.          60  58  54  62  59  57
9WILSØN, RICHARD F.      100  92  80  76  78  75
```

FIG. 12-11

The code for a character is stored as a number, and arithmetic statements such as

```
N = X
```

or

```
Q = J
```

change the form of the number. Therefore an arithmetic statement of one of these types should not be used when the number stored represents the code for a character. The statements

```
    READ(5,72)X
 72 FORMAT(1X,A1)
    N = X
    WRITE(6,72)N
```

would *not* print the character read from the data card. **A** codes stored in locations specified by real-variable names should only be transferred to locations specified by other real-variable names, and **A** codes stored in locations specified by integer-variable names should only be transferred to locations specified by integer-variable names.

Most computers permit the storage of a maximum of four characters in one memory location. Therefore **A1**, **A2**, **A3**, or **A4** specifications may be used. There are exceptions however. One small computer permits the storage of a maximum of two characters in a location specified by an integer-variable name and the storage of a maximum of four characters in a location specified by a real-variable name. Some other computers permit six or even eight characters to be stored in each location. The programmer is usually safe if he limits himself to no more than four characters per location.

An instructor wishes to make an average for each student in a class on the basis of 15 percent on each of five quiz grades and 25 percent on the final examination grade. An A is to be assigned if the average is 100 or is in the 90's, a B if the average is in the 80's, a C if in the 70's, a D if in the 60's, and an F if below 60. The program shown in Fig. 12-11 reads the characters to be used for the letter grades from a card into array **L** using **A1** specifications, reads the student name and six grades, computes the average, and prints the student name, average, and letter grade. The first column of each data card is used as described in Sec. 6-1 to indicate when the last card has been read. Twenty columns are reserved for the student name. Since the maximum number of characters that may be stored in one location with many computers is four, five such locations, **X(1)**, **X(2)**, **X(3)**, **X(4)**, and **X(5)**, are required to store these 20 characters. The variable **M** is computed which indicates which letter grade character is to be printed for the student. Figure 12-12 shows the output of this program.

NAME	AVERAGE	GRADE
ALLEN, ROBERT J.	83.0	B
BEAM, DAVID R.	76.7	C
FOX, ADOLF W.	72.8	C
JONES, SUSAN B.	95.4	A
MARTIN, WILLIAM P.	44.7	F
MC NEAL, EDWARD E.	98.4	A
SCOTT, CARL D.	63.1	D
TAYLOR, JANET R.	58.1	F
WILSON, RICHARD F.	82.6	B

Fig. 12-12

12-3. Overflow, Underflow, and Divide by Zero

If the mileage indicator on an automobile indicates 99999.9 miles and the car is driven one more mile, the indicator should show 100000.9 miles, but since there is no number wheel to contain the one, the indication will be 00000.9 miles. We say that there has been an "overflow," and the indicator does not give a correct indication of the distance the automobile has traveled. The indicator will show mileages between 00000.0 and 99999.9 miles. When the mileage goes beyond the maximum the indicator starts around again.

Several computers are able to store integer numbers from **−2147483648** to **+2147483647** and if an arithmetic statement causes a number to be computed outside this range, the "indicator" starts around again. If a value equal to **+2147483647** is stored in **J**, the statement

$$J = J + 1$$

would leave **−2147483648** stored in **J**. There is no way in which the computer may be made to tell us that an overflow in the integer mode has occurred (other than its giving us unexpected answers). Other computers have different ranges but any computer will give an overflow if a calculation would produce an integer number outside its range.

A statement that requires the computer to divide by zero will also give incorrect results. A statement such as

$$M = (J - K) / (N - 6)$$

would give incorrect results when **N** was equal to six. In this case the value stored in **M** by this statement would depend on the value of **J-K**, but since the computer is unable to store infinity, the value stored could never be correct. Again, there is no way that the computer can be made to tell us that a divide by zero has been attempted in the integer mode.

Computers are able to store real numbers whose absolute values are much greater than the maximum integer number they are able to store, but there is a definite maximum for each computer; 10^{38} is a typical value. If a statement causes a real number larger than this limit to be produced, an overflow will occur, and the "indicator" will start around again producing incorrect results.

Computers are able to store a real number whose value is zero. Typically the smallest absolute value that it is able to store as a real number (other than zero) is approximately 10^{-39}. If a real number is produced whose absolute value is smaller than this limit, an "underflow" occurs, and the value of this number is set equal to zero by the computer.

A statement that causes a divide by zero in the real mode will also produce incorrect results. A programmer may avoid an error caused by dividing by zero in either mode by using an **IF** statement to determine whether or not the divisor is zero before making the division.

A few FORTRAN systems contain the necessary hardware and library subroutines that permit the programmer to ask the computer if any overflows, underflows, or divide by zeros in the real mode have occurred. There are other systems that print an error message and halt the computation if an overflow or divide by zero in the real mode occurs.

12-4. The **PAUSE** Statement

The **PAUSE** statement is a control statement that causes the computer to stop computing and wait for operator intervention. Pressing the start key on the console causes the computer to resume computation starting at the first executable statement after the **PAUSE** statement. This statement should not be used when a group of programs is being batch processed.

The pause statement consists of the one word **PAUSE** written in the usual columns (starting at column 7).

The **PAUSE** statement is used when it is desirable to examine the output of the program at a certain point in order to decide whether or not the program should be continued or which of several possible sets of data should be loaded. The **PAUSE** statement may be used to permit the operator to change the paper loaded in the printer, to load new cards in the hopper of the card reader, or to make any other adjustments necessary.

12-5. CONCLUSION

Every programmer must remember that his FORTRAN program must be translated into a machine-language program before the computer is capable of performing the computations desired. This translation or compiling is carried out by the execution of a program known as a FORTRAN *compiler*. This program uses the programmer's FORTRAN program as input and produces the machine-language program that is executed.

The exact form that certain FORTRAN statements must take in order to be acceptable is more a function of the compiler than it is of what model computer is used. The limitations as to word length, wiring, and other computer configurations will of course affect the details of the operations performed by the compiler.

The compiler is a program that must be read into the computer in order to be used. This program may be changed. The computer's manufacturer may make changes in the compiler if more efficient ways of performing certain functions are discovered or if errors are found. The programmers at a particular university or company using a computer may make changes that they feel make the compiler better for their particular uses.

A programmer may discover that the compiler at one particular computer installation ignores blanks in certain positions in arithmetic statements, while the compiler at a different installation using the same model computer treats blanks in the same positions in the same statements as zeros. What is more, the programmer may find that the treatment of these blanks may be changed at one installation from time to time.

These differences are usually minor and normally cause little difficulty unless the programmer attempts to use "tricks" that take advantage of certain peculiarities of a particular compiler.

The FORTRAN manuals are brought up to date periodically, but often these revisions are months behind the changes made in the compiler.

Above all the programmer must remember that while the computer will make arithmetic computations very rapidly it must be told exactly what computations to make. The programmer must do the thinking and supply the logic.

PROBLEMS

12-1. Write a **SUBRØUTINE** subprogram that will compute

$$a = c^2 + d^2 \quad \text{and} \quad b = c^2 - d^2$$

Write a main-line program that uses this **SUBRØUTINE**. The main-line program is to set x, y, and z equal to 82.0, 5.5, and 101.0 respectively, and calculate q such that

$$q = \frac{(x^2 + y^2)}{(z^2 - x^2)} + \frac{(x^2 - y^2)}{(z^2 + x^2)}$$

and print the value of q.

12-2. Write a **SUBRØUTINE** subprogram to find the largest value and the smallest value in the first n elements of a real array. Write a main-line program that uses this **SUBRØUTINE**. The main-line program is to calculate the values of the elements of two arrays according to the formulas

$$x(j) = j^3 - 14j^2 + 56j - 64 \qquad \text{for } j = 1 \text{ to } 10$$
$$y(k) = k^2 - 19k + 70 \qquad \text{for } k = 1 \text{ to } 20$$

The main-line program should print the largest and smallest value of each of these arrays.

12-3. Solve Prob. 12-2 having the **SUBRØUTINE** do the printing. No values are to be returned to the main-line program by the **SUBRØUTINE**.

12-4. Write a **SUBRØUTINE** subprogram that examines the first n elements of an array **A** and places all positive nonzero elements in a new condensed array **B**. This new array and the number m of its elements should be returned to the main program. Write a program that calculates the values of the elements of arrays **X** and **Y** according to the formulas given in Prob. 12-2, calls the **SUBRØUTINE** to produce the condensed arrays, and prints the condensed arrays.

12-5. The sine and cosine of an angle may be obtained from the series

$$\sin x = x - \frac{x^3}{3!} + \frac{x^5}{5!} - \frac{x^7}{7!} + \frac{x^9}{9!} - \cdots$$
$$\cos x = 1 - \frac{x^2}{2!} + \frac{x^4}{4!} - \frac{x^6}{6!} + \frac{x^8}{8!} - \cdots$$

where x is measured in radians. Write a **SUBRØUTINE** that uses the first five terms of each of these series to compute the sine and cosine of an angle measured in radians. Write a main-line program that uses this **SUBRØUTINE** in producing a table of sines and cosines for angles of 0.1, 0.2, 0.3, 0.4, 0.5, ..., 2.0 radians.

12-6. Write a program that will place the character **X** in each of the shaded elements of the matrix shown in Prob. 8-6 and blanks in the unshaded elements and print the matrix. Use **A** specifications and a relationship involving **J** and **M** to determine whether an element is to contain an **X** or a blank.

12-7. Write a program that will read one integer number from a card, determine whether or not it is prime (not exactly divisible by any positive integer other than one or itself), and print the number with a statement of the form

127bbISbPRIME

or

1365bNØTbPRIME

The program is to be written so that any number of numbers may be read one at a time. Use an **A** specification to put b**IS** or **NØT** in the printed statement. Use the following numbers for input data: 127, 1013, 1036, 1617, 1807, 4211.

12-8. Write a program that will place **A FØRMAT** characters in each of the elements of the matrix shown and print the matrix. The character placed in any one element should be +, 0, or − depending on whether $m(3 - m) + (j - 4)^2$ is positive, zero, or negative for that element.

$$J$$

	1	2	3	4	5	6	7
1							
2							
3							
4							
5							
6							
7							

(M labels the rows)

12-9. Write a program that reads 15 cards, each containing one person's name and his birth date (name in columns 1 through 20, number of month right-justified in columns 22 and 23, day of month right-justified in columns 25 and 26, and year in columns 28 through 31), and prints a table of the names and birth dates. The name of the month should be printed as **JAN., FEB., MAR., APR., MAYb, JUNE, JULY, AUG., SEPT, ØCT., NØV.,** or **DEC..** Note that SEPT does not use a period to permit all names to use four characters each. Run the program using the following names and dates for the first 14 and your own name and birth date for the 15th.

Charles Babbage	12-26-1791	Blaise Pascal	6-19-1623
Gottfried Leibnitz	7-1-1646	Alan M. Turing	6-23-1912
Sir Isaac Newton	12-25-1642	Orvill Wright	8-19-1871
Albert Einstein	3-14-1879	Nellie Melba	5-19-1859
Wolfgang A. Mozart	1-27-1756	Samuel Johnson	9-18-1709
Sir W. S. Gilbert	11-18-1836	Abraham Lincoln	2-12-1809
Washington Irving	4-3-1783	Giuseppe Verdi	10-10-1813

DOUBLE-PRECISION OPERATIONS

Figure 2-2 showed how the clerk wrote real numbers on his blackboard. He was able to write six significant digits of a number and had to write

$$+333333+00$$

and

$$+314159+01$$

if he wished to represent one third and π. Most computers represent real numbers in their memories using binary arithmetic and permit the equivalent of approximately seven significant decimal digits.

Most FORTRAN systems include something called *double-precision operations*, which permit numbers with approximately sixteen significant decimal digits for use in problems where more accuracy is required. Suppose that the clerk is told that if a number is designated as a double-precision number he is to use two rectangles to write it on his table. He is to use the first compartment of the first word for the sign of the number and the last three compartments of the second rectangle for one sign and two digits of the exponent. This leaves enough compartments for him to write sixteen significant decimal digits as shown in Fig. A-1. Locations **040** and **041** contain the double-precision

040	041
+|3|3|3|3|3|3|3|3	3|3|3|3|3|3|3|+|0|0
042	043
+|3|1|4|1|5|9|2|6|5	3|5|8|9|7|9|3|+|0|1
044	045
+|2|7|1|8|2|8|1|8|2	8|4|5|9|0|4|5|+|0|1
046	047
-|6|7|3|0|8|5|7|1|2	0|8|6|4|6|2|7|-|0|9
048	049
-|4|6|5|1|0|8|1|2|5	4|5|7|7|6|4|2|+|3|6

FIG. A-1

representation of one-third. The next two numbers in Fig. A-1 (locations **042** and **043**, locations **044** and **045**) represent π and e (the base of the natural logarithms). These numbers are still not exact but

$$+0.3333333333333333 \quad \text{and} \quad +3.141592653589793$$

represent one-third and π with more precision than

$$+0.333333 \quad \text{and} \quad +3.14159.$$

A variable name is designated as the name of a double-precision variable by the use of a type statement. The statement

```
DOUBLE PRECISION RUM,J,R(3,5)
```

tells the computer that the values stored at locations **RUM** and **J** as well as all the elements of the array **R** are to be stored as double-precision numbers. The double-precision type statement is placed in the program along with the **REAL** and **INTEGER** type statements.

A constant in a FORTRAN program is made a double-precision constant by writing it in a form similar to the **E** format method of writing real constants described in Sec. 3-1 with a letter **D** replacing the letter **E**. The statements

```
DOUBLE PRECISION BAA,HECK
BAA=56.D+00
HECK=4.5D+05+BAA/3.2D-06
```

show the use of double-precision constants **56.D+00**, **4.5D+05**, and **3.2D−06**. The constant **4.5D+03** would of course represent a number equal to

$$4.5 \times 10^3 = 4500.$$

This constant would be stored in the computer memory in a binary equivalent of **+4500000000000000+03**. Note that since the decimal number 0.1 may not be exactly represented by a binary number, 0.1 and many other decimal numbers may be more precisely represented in the computer memory when written as double-precision constants than when written as real constants.

Double-precision constants and variables and single-precision real constants and variables may be used in the same arithmetic expressions. When this occurs the single-precision numbers are converted to double-precision form before the computation is made. The clerk would convert **+314159+01** to **+3141590000000000+01** before multiplying it by **+2718281828459045+01**.

Input and output of double-precision numbers is done by use of a **D** specification which works exactly as the **E** specification except that the **D** is used and printed with double-precision where the **E** was used with real numbers. For example,

```
    WRITE(6,18)BAA,HECK
 18 FORMAT(D24.11,D25.13)
```

The FORTRAN systems that permit the use of double-precision operations contain double-precision library functions which use double-precision arguments and return a double-precision value. The names of these functions are the same as those used with real numbers with the letter **D** added. The function **SQRT** is used with a real argument to obtain a real square root. The function **DSQRT** is used with a double-precision argument to obtain a double-precision square root.

An arithmetic statement function as described in Sec. 10-1 may be made double-precision by placing its name in a type statement.

A **FUNCTIØN** subprogram as described in Sec. 11-1 may be made double-precision by using the words **DØUBLE PRECISIØN FUNCTIØN** instead of just the word **FUNCTIØN** in the first statement of the subprogram.

COMPLEX OPERATIONS

Some FORTRAN systems include a **CØMPLEX** mode for use with complex variables. The description of this mode will be of little use to those unfamiliar with complex arithmetic.

We can mathematically consider a complex number as having the form $a + bi$ where a and b are real numbers and i, called the "imaginary unit," is a number which satisfies the equation

$$i^2 = -1$$

When a complex number z is such that

$$z = a + bi$$

a is called the *real part* of z and b is called the *imaginary part* of z.

If the computer is informed that a variable is complex by the use of a type statement

```
COMPLEX Z
```

the computer will assign two storage locations for the variable **Z**, the first to hold the real part of **Z** and the second to hold the imaginary part of **Z**. Both of these numbers are stored in the **REAL** form. The clerk would put **+300000+01** and **+400000+01** on his blackboard when asked to store a number equal to $3 + 4i$. A complex variable may also be subscripted:

```
COMPLEX Z,KY,WD(70),PU(5,2)
```

Complex constants are written in the arithmetic and **IF** statements as a pair of **REAL** constants enclosed in parentheses and separated by a comma. The following are valid complex constants.

Constant	Meaning
(3.0,4.0)	$3.0 + 4.0i$
(5.206,0.0)	$5.206 + 0.0i$
(0.0,6.5E3)	$0.0 + 6500.i$

Complex constants, complex variables, **REAL** constants, and **REAL** variables may be combined with the operation symbols $+$, $-$, $*$, and $/$ to form arithmetic expressions. When a complex number is raised to a power by use of the operation symbol $**$ the exponent must be integer.

Input and output for complex variables are very simple. Each complex-variable name represents two **REAL** numbers and therefore requires two **F** or **E** specifications.

The statements

```
          COMPLEX A,B,C
          A=(3.0,4.5)
          B=(2.0,1.2)
          C=A-B
          WRITE(6,9)C
        9 FORMAT(1X,F5.2,E12.3)
          STOP
          END
```

would produce the output

$$1.00 \qquad 0.330E \ 01$$

with the real part of C being printed with the **F5.2** specification and the imaginary part of C being printed with the **E12.3**.

The names of complex library functions include the letter **C** and require complex arguments. The mode of these functions is also complex except for the function **CABS** since the absolute value of a complex number is real.

An arithmetic statement function as described in Sec. 10-1 may be made complex by including its name in a type statement.

A **FUNCTIØN** subprogram as described in Sec. 11-1 may be made complex by using the words **CØMPLEX FUNCTIØN** instead of just the word **FUNCTIØN** in the first statement of the subprogram.

LOGICAL OPERATIONS

There are only two possible values of *logical constants*. These values are

```
.TRUE.
```

and

```
.FALSE.
```

The decimal points before and after the letters are a necessary part of the constants.

Variable names may be declared to be the names of *logical variables* by the use of a **LØGICAL** type statement:

```
LOGICAL J25,TAN,WA2(55)
```

Logical variables may be assigned the value "true" or the value "false" either by reading a value from a data card or by the use of a *logical assignment statement*. The simplest logical assignment statement consists of a logical-variable name, an equals sign, and a logical constant. For example,

```
LA=.TRUE.
```

and

```
LB=.FALSE.
```

would be valid logical assignment statements if **LA** and **LB** had been made logical-variable names.

A logical assignment statement may consist of a logical-variable name, and equals sign, and a logical-variable name. The statement

```
LC=LB
```

would cause the logical value "false" to be stored in location **LC** if the value "false" had previously been stored in location **LB**.

The assignment statement may contain a *logical expression* following the equals sign. The logical expression is an assertion that may or may not be true. This may be a *relational expression* which uses one of the relational operators **.EQ., .NE., .GT., .GE., .LT.,** or **.LE.** discussed in Sec. 7-3. The expression

```
X .GT. Y
```

asserts that **X** is greater than **Y**. This assertion would be true if **X** and **Y** had the values **50.2** and **47.3** respectively but would not be true if **X** and **Y** were both **50.**, or if **X** and **Y** had the values **50.2** and **81.8** respectively. The statement

```
LA=X .GT. Y
```

would thus cause either a "true" or a "false" to be stored at location **LA** depending on the values of **X** and **Y**. The items before and after the relational operator may be any valid arithmetic expressions. The statements

```
LB=X .NE. 50.2

LC=X-A .LT. R*Y-COS(Q)
```

and

```
LD= 5 .EQ. J-2
```

would be valid. These expressions before and after the relational operator may both be integer, both be real, or both be double precision. They may not be complex.

Relational expressions and/or logical-variable names may be combined in more complex logical expressions by using the *logical operators* .AND., .ØR., and .NØT..

All relational expressions and logical variables connected by the operator .AND. must be true in order for the logical expression to be true. The expression

```
G .GT. W .AND. LE
```

would only be true if both **G** .**GT.** **W** were true and the value "true" were stored at location **LE.** The expression

```
RUB .AND. X-Z*T .GE. 5.6 .AND. W .EQ. T
```

would be false if one or more of the three items **RUB**, **X−Z∗T** .**GE.** **5.6**, or **W** .**EQ.** **T** produced a "false" value.

If one or more of the items connected by the operator .**ØR.** produced a "true" value the entire expression will be true. The expression

```
RUB .OR. X-Z*T .GE. 5.6 .OR. W .EQ. T
```

would be true if one or more of the three items produced a "true."

The logical operator .**NØT.** reverses the truth value of the expression or variable it precedes. For example, if **RUB** has the value "true" .**NØT.** **RUB** has the value "false." If **W** .**GT.** **X** is false, .**NØT.** **W** .**GT.** **X** is true. The .**AND..NØT.** and .**ØR..NØT.** combinations are the only ones in which two operation symbols may appear together.

Parentheses may be used in logical expressions as well as in arithmetic expressions to control the order in which the operations are executed. Thus the expression

```
(LA .AND. LB) .OR. LC
```

would be true while the expression

```
LA .AND. (LB .OR. LC)
```

would be false if **LA** and **LC** had the value "true" and **LB** had the value "false."

When the order of operations is not indicated by parentheses, the precedence of execution is

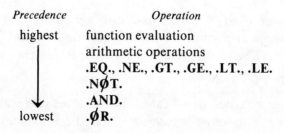

Precedence	*Operation*
highest	function evaluation
	arithmetic operations
	.EQ., .NE., .GT., .GE., .LT., .LE.
	.NØT.
	.AND.
lowest	.ØR.

Any of the logical expressions may be used in a logical assignment statement or in a logical **IF** statement.

Values of "true" and "false" may be read into locations designated by logical-variable names by use of an **L** specification. The statements

```
    LOGICAL Z,K
    READ(5,53)Z,K
53  FORMAT(L4,L5)
```

tell the computer to examine fields of 4 columns and 5 columns. If the first (leftmost) nonblank character in the **L** field is the letter **T** a value "true" will be assigned. If the first nonblank character is the letter **F** a value "false" will be assigned. If the entire field is blank a value "false" is assigned. If the first nonblank character is any character other than **T** or **F** an error condition occurs. Any remaining columns after the first nonblank column are ignored.

Logical values are printed using the **L** specification. The letter **T** or the letter **F** is printed right-justified in the **L** field.

THE CØMMØN STATEMENT

The **FUNCTIØN** and **SUBRØUTINE** subprograms shown in Secs. 11-1 and 12-1 all contained a list of dummy arguments, and the programs that called for the execution of these subprograms contained a list of arguments. These lists told the computer what memory locations were to be used when numerical information was to be transmitted between the subprogram and the calling program. This method of transmitting numerical information between programs will always work, but there is another method that may be used.

A statement that consists of the word **CØMMØN** followed by a variable name list tells the computer to use locations in a special part of the memory it is to designate as the common area for the storage of the variables named in the **CØMMØN** statement. Think of the clerk being told that if the program he is executing contains the statement

        COMMON Q,R,T,V

he is to use the first rectangle in the area called "common" on his blackboard to store the variable **Q**, the second rectangle of this area for **R**, the third for **T**, and the fourth for **V**. This would be of no help to him if he was only working with one program, but a **CØMMØN** statement, like one scissors blade, is normally not used alone. A **CØMMØN** statement in one program will usually have at least one counterpart in the program that either calls for, or is called by, the first program.

If the program the clerk is executing contained the statement

        COMMON Q,R,T,V

and the statement

        R=50.

he would write a real number equal to **50.** in the second rectangle of the common area of his blackboard. If this program also contained the statement

        CALL SUB(W)

he would begin executing the **SUBRØUTINE SUB** without erasing any numbers written on his blackboard. If this **SUBRØUTINE** contained the statements

        COMMON A,B,C,D

and

        C=25.+B

the clerk would go to the second rectangle of common to find the value he is to use for **B** since **B** is the second variable listed in the **CØMMØN** statement in the program he is *now* executing. He would then add **25.** to the **50.** he found on the blackboard for **B** and write a real number **75.** in the third rectangle of common, the location he is told to use for **C** when executing this subprogram. After he reached a **RETURN** statement in the subprogram he would go back to the instructions of the first program. The numbers **50.** and **75.** would still be written in the second and third rectangles of common and he would find these numbers if this first program asked him to use **R** or **T** in a calculation. The clerk is told to think of the first four rectangles of common as **Q, R, T,** and **V** when he is executing instructions from the first program and to think of these same four rectangles as **A, B, C,** and **D** when he is executing the instructions of the **SUB-RØUTINE SUB.** There would be no need for him to have any of the letters **A, B, C,** or **D** appear as dummy arguments in the subprogram or any of the letters **Q, R, T,** or **V** appear as arguments in a **CALL** statement in the first program since the locations in common are already available to both programs.

   If a subprogram began with the statement

```
        SUBROUTINE SUB(B,C,UP)
```

and the main-line program contained the statements

```
        CALL  SUB(R,T,W)
        CALL  SUB(R,T,S)
        CALL  SUB(R,T,P2)
```

and

```
        CALL  SUB(R,T,DAB)
```

all of the numeric information would be transmitted between the two programs by the use of the arguments and dummy arguments. The two programs could be revised so that the common area is used for the transmission of the information that does not change from call to call. The statement

```
        COMMON R,T
```

could be put in the main-line program. The calling statements could then be

```
        CALL  SUB(W)
        CALL  SUB(S)
        CALL  SUB(P2)
```

and

```
        CALL  SUB(DAB)
```

if the subprogram began with the statements

```
        SUBROUTINE  SUB(UP)
        COMMON B,C
```

The third argument in this program could not be transmitted by the use of the **CØMMØN** statements since it is not the same in each call. There are cases where all of the numeric information may be transmitted between a **SUBRØUTINE** and a program that calls for it. In such a case the first statement of the **SUBRØUTINE** would contain the word **SUBRØUTINE** and the subprogram name but would not contain any dummy arguments. The calling statement would contain the word **CALL** and the subprogram name without any arguments.

   The above examples have shown **CØMMØN** statements used in connection with **SUBRØUTINE** subprograms.   A **FUNCTIØN** subprogram may also contain a

CØMMØN statement and use the common area to transmit numerical information. Unlike the **SUBRØUTINE** however, a **FUNCTIØN** subprogram must have at least one dummy argument.

When array names are placed in **CØMMØN** they may be dimensioned by either putting the dimension information in the **CØMMØN** statement

```
COMMON PEP(6,9)
```

or by putting the dimension information in the **DIMENSIØN** statement and having the array name without dimensions appear in the **CØMMØN** statement

```
DIMENSION PEP(6,9)
COMMON PEP
```

An array with adjustable dimensions must not be in common.

Some complications may arise in connection with **CØMMØN** if more than two programs are involved. A main-line program may call two or more subprograms at different times, or a main-line program may call a subprogram which calls another subprogram. The statement

```
COMMON X1,X2,X3,X4,X5
```

in the main-line program would tell the computer to use the first five locations in the common area for the five variables **X1**, **X2**, **X3**, **X4**, and **X5** when the main-line program is being executed. If this main-line program calls either a **FUNCTIØN** subprogram or a **SUBRØUTINE** subprogram named **SUB1** that contains the statement

```
COMMON U,V,W
```

a correspondence between **X1** in the main-line program and **U** in **SUB1** is set up. Correspondences between **X2** and **V** and between **X3** and **W** in the two programs are also achieved. The program that is called may have fewer locations listed in its **CØMMØN** statement than are listed in the calling program but may not have more. If the main-line program also calls for a subprogram **SUB2** and the programmer wishes to set up a correspondence between **F** and **G** in **SUB2** with **X4** and **X5** in the main-line program he could not use the statement

```
COMMON F,G
```

in **SUB2** to set up this correspondence since this would make **F** refer to the first location of common and not to the fourth as is desired. The statement

```
COMMON E1,E2,E3,F,G
```

in **SUB2** would accomplish the desired relationships. The variable names **E1**, **E2**, and **E3** are used as dummy place holders and may be any variable names of the correct mode not used elsewhere in the program in which this **CØMMØN** statement occurs.

Many FORTRAN systems permit the use of more than one common block in storage in which each block is given a name. These blocks are known as *labeled* **CØMMØN**. The statement

```
COMMON/BL1/X1,X2,X3/BL2/X4,X5
```

in the main-line program would tell the computer to set up two different **CØMMØN** areas or blocks in memory. The first three locations of a block called **BL1** are to be known as **X1**, **X2**, and **X3** and the first two locations of a block called **BL2** are to be known as **X4** and **X5** when the main-line program is being executed. The statement

COMMON/BL1/U,V,W

in program **SUB1** and the statement

COMMON/BL2/F,G

would set up the relationships mentioned above. Note that the name of the **CØMMØN** block, the label, is enclosed in slashes and precedes the names of the variables to be included in this block. A block of **CØMMØN** without a name called either *blank* **CØMMØN** or *unlabeled* **CØMMØN** may be included by placing the variable names list first or by giving two slashes with no label between. Either the statement

COMMON VASE,PAN/BL1/X1,X2,X3/BL2/X4,X5

or the statement

COMMON/BL1/X1,X2,X3//VASE,PAN/BL2/X4,X5

would place **VASE** and **PAN** in blank **CØMMØN**, **X1, X2,** and **X3** in the block labeled **BL1**, and **X4** and **X5** in the block labeled **BL2**. When two or more programs are used with labeled **CØMMØN** blocks with the same name the blocks must be of the same size. If a block named **BL1** in the main-line program refers to three locations, a block named **BL1** in program **SUB1** must refer to three locations.

Two **CØMMØN** statements establish equivalence between variable names in two different programs. An **EQUIVALENCE** statement establishes equivalence between two variable names that both appear in the same program. If any names in the **CØMMØN** statement appear in an **EQUIVALENCE** statement in the same program, complications may occur. A beginning programmer should avoid this condition.

One of the reasons for using **CØMMØN** statements is to make it unnecessary to include a large number of arguments in the **CALL** statement. Another reason for using **CØMMØN** statements is that memory locations may be saved by their use.

THE **DATA** STATEMENT

The first step in many computations is the assigning of initial values to a number of variables. The arithmetic statements

```
SUM=0.
J=0
```

at the beginning of the program of Fig. 5-21 are to perform this "initialization." More complicated problems may require many more variables to be initialized, and many of the initial values may not be zero.

Most FORTRAN systems contain a specification statement known as a **DATA** statement that is used to store initial values in specified memory locations at compilation time, the time the computer is writing the machine-language program. Specification statements are statements that do not tell the computer to do any computation but give it information about how the other statements in the program are to be carried out. Some other specification statements already covered are **INTEGER**, **REAL**, **DIMEN-SIØN**, **CØMMØN**, and **EQUIVALENCE** statements.

The statement

```
DATA J2,SUM,QR,NEG/20,0.,-10.5,-15/
```

would cause **20** to be stored in location **J2**, **0.** in location **SUM**, **−10.5** in **QR**, and **−15** in **NEG** before the computation started. The constants may be positive or negative but must agree in mode with the variable name: the constant must contain a decimal point if it is to be stored in a location specified by a real-variable name and must not contain a decimal point if it is to be stored in a location specified by an integer-variable name. The statement

```
DATA J2,SUM,QR,NEG/20,0,-10.5,-15/
```

would not be valid since the statement asks for the integer constant zero (without a decimal point) to be stored in the real location **SUM**.

There must be the same number of variable names in the list as there are constants. The statement

```
DATA A,B,C/2.5,3./
```

would give an error indication, since it contains three variable names and only two constants. Three constants and two variable names would also be invalid.

Elements of an array may be initialized by including the subscripted array names in the variable-name list. In this case the subscript *must* be an integer constant.

```
DIMENSION JK(8)
DATA A,JK(3),P,JK(7)/2.5,-7,0.2,0/
```

This statement would not initialize the other elements, **JK(1)**, **JK(2)**, **JK(4)**, **JK(5)**, **JK(6)**, and **JK(8)** of the array.

An unsigned integer constant and an asterisk are used to indicate that constants are to be repeated. The statement

```
DATA J,K,L,M/3*5,4/
```

is equivalent to the statement

```
DATA J,K,L,M/5,5,5,4/
```

If an array name without a subscript is included in the variable-name list of a **DATA** statement, the constants are assigned to the elements of this array in order starting with the first element. The statements

```
DIMENSION R(5),T(4)
DATA R,X,T/3*0.,5*7.6/
```

would cause the constants to be stored as follows:

R(1)	R(2)	R(3)	R(4)	R(5)	X	T(1)	T(2)	T(3)	T(4)
0.0	0.0	0.0	7.6	7.6	7.6	7.6	7.6		

If the last item in the variable-name list is an unsubscripted array name enough constants must be specified so that at least one element of this array is initialized, but it is not necessary to initialize every element of this array. The **DATA** statement above must specify at least seven and not more than ten constants.

Most but not all systems which permit the use of the **DATA** statement permit the use of the implied **DØ**-loop in the variable-name list. The parameters of the implied loop must be constants.

```
DIMENSION FUSS(20)
DATA (FUSS(J),J=1,15)/15*4.5/
```

One FORTRAN program may contain more than one **DATA** statement. A comma, an additional variable-name list, and an additional list of constants enclosed by slashes may be added to the end of a **DATA** statement. Three equivalent ways of initializing **A, B, J,** and **N** are

```
DATA A,B,J,N/2.5,0.0,-1,0/
```

```
DATA A,B/2.5,0.0/
DATA J,N/-1,0/
```

```
DATA A,B/2.5,0.0/,J,N/-1,0/
```

Real constants in the **DATA** statement may be written using the **E FØRMAT**:

```
DATA X,Q,Z/4.3E3,7.5,-0.23E-5/
```

Logical constants in the **DATA** statement may be written as **T** and **F** or as **.TRUE.** and **.FALSE.**.

```
LOGICAL TY,L5
DATA TY,X,L5/F,78.6,.TRUE./
```

The letter **D** is used when using double-precision constants.

```
DOUBLE PRECISION DB
DATA DB/56.7D3/
```

A complex variable appearing in a **DATA** statement requires two constants.

```
COMPLEX YELL
DATA YELL/5.67,-34.89/
```

Literal data may be included with the constants in the **DATA** statement by the use of Hollerith fields. The statement

```
DATA J,X,Y/2HRT,3HA3F,4HGT29/
```

would store the characters **RT** in location **J**, **A3F** in location **X**, and **GT29** in **Y**. These characters would normally be printed at some time in the program using **A2**, **A3**, and **A4** **FØRMAT** specifications. The program shown in Fig. 12-11 could have included the statement

```
DATA L/1HF,1HF,1HF,1HF,1HF,1HD,1HC,1HB,1HA,1HA/
```

instead of the statements

```
READ(5,4)(L(J),J=1,10)
4 FORMAT(10A1)
```

The first data card containing the **FFFFFDCBAA** would also not be needed. (The **DIMENSIØN** statement including the array **L** would be required as before.)

If the FORTRAN system being used accepts literal data inclosed by apostrophes, literal data in this form may be included in the **DATA** statement.

```
DATA J,X,Y/'RT','A3F','GT29'/
```

In some systems several variables may be filled with literal characters by writing the data as one long literal constant. Each variable in turn is filled with the maximum number of characters until all have been stored. The statement

```
DATA X,Y,Z/15HNOW IS THE TIME/
```

used such a system that permits a maximum of six characters per real storage location would store **NØWbIS** in **X**, **bTHEbT** in **Y**, and **IME** in **Z**. A blank is a valid character.

The **DATA** statement is a specification statement and is not executed. It therefore should not have a statement number and may not be referred to by a transfer statement such as an **IF**, **GØ TØ**, or **DØ** statement. If the programmer wishes certain values to be assigned more than once either during one execution of a program or during several executions without recompiling, he must use **READ** or arithmetic statements instead of a **DATA** statement.

The **DATA** statement is often simpler to write than the series of arithmetic statements that could be used to achieve the same initialization. It is particularly useful in initializing literal data since otherwise this data must be read from data cards. An additional advantage of the **DATA** statement over the arithmetic statements is that the **DATA** statement produces no machine-language instructions that require memory space.

There is no way in which to preassign values to variables in the unlabeled **CØMMØN**, and a special subprogram beginning with the words **BLØCK DATA** must be used to preassign values to variables in labeled **CØMMØN**. A **BLØCK DATA** subprogram is composed of **CØMMØN**, **DIMENSIØN**, type, and **DATA** statements with an **END** statement. The program

```
BLOCK DATA
COMMON/BL1/X1,X2,X3
COMMON/BL2/X4,X5
DATA X1,X2,X3,X4,X5/1.2,0.0,4.2,-2.89,6.3/
END
```

could be used with the main-line program and the subprograms **SUB1** and **SUB2** discussed in Appendix D.

The **EXTERNAL** Statement

The argument in a statement that calls a subprogram and the dummy arguments in the subprogram are usually used to transmit numerical information between the two programs. In most FORTRAN systems it is also possible to use an argument and a dummy argument to transmit the name of a subprogram from the calling program to the called program if the names to be transmitted appear in an **EXTERNAL** statement in the calling program.

A programmer might wish a **SUBRØUTINE WAFF** to execute a statement equivalent to

    X=Y*SIN(Q)

the first time it is called and a statement equivalent to

    X=Y*COS(Q)

the second time it is called. This could be accomplished by including the statements

    EXTERNAL SIN,COS

    CALL WAFF (A,B,SIN,C)

and

    CALL WAFF (D,R,COS,W)

in the main-line program. The subprogram would contain the statements

    SUBROUTINE WAFF(Q,Y,PRO,X)

and

    X=Y*PRO(Q)

The third argument in the calling statements and the third dummy argument in the **SUBRØUTINE** are used to transmit the names of functions **SIN** and **CØS** from program to program. The name **PRØ** is used as a dummy argument—there is no subprogram named **PRØ**. The other arguments and dummy arguments would transmit the usual numerical information.

The statement

    CALL WAFF (R,T,SQRT,P)

in the main-line program would not work unless the name **SQRT** were included in the **EXTERNAL** statement.

The names of subprograms included in the **EXTERNAL** statement and transmitted to the subprograms may include the names of library functions, names of **FUNCTIØN** subprograms written by the programmer, or names of **SUBRØUTINE** subprograms. These names may be transmitted to either **FUNCTIØN** subprograms or to **SUBRØUTINE** subprograms.

SCALE FACTOR IN FØRMAT

A scale factor may be used with **F**, **E**, or **D** specifications in a **FØRMAT** statement. This is accomplished by placing a positive or negative integer constant and the letter **P** in front of the specification. The statement

```
16 FORMAT(2P3F10.2,1PE16.5,4P5D18.7)
```

tells the computer to use a scale factor of **2** with the **3F10.2** specification, a scale factor of **1** with the **E16.5**, and a factor of **4** with the **5D18.7**.

When a scale factor of **2** is used with an **F** specification with a **WRITE** statement, the number written will be 10^2 times the number in the computer memory. The statements

```
X=25.798
Y=0.07865
WRITE(6,27)X,Y
27 FORMAT(1X,2PF10.1,3PF6.2)
```

would cause the computer to print

```
2579.8 78.65
```

since $25.798 \times 10^2 = 2579.8$ and $0.07865 \times 10^3 = 78.65$. The numbers stored in locations **X** and **Y** would not be changed by the execution of the **WRITE** statement.

A scale factor of **2** used with an **F** specification with a **READ** statement causes the number read to be multiplied by 10^{-2} before it is stored. Scale factors, however, are seldom used with input.

The use of a scale factor with an **E** or **D** specification with a **WRITE** statement does not change the magnitude of the number printed but changes its form. The statements

```
R=5.239
T=8967.36
WRITE(6,33)R,T
33 FORMAT(1X,E12.4,E14.6)
```

would cause the computer to print

```
0.5239E 01   0.896736E 04
```

while the statements

```
R=5.239
T=8967.36
WRITE(6,34)R,T
34 FORMAT(1X,3PE12.1,1PE13.5)
```

would print

```
523.9E-02   8.96736E 03
```

The number that would be printed in front of the letter if no scale factor were used is multiplied by 10 raised to the power indicated by the scale factor, and the exponent that would be printed after the letter **E** is reduced by the scale factor. A scale factor used with a **D** specification with a **WRITE** statement operates in exactly the same way as with the **E** specification.

A scale factor used with an **E** or **D** specification has no effect when used with a **READ** statement.

A scale factor in a **FØRMAT** statement applies to all of the **F**, **E**, and **D** specifications following it if no other scale factors appear in the statement. The statement

```
35 FORMAT(2PE16.5,I5,F10.4,E17.7,3PE16.5)
```

would assign the **2P** factor to the **E16.5**, **F10.4**, and **E17.7** specifications. A **0P** factor may be used if the **2P** is only to apply to the **E16.5** specification:

```
35 FORMAT(2PE16.5,I5,0PF10.4,E17.7,3PE16.5)
```

Scale factors are not used with **I**, **A**, or **H** specifications.

INDEX

DATE DUE

DEC 0 7 1995	